W9-ACY-095

WITHDRAWN

Gramley Library
Salem Academy and College
Winston-Salem, N.C. 27108

GENDER, DESIRE, AND SEXUALITY IN T. S. ELIOT

This collection of new essays brings together scholars from a wide range of critical approaches to study T. S. Eliot's engagement with desire, homoeroticism, and early twentieth-century feminism in his poetry, prose, and drama. Ranging from historical and formalist literary criticism to psychological and psychoanalytic theory and cultural studies, *Gender, Desire, and Sexuality in T. S. Eliot* illuminates such topics as the influence of Eliot's mother – a poet and social reformer – on his art; the aesthetic function of physical desire; the dynamic of homosexuality in his poetry and prose; and his identification with passive or "feminine" desire in his poetry and drama. The book also charts his reception by female critics from the early twentieth century to the present. This book should be essential reading for students of Eliot and modernism, as well as queer theory and gender studies.

CASSANDRA LAITY is Associate Professor of English at Drew University and coeditor of *Modernism/Modernity*. She has published widely on British and American modernism and is the author of *H.D. and the Victorian Fin de Siècle: Gender, Modernism, Decadence* (Cambridge, 1996).

NANCY K. GISH is Professor of English and Women's Studies at the University of Southern Maine. She is the author of books and articles on twentieth-century poetry and on T. S. Eliot, including *Time in the Poetry of T. S. Eliot* (1981) and *The Waste Land: A Poem of Memory and Desire* (1988).

GENDER, DESIRE, AND SEXUALITY IN T. S. ELIOT

EDITED BY

CASSANDRA LAITY AND NANCY K. GISH

CAMBRIDGE
UNIVERSITY PRESS

Gramley Library
Salem Academy and College
Winston-Salem, N.C. 27108

CAMBRIDGE UNIVERSITY PRESS
Cambridge, New York, Melbourne, Madrid, Cape Town, Singapore, São Paulo

Cambridge University Press
The Edinburgh Building, Cambridge CB2 2RU, UK

Published in the United States of America by Cambridge University Press, New York

www.cambridge.org
Information on this title: www.cambridge.org/9780521806886

© Cambridge University Press 2004

This publication is in copyright. Subject to statutory exception
and to the provisions of relevant collective licensing agreements,
no reproduction of any part may take place without
the written permission of Cambridge University Press.

First published 2004

A catalogue record for this publication is available from the British Library

Library of Congress Cataloguing in Publication data
Gender, desire, and sexuality in T. S. Eliot / co-edited by Cassandra Laity and Nancy K. Gish.
p. cm.
ISBN 0 521 80688 7
1. Eliot, T. S. (Thomas Stearns), 1888–1965 – Criticism and interpretation.   2. Homosexuality and
literature – United States – History – 20th century.   3. Homosexuality and literature – England –
History – 20th century.   4. Feminism and literature – United States – History – 20th century.
5. Feminism and literature – England – History – 20th century.   6. Erotic poetry, American –
History and criticism.   7. Sexual orientation in literature.   8. Gender identity in literature.
9. Body, Human, in literature.   10. Desire in literature.   11. Sex in literature.   I. Laity, Cassandra.
II. Gish, Nancy K., 1942–
PS3509.L43Z6765   2004
821′.912 – dc22   2004040760

ISBN-13 978-0-521-80688-6 hardback
ISBN-10 0-521-80688-7 hardback

Transferred to digital printing 2006

The publisher has used its best endeavours to ensure that the URLs for external websites referred to in
this publication are correct and active at the time of going to press. However, the publisher has no
responsibility for the websites and can make no guarantee that a site will remain live or that the
content is or will remain appropriate.

*This book is dedicated in memory of my great-uncle, John Hall
Wheelock – Cassandra Laity
This book is dedicated to George Gish for many years of
support – Nancy Gish*

Contents

Acknowledgments

We wish to thank Dominique Bartels and Rebecca Wisor for their invaluable editorial and computer work in preparation of the text.

Notes on contributors

CHARLES ALTIERI teaches modern American poetry at the University of California-Berkeley. His most recent book is *The Particulars of Rapture: An Aesthetics of the Affects* (Cornell University Press, 2003).

RICHARD BADENHAUSEN is Associate Professor and Kim T. Adamson Chair at Westminster College in Salt Lake City, where he also directs the honors program. He has published numerous essays on Eliot and other writers. He is the author of *T. S. Eliot and the Art of Collaboration*, which is forthcoming at Cambridge University Press.

JEWEL SPEARS BROOKER, Professor of Literature at Eckerd College, is the author or editor of several books, including *Mastery and Escape: T. S. Eliot and the Dialectic of Modernism* and, with Joseph Bentley, of *Reading* The Waste Land*: Modernism and the Limits of Interpretation*. Her most recent book is *T. S. Eliot: The Contemporary Reviews* (Cambridge University Press, 2003).

ELISABETH DÄUMER is a professor of literature at Eastern Michigan University. She wrote her dissertation on the impact of Charlotte Stearns Eliot on her son's work and is presently writing on T. S. Eliot's reception in Germany.

TIM DEAN teaches in the English department and the Center for the Study of Psychoanalysis and Culture at the University of Buffalo (SUNY). He is the author of *Beyond Sexuality* and coeditor of *Homosexuality and Psychoanalysis*. He is currently completing two book manuscripts, one on aesthetic theory and the other on barebacking.

NANCY K. GISH teaches modern literature and women's studies at the University of Southern Maine. Her publications include *Time in the Poetry of T. S. Eliot* and *Hugh MacDiarmaid: Man and Poet* as well as articles on contemporary Scottish poets. She is currently working on modernism and dissociation.

CASSANDRA LAITY teaches modern literature and critical theory at Drew University. She is coeditor of *Modernism/Modernity* and a founder of the Modernist Studies Association. She is the author of *H.D. and the Victorian Fin de Siècle: Gender, Modernism, Decadence* and is currently working on a manuscript entitled *T. S. Eliot's Pagan Bodies: Modernism, Desire, and British Decadence.*

COLLEEN LAMOS is Associate Professor of English at Rice University. She is the author of *Deviant Modernism: Sexual and Textual Errancy in T. S. Eliot, James Joyce, and Marcel Proust* and is coeditor of *Masculinities in Joyce: Postcolonial Constructions.* She has published widely in queer theory.

GAIL MCDONALD is Associate Professor of English at the University of North Carolina-Greensboro. She is the author of *Learning to be Modern: Pound, Eliot, and the American University.* Her current projects include *Collaborative Sin: American Naturalism and the Languages of Responsibility* and, for Blackwell Publishing, *American Literature and Culture: 1900– 1960.*

PETER MIDDLETON is Reader in English at the University of Southampton and the author of *The Inward Gaze: Masculinity and Subjectivity in Modern Culture* and, with Tim Woods, of *Literatures of Memory: History, Time and Space in Postwar Writing.* His most recent book is *Distant Reading: Performance, Readership, and Consumption* (Alabama University Press, 2004).

DR. RACHEL POTTER is Lecturer in modernist literature at Queen Mary, University of London where she teaches courses on modernist literature and literary theory. Her book, *Unacknowledged Legislators: Modernism and Democracy,* is forthcoming at Oxford University Press.

MICHELE TEPPER received a Ph.D. in English from the University of Michigan in 1998. She has published articles on modernist poetry, detective fiction, academia, and internet culture. A writer, independent scholar, and journalist, she lives in Brooklyn, New York.

Introduction: Eliot, gender, and modernity

Cassandra Laity

Eliot's female contemporary, poet Kathleen Raine, recalled the impact of her first encounter with Eliot's poetry as "instantaneous and tremendous."[1] Muriel Bradbrook similarly exclaimed, "the effect of *The Waste Land* was not gloomy but exhilarating and intensely stimulating . . . [the poem] gave us a new world . . . 'Bliss was it in that dawn to be alive!'"[2] May Sinclair admired Eliot particularly for his "disturbing" "genius." He is "dangerous," she remarked, not a poet whom "comfortable and respectable people can see, in the first moment after dinner."[3] And, as Gail McDonald's study of Eliot's reception by first-generation college women in this volume establishes, his rise in the academy was concurrent with the influx of women into universities, and many saw "their [own] pioneering energies mirrored in his work." Similarly, with the recent flourishing of queer theory (beginning mainly in the 1990s), gender studies of alternative "masculinities," and the expansion of feminist criticism into issues of race, class, and male sexuality, contemporary women critics are beginning to echo these early perceptions of Eliot's poetry as startlingly rebellious, "dangerous," and compelling. Queer theorist Colleen Lamos observes in *Deviant Modernism* that readers must "fac[e] up to the errant female sexual energies within his . . . poems if we are to continue to read Eliot with something other than hostility or incomprehension."[4] Feminist critic Bonnie Kime Scott comments in *Refiguring Modernism*, "The subjects of the emotions, the feminine, and the disorder of sexuality recur in Eliot's writing and make him a more confused figure than we found in . . . accounts that cite only his violent texts on women."[5] And poetry critic Marjorie Perloff concedes in her recent book's defining first chapter, "Avant-Garde Eliot," that whereas she formerly fixed Eliot as the static "symboliste" – against which she posited the more fluid, contemporary "poetics of indeterminacy" – she now encounters a "constructivist" poet in the early Eliot who uses language "as an active compositional agent, impelling the reader to participate in the process of construction."[6] Both generations of readers, separated by the critical gap of feminist criticism/theory, postmodernism, and cultural studies, perceive radical experiment and vitality in the sexual, "feminine," and linguistic currents of his poetry.

Despite such enthusiastic acknowledgments, however, Eliot's relation to the early modernist spheres of feminism, alternative masculinities, the feminine, and homoeroticism remains largely unexamined. By contrast, other "hypermasculine" male modernists such as Yeats and Joyce have been substantially reclaimed for sex/gender nuance and careful articulation in the complex gender phenomena of their time (perhaps because their clear association with Irish politics has proffered critics an easy transition to other social concerns).[7] Eliot's unusually prolonged association with a monolithically elitist, masculinist, and reactionary conception of early modernist culture may be among the chief critical obstacles to his resituation in the sex/gender/erotic contradictions of his own milieu. However, increasing critical attention to a refocused "modernity" which reenters early modernism alternatively from the perspective of its complex gender dynamics as well as its negotiations between high and low culture brings to view, in this volume, Eliot's largely unexplored engagement with various public and private worlds of women, eroticism, and the feminine.

Important studies seeking to move beyond polarized versions of modernism and postmodernism toward a redefinition of "the modern" encompassing – among other things – both popular and high culture, misogyny, and new attitudes toward women and "the feminine" include Michael North's *Reading 1922: A Return to the Scene of the Modern* (1999), Janet Lyon's *Manifestoes: Provocations of the Modern* (1999), Lawrence Rainey's *Institutions of Modernism: Literary Elites and Popular Culture* (1998), and Rita Felski's *Doing Time: Feminist Theory and Postmodern Culture* (2000).[8] As Rainey observes, for example, postmodern studies of mass culture created a false opposition between an "emancipatory" postmodernism that negotiated between the claims of high art and mass culture and a uniformly elitist, "naive and irremediably reactionary" modernism.[9] Similarly, in sex/gender scholarship, fluid, "feminine," and nontraditional definitions of desire equated with the postmodern were celebrated over homophobic, misogynist, and hypermasculine forms of desire ascribed to the modern. Accordingly, the era of postmodernism saw a backlash against Eliot who was largely perceived as the progenitor of New Criticism and the exemplar of a "reactionary" modernism.

As more inclusive conceptions of modernism gain currency, however, the critical climate becomes ripe for explorations of Eliot's connection to a modernity characterized not by rigid binaries, but rather as an "event" extending from early modernism into the present and "subject to the very discontinuities of time that its narratives seek to disguise: different 'times' co-exist within the same discrete historical moment" (*M*, 203). Such wider-ranging views of modernity restore to early modernism the gender-multiplicity and cross-fertilization between high and low culture formerly considered the preserve of postmodernism.

In his brief history tracing the politically volatile reception of Eliot's work, Jeffrey Perl perceives the forces gathering behind present redefinitions of modernity, claiming that "a reconsideration of anti-modernist postmod-ernism has in fact begun."[10] Indeed, debating and/or redefining Eliot's rela-tion to "low" culture, gender/sexuality, and race (specifically anti-Semitism) has become a means of defining the nature and shape of literary experience and expression itself for the last two generations. And at this writing, both new articulations of the debate regarding Eliot and anti-Semitism and the first full-length study of Eliot and popular culture, David Chinitz's *T. S. Eliot and the Cultural Divide* (2003), have just appeared.[11] Such reconsid-erations offer new insights into modernism and further complicate Eliot, treating him as a receptive observer of modern social and cultural phe-nomena and, as David Chinitz observes, "a multidimensional thinker and artist whose approach to [modern culture] is supple, frequently insightful, and always deeply ambivalent."[12] Thus, while he formulated a high mod-ernism eschewing "low" culture, Eliot embraced the "modern popular" in his poetry and critical essays; he could be brutally anti-Semitic, yet ponder the cultural/religious complexities surrounding ideas of a Jewish society.[13] *Gender, Desire, and Sexuality in T. S. Eliot* joins such efforts to recontex-tualize Eliot's work and thought, acknowledging that Eliot's poems, plays, and critical essays are often blatantly misogynist and homophobic, but also seeking to trace their intricate engagements with multiple forms and degrees of desire, contemporary feminism, the feminine, and homoeroticism.

TOWARD MODERNITY: CRITICAL OVERVIEW

Eliot's critical reception has evolved through a markedly long series of seemingly contradictory yet often similarly exiling phases toward a moder-nity capable of resituating him in the sex/gender/erotic ferment of his own time. Purist New Critics first isolated Eliot from social, historical, and biographical concerns, restricting readers to "the words on the page" and the "impersonal" realm of a transcendent art. Subsequently, first-wave feminism consigned Eliot and the male tradition to a masculinist limbo, emptied of women writers, feminist protestors, and the feminine.

As Michael North notes, Sandra Gilbert and Susan Gubar's *No Man's Land* "had to begin by addressing a [male-defined] version of twentieth-century literature in which there were virtually no women" in order to accomplish "the repair work necessary to bring[ing] . . . Anglo-American women back into the canon" (*RSM*, 10).[14] Confined to the conceptual trope of an entirely male-defined modernism, therefore, early in-depth studies of Eliot focused almost exclusively on his patriarchal images of women, violence against women, and aversions to the female body.[15] Further, perhaps because of the removal from space and time effected by New Critical impersonality and his role as a stock figure for misogyny in feminist overviews, the first full-length studies to consider Eliot's complex relation to women and errant sexuality were biographical. In her first two biographies, Lyndall Gordon traced the opposing projections of Vivien Haigh-Wood and Emily Hale as, respectively, the demonic female and the exalted "higher dream" presiding over Eliot's spiritual journey through the temptations of sickness and sin (Vivien) to the transmutation of personal agony "into something universal and holy" (Emily).[16] James E. Miller first broached at length the subject of Eliot's homoeroticism in his then controversial psychobiography *T. S. Eliot's Personal Waste Land: Exorcism of the Demons*, which interpreted the poem as an elegy to Jean Verdenal. Published in a relatively conservative critical climate, Miller's book was met with outrage and indignation for its "vulgar" impugning of Eliot's memory. More recently, Carole Seymour-Jones's biography of Vivien Eliot, *Painted Shadow*, largely attributes the failure of Eliot's marriage to his homosexual desires.[17]

Postmodernism's recasting of Eliot (and modernism) as a reactionary "elitist" foil for its social, political, and linguistic agendas further insulated Eliot from the rich gender phenomena of his own time.[18] However, psychoanalytic, postmodernist reassessments of Eliot first accessed powerful libidinal currents in his work, albeit through the circuitous route of discovering "the postmodern" in the modern. Thus Christine Froula juxtaposed the overweening desire of *The Waste Land*'s homoerotic "lover" "to become . . . woman" against his (self-policed) obligation to enter the patriarchal order of the Law of the Father.[19] Wayne Koestenbaum's study of Eliot and Pound's homosocial collaboration over the hysterical "feminine" text/body of *The Waste Land* explored the conflicted strains of homosociality, homoeroticism, and feminine self-identification fueling that creative combination. And both Maud Ellmann's *Poetics of Impersonality* and Andrew Ross's *The Failure of Modernism* argued that his poetry's perpetuation of narcissistic, "abject," and deferred desires undermined Eliot's rigid, authoritarian identity politics of impersonality.[20] Such *post*-modern assessments, however – launched, by definition, from a later, emancipatory advantage – left relatively unchallenged the mainstream view of modernism as a "naive and irremediably reactionary" period.[21] (Ross's argument for the "failure of modernism" and thus the inevitable reinstatement of Eliot's authoritarianism is particularly representative of this view.[22])

Until recently, therefore, Eliot scholarship frequently required the critic to maneuver around Eliot's fixed association with the oppressive first term in a series of binary divides – *male*/female, *reactionary*/progressive, *high*/low – against which feminism, postmodernism, and cultural studies were articulated. Indeed, paradoxically, his fixed symbolic role in the overpowering imaginaries, "male modernism," "high modernism," and "reactionary modernism," served to legitimate the alternative, vital worlds of the feminine, popular, and postmodern spheres by disallowing Eliot himself direct access to them. I will suggest that modernity's reentry into early modernism from the vantage point of these worlds, "peopled," as Rita Felski observes, by multitudes of "previously invisible figures" – "suffragettes and shoppers, actresses and rap artists, Indian cricketers and gay *flaneurs*" among them – has enabled this first full-length study exploring Eliot's interaction with various public and interior sectors of women, desire, and the feminine (*DT*, 57). Moreover, Eliot's increasing dissociation from New Critical aesthetic transcendence has freed up diverse methodologies – formalist, psychoanalytic, cultural, linguistic – for new readings of Eliot's life and art both within this collection and elsewhere. The second part of this introduction will suggest that Eliot's reinsertion into modernity corresponds with a larger, all-encompassing project (of which this anthology forms a part) to dissolve the boundary between aesthetics and society in various venues, including the academy's methodological divides, for which Eliot long stood.

MODERNITY

Feminist and postmodern binary oppositions crucially made visible the subordinate second term – male/*female*, high/*low*, then/*now* – enabling, still further, the more finely articulated coexistence of both at different "times" in the reconceived stream of a modernity-at-large. This restoration of gender multiplicity and cross-fertilizations between "high" and mass culture formerly reserved for postmodernism now requires critics to entertain the possibility of Eliot's direct access to the sex/gender complexities and popular culture of his own time.[23] Moreover, such a conjoining of once opposed worlds keeps Eliot's, and modernism's, contradictions in play, generating unexpected juxtapositions and startling congruencies.

Chafing at the strict division between "male" and "female" modernism, for example, feminist critic Janet Lyon, in *Manifestoes*, discerns "strange bedfellows" in such early modern movements as militant suffrage and a vehemently masculinist Vorticism deploring "feminism and women as a category" (*M*, 101). Lyon not only superimposes the two groups' "energy," "iconoclasm," and "revolutionary discourse," but offers visible evidence of their colliding worlds at, for example, Marinetti's speeches, which collected "suffrage supporters as well as nascent avant-gardists" (*M*, 100, 101). "From this angle," Lyon concludes, readjusting the limited time frame and oppositional spatialization of earlier modernist scholarship to a more inclusive modernity, "femininity and modernity *are* locked in an antithetical – albeit dialectical – relation" (*M*, 113; emphasis added). Modernity's redefinition, as a charged nexus of intersecting cultural sectors persisting to the present, has uncovered similarly surprising contiguities and dialectical relations in recent Eliot studies. Thus Lawrence Rainey's inquiry into the marketing and dissemination of Eliot's work (among that of other modernists) concludes that while modernism entailed "a certain retreat from . . . public culture," it also "continued to overlap and intersect with the public realm in a variety of contradictory ways."[24] Michael North's *Reading 1922* notes the paradox that Eliot could simultaneously make "American popular culture a legitimate object of criticism" and a subject for art while "formulating the public definition of literary modernism" that would come to exclude mass culture (*RSM*, 141). David Chinitz's abovementioned *T. S. Eliot and the Cultural Divide* plies the once unthinkable "natural associat[ion]" of modernism and popular culture.[25] And building on Maud Ellmann's study of Kristevean, "abject" waste in *The Waste Land*, Tim Armstrong demonstrates Eliot's engagement with modern technology and the body, cataloguing the poem's crammed materials of mass culture – gramophones, popular songs, pubs, the throbbing taxi, even the "human engine" – by which Eliot is "simultaneously fascinated and repelled."[26]

Such dissolutions between high and low, masculine and feminine, then and now, have made possible this collection's sustained attention to Eliot's intricate and multifaceted engagement with various worlds of women, the feminine, homoeroticism, and desire. Organized accordingly under the headings "Homoeroticisms," "Desire," and "Modern Women," questions directing the lines of inquiry in this anthology include the following: what was the impact on Eliot's work of phenomena such as the New Woman? What personae, motifs, configurations of the body, psychoanalytic or psychological discourses, and language practices informed

Eliot's pervasive identification with the feminine, his complex negotiations between "thought" and "feeling," erotic attraction and revulsion, or the dynamic of male-male love in his work? How did Eliot's work reflect war trauma and the homoerotic mourning for masculinities lost in the carnage of war? How has Eliot's reputation been shaped by the changing reception of his academic women readers who initially perceived him as empowering to their scholarly and literary pursuits? And what influence did Eliot's mother, Charlotte Stearns Eliot – social reformer, poet, and vital, problematic force in her son's life – have on the maternal characters of Eliot's drawing room plays?

The authors' attention to differentiating Eliot's place in the frequently contradictory gendered spheres and discourses of modernity often yields elective affinities and "strange bedfellows" resembling Lyon's unexpected superimposition of suffragettes and Vorticists or the image of an Eliot mingling with crowds of "suffragettes and shoppers, actresses . . . and gay *flaneurs.*" Thus, while Gilbert and Gubar sequestered Eliot as the oppressor of modernist women's writing, Gail McDonald resituates him among early women academics who found his transgressive attitudes toward domesticity and marriage uniquely inspiring. Further, citing Eliot's subversive protestation of the "old," exclusively classical (male) curriculum in favor of more contemporary electives such as contemporary literature, McDonald unsettles Woolf's image of the exclusionary male academic. Rachel Potter links Eliot's career-long critique of liberal democracy with *The Waste Land's* poetic appeal to mass culture and (working) class/gender-inflected idioms she claims he paradoxically employs to flaunt the pretensions of the bourgeoisie. Elisabeth Däumer shows how male anxieties over the social gains of the New Woman clash with the Victorian, spiritually based feminism Eliot gleaned from his mother and expressed in the hieratic women and "richly pagan world of natural forces" of his later plays. Redefining *Four Quartets* as a "serial war poem" mourning the lost masculinities of World War II, Peter Middleton's response to Margaret Higonnet's well-known description of war as a gendering activity yields striking analogies between Eliot's poem and the war writings of Wilfred Owen, Siegfried Sassoon, and D. H. Lawrence.[27] Michele Tepper discerns competing discourses of imperialism/ postcolonialism and homosociality/homoeroticism in the metaphoric "bodies" circulating through two of Eliot's little-known essays. Such proliferating bodies enact by turns conflicting desires to consume, to be consumed, to encompass, and "to lose oneself in 'something greater.'"

COEXISTING METHODOLOGIES: THE RETURN
TO THE AESTHETIC

The enormous expansion of modernist studies brought about by a more inclusive, all-encompassing modernity thus reaches backward to restore and enrich early modernism's thriving social, ideological, and cultural milieu. However, it appears to be working forward as well. Recent critics, from Marjorie Perloff and Elaine Scarry to Rachel Blau DuPlessis and Andreas Huyssen, are calling for a return to aesthetic issues coupled with postmodern, cultural, or social critique.[28] The recent announcement of PMLA's forthcoming special topic "On Poetry," for an issue scheduled to appear in January 2005, anticipates such an aesthetic revival:

Although many psychoanalytic and poststructuralist theories are grounded in poetic discourse, critics . . . [invoking] these paradigms have seemed reluctant to take poems as objects of analysis. Has the time come to revisit the relevance of poetry and the pleasures of the poetic in this changed interpretive universe?[29]

In answer, I will demonstrate that critics of modernity are already theorizing ways to intermesh attention to the text as aesthetic "object" with postmodernist and cultural approaches. Bridging the time-honored gap in literary history between aesthetics and the social, critics are seeking to regain what Rachel DuPlessis has described as "the nuanced pleasurable textiness of texts" and/or to rescue a rapidly (globally) expanding field from incoherence and superficiality.[30] Outside the academy, the recently termed "poetry renaissance of the 1990s" indicates the larger, all-embracing project under way to break down the conceptual divide between aesthetics and the social. Marjorie Perloff, Jan Clausen, and others have written on the contemporary flourishing of poetry in "extra-academic venues." Clausen's "The Speed of Poetry" pronounces poetry a "star of popular culture," citing the proliferation of internet poetry and websites, the success of US poet laureate Robert Pinksy's Favorite Poems Project, television documentaries on poetry, and the popularity of "slams."[31]

Perhaps the inauguration of Eliot – New Criticism's last stronghold – into modernity proffers an index to the revival of poetry both within and outside the academy. Indeed, Eliot serves as a pivotal figure for the changing attitude of literary criticism toward the poem/literary text's value as an aesthetic "object." The reluctance of postmodernism (and I would add cultural studies) "to take poems as objects of analysis" frequently turned on its disenchantment with transcendent conceptions of art linked to his "impersonality" and "objective correlative." Correspondingly, the present, increasing desire to revalue the textual "object" without regressing to notions of aesthetic transcendence, I will argue, has liberated mixed methodologies – formalist, historical, postmodern, social – affording new readings of Eliot's poetry and provocative redefinitions of aesthetic doctrines such as impersonality, dissociation, and the "unified" sensibility in this collection and elsewhere. I begin here by summarizing postmodern and cultural indictments of the aesthetic that turned on the axis of Eliotic impersonality and the objective correlative. I then briefly illustrate the turnabout in some contemporary propositions for modernity and move to ways in which this anthology joins endeavors to bring Eliot full circle.

It has become a critical commonplace that the purist New Critics considered incursions of the author's biography, personal feelings, or politics detrimental to the "impersonal" creative process whereby the author's disinterested discovery of a form (objective correlative) exactly matches an "aesthetic emotion." On the other side, as Tim Dean lucidly demonstrates in this volume, postmodern interpretations of Eliotic impersonality frequently evacuated the doctrine of its aesthetic value, interpreting impersonality rather as a pretense or "ruse" devised to deflect readers from the author's personal "deviant" desires or to exclude (sex, gender, race) difference from art. Epitomizing the former approach, James E. Miller suggested that Eliot's evocation of poetry as "an escape from emotion" "seems not shaped by the 'impersonal theory' but by a personal anguish (and the possible need for concealment)" caused by obsessive homoerotic desires.[32] Similarly, for Terry Eagleton, the impersonal "escape from emotion" masked "an extreme right-wing authoritarianism," potentially culminating in fascism.[33] And Maud Ellmann stressed impersonality's inborn "conservative" nature.[34]

By extension, postmodern readers frequently condemned the objective correlative's insistence on the "exact" correspondence between "word" and "thing" as a further policing of sexual/textual free-play that ensured entry into the oppressive symbolic order and the Law of the Father. Edward Larissy impugned the objective correlative's emphasis on "immediate presence of meaning" for halting "the difference and deferral of the signifying chain," adding that the "application of word to thing" is synonymous with "the law of the phallus and phallic sexuality."[35] Entitling a chapter of his *Discovering Modernism* "Problems about Objects," Louis Menand similarly objected to Eliot's implication that language aims straight for the object of its desire "like an arrow" (and thus suggested the phallic association).[36] For purist New Critics, then, social issues and biographical particularities encroached upon aesthetic creativity, while for many postmodernists and cultural critics formalist aesthetics merely camouflaged social prejudice.

From either perspective society canceled out art, and both pivoted, albeit at different angles of incidence, on Eliot's doctrines.

However, cultural and postmodern critics are increasingly concluding that a text's association with a socially prejudiced author need not contaminate its value as an aesthetic object or negate its attendant poetics.[37] Indeed, without attention to "what is said *as* poetry," the poem risks lapsing into a "message system for delivering ideas" ("PMM," 389). Seeking to "appreciate" modernism – both in the market and aesthetic sense – or to infuse an expanding field with aesthetic depth and coherence, therefore, current scholars of modernity are consciously formulating previously unthinkable merges of (New Critical) formalism with social critique.[38] Thus, in her recent book on modern poetry, DuPlessis urges a postformalist poetics she terms "a social philology," "offering reading strategies that can mediate between the [social,] historical terrain and the intimate poetic textures of a work."[39] Protesting that cultural criticism often sacrifices the joy of the unparaphrasable, she advocates a poetics that specifically links formal moves rejected by New Criticism – "social substance, biographical traces [and] historical debates" – with "New Critical care" and technique ("PMM," 389). DuPlessis's social philology embraces the intricate and proliferating mechanics of "the words on the page" first formalized by the New Critics and containing the following:

line break, stanza break and other segmentivities, caesurae, visual image and semantic image, etymology, phonemes, lateral associations, puns . . . including translingual puns, its own particular genres, the diegesis with its actors and pronouns, and the whole text with its speaker or persona.[40]

Her ensuing analysis of the subtle, intertwining misogynist and racist strands within the "textures and fabric" of Eliot's poetic language demonstrates that artistry can accompany, even inform, the warp and weave of social prejudice. Indeed, Anthony Julius's *T. S. Eliot, Anti-Semitism and Literary Form* similarly converges social concerns with aesthetics, arguing controversially that Eliot's genius animated stale, racist clichés into art.[41] And Marjorie Perloff, who formerly dismissed Eliot as a racist, misogynist, and linguistically fixed, Symbolist poet, now yokes the early "avant-garde Eliot" with cubism, surrealism, and postmodern linguistic free-play, reinstating him as a precursor to Gertrude Stein and contemporary artists.[42]

Such crossings of art and society are also occurring at the furthest reaches from the canon, in modernity studies of non-Western mass culture. Gesturing toward recent materialist studies – the abovementioned works on Eliot among them – Andreas Huyssen acknowledges the dissolution of the conceptual divide between high modernism and mass culture he mapped in *After the Great Divide* (and thus helped to deconstruct).[43] Affirming that cultural studies has "won the battle" in the academy, Huyssen warns that its self-imposed ban on important issues and cultural praxes associated with the elite, such as "aesthetic quality and form" and "our reading skills" ("what we do best"), risks "the danger" of rendering the field "superficial" or "incoherent" in global studies of non-Western, peripheral cultures ("HL," 365, 373). Rather he advocates combining the best of the old with the new, "recent theory [and cultural studies] with traditional critical practices of the disciplines . . . focusing, for example, on the complexity of repetition, rewriting and bricolage" ("HL," 365, 371). Denying the automatic assumption that elitism necessarily taints (high modernist) aesthetics, Huyssen would seem, in a global context, to answer the question posed by PMLA's call for papers "On Poetry" – "has the time come to revisit the relevance of the poetic text in this changed interpretive universe?" – by concluding that "the time has come to rescue [questions] of aesthetic value" posed by high culture for "all culture" ("HL," 373).

In keeping with modernity's inclination toward cross-methodological, cross-generational approaches, the authors in this collection speak across the divides in the academy. "Older" Eliot scholars rethink Eliot from new critical angles, bringing their total recall of his work and long acquaintance with its changing lights to bear in unexpected juxtapositions and surprising congruencies. "Newer" scholars who have served their apprenticeship in critical theory contribute their expertise to a poet often regarded as methodologically depleted. Thus queer theorist Tim Dean's important reassessment of Eliot's impersonality ushers this pivotal doctrine into modernity. Closing the gap between aesthetics and society, he redefines impersonality as an aesthetics not of "concealment" but of "access" that taps into socially marginal, "feminine," and homoerotic modes of creative receptivity. Like DuPlessis, Huyssen, and others, Dean calls upon both "old" and "new" literary approaches with the conscious intent to show "that something fundamental remains to be learned from the relation between transhistorical concepts of poetic utterance and modern forms of sexuality." Thus Dean's illumination of Eliot's doctrine combines traditional, literary linkages between the myth of the violated Philomel and the accession to poetic voice – from Ovid through the British Romantic poets – with Leo Bersani's Queer Theory of an ecstatic, "self-shattering" male passivity.[44]

Taking as his point of departure Eliot's response to "dissociated sensibility," Charles Altieri provocatively redefines Eliot's poetic innovations as the

Gramley Library
Salem Academy and College
Winston-Salem, N.C. 27108

creation of "an abstract modern imaginative space radically new for English poetry." Aligning Eliot with Lacan in his resistance to romantic notions of identity as a unified core self, Altieri argues that Eliot offered, in place of narrative causality for affective life, a language of emotions paralleling non-representational works in other modernist art. While Altieri reframes Eliot's modernist aesthetics in terms of philosophical conceptions of emotion, reason, and agency, Nancy K. Gish demonstrates that Eliot's early aesthetic theories are inseparable from psychological theories of self, identity, and personal as well as social functions of art. Tracing the sources in pre-Freudian, early twentieth-century psychology of multiple personality behind Eliot's notion of a "dissociation of sensibility" and his own use of then-current psychological terminology, she reveals in his early work a complex aesthetics fusing immediacy and abstraction, personal and "impersonal" in ways that remain indefinable without such a revised history. And Jewel Spears Brooker reads the volatile operations of mimetic desire in *The Waste Land* through the lens of René Girard's cultural analysis and the modernist return to origins, demonstrating how Eliot's employment of myth interwoven with his use of biography creates a poetics of escalating desire, violence, and crisis. Other essays combine cultural and theoretical approaches with close attention to the particularities of Eliot's language. Richard Badenhausen applies the richly metaphoric French feminist *écriture féminine* to the intricacies of Eliot's "feminine" bodily, experiential writing in the later plays. Colleen Lamos's inquiry into Eliot's elegiac homoeroticism yokes at once Judith Butler's psychoanalytic theory of melancholia and "the melancholic homoeroticism between men characteristic of the early twentieth century" with the intent to show how homoerotic "desires are woven into . . . the fabric [of Eliot's poetry] and displayed on its most innocent surfaces."

"AVANT-GARDE ELIOT"

Eliot's equations between poetry and culture, his role as "innovator" in the academy, and his initial mass appeal suggest his own progress toward dissolving the boundaries between art and society. As Gail McDonald's *Learning to be Modern: Pound, Eliot, and the American University* lucidly demonstrates, Eliot (like critics such as Huyssen) felt compelled to imbue his potentially sprawling, controversial field with cultural resonance, history, and intellectual/aesthetic depth. In the equally changing academy of early twentieth-century modernity, Eliot the outspoken proponent of contemporary poetry faced issues of aesthetics and cultural relevance which still resound a century later. He sided with the subversive vanguard during the historic and bitterly contested shift in the university from an exclusively classical, "scholarly" curriculum to one including more diverse electives such as contemporary literature in "the mother tongue." And just as 21st-century critics continue to fend off the unavailing legacies of high modernism, Eliot defended his field as socially responsive at a time when the prevailing literary criticism remained indiscriminately reverent, and literature the province of the elite, ineffectual, gentleman scholar.[45]

In perhaps another paradoxical alignment brought about by current redefinitions of modernity, Eliot's early theories of contemporary poetry bear on claims made by 1930s aesthetic/social theorist Walter Benjamin for the correspondence between history, experience, and aesthetics. Asserting that certain artistic forms (Baudelaire's poetry, Proust's narrative, or the film medium, for example) meet the changing perceptual/aesthetic needs of a public assaulted by the speed and sensory "shocks" of modern life, Benjamin lends new resonance to Eliot's famous words on the genesis and demands of contemporary poetry: "Our civilization comprehends great variety and complexity, and this variety and complexity playing upon a refined sensibility, must produce various and complex results . . . [requiring the poet] to force, to dislocate if necessary, language into his meaning."[46] Further, as the "spokesman for his generation," Eliot gained an initial reputation for directly translating the conditions of modern life into art roughly paralleled in "the poetry renaissance of the 1990s" described by Jan Clausen's "The Speed of Poetry" (the title of which links Benjamin's aesthetics of speed and sensory shocks to our own highly technological era).[47] Indeed, Muriel Bradbrook's evocation of her immediate response to *The Waste Land*, with which this introduction began, as "exhilarating," and "intensely stimulating," evinces just such an emotional/aesthetic seizure. Bradbrook further elaborated on the direct, experiential, and enduring impact Eliot continued to exert:

Our confusion was understood, our time had found a voice . . . great contemporary poetry met in youth . . . not only interprets experience but is itself an experience. It [*The Waste Land*] grew within my privileged generation, became part of ourselves, and has remained so.[48]

Felling a god in "Eliot at 101," Cynthia Ozick attributed Eliot's unprecedented popularity to the lure of an "unfamiliar," inaccessible poetry "bound by ribbons of ennui." But her vivid images of dormitory rooms where Eliot's poetry competed with pinups of Picasso, or of a football stadium filled with fourteen thousand people gathered to hear him lecture on criticism and poetry, conjure, perhaps unwittingly, his sudden electrifying effect on the public and academic imagination.[49]

NOTES

1. Quoted by Muriel Bradbrook in "Growing Up with T. S. Eliot," *DLB Yearbook* (Detroit: Gale Research Co., 1988), 110.
2. M. C. Bradbrook, "My Cambridge," in *Women and Literature 1779–1982*, (Brighton, Sussex: Harvester Press, 1982), 115.
3. May Sinclair's 1917 review of *Prufrock and Other Observations*, reprinted in *The Gender of Modernism*, ed. Bonnie Kime Scott (Bloomington: Indiana University Press, 1990), 448–53.
4. Colleen Lamos, *Deviant Modernism: Sexual and Textual Errancy in T. S. Eliot, James Joyce and Marcel Proust* (New York: Cambridge University Press, 1998), 103. Lamos's book constitutes the fullest, most up-to-date, and most varied study of Eliot's transgressive sex/gender energies. For an inquiry into the impact of the British Decadents on modes of eros in Eliot's poetry and poetics, see my "T. S. Eliot and A. C. Swinburne: Decadence, Desire, and Modern Modes of Perception," *Modernism/Modernity* 11, no. 3 (forthcoming September 2004).
5. Bonnie Kime Scott, "The Men of 1914," in *Refiguring Modernism*, vol. 1: *Women of 1928* (Bloomington: Indiana University Press, 1995). Scott argues for a webbing of influences between modernist women writers and their male contemporaries; she focuses on Eliot's ties to literary women, his impact on women writers, and his promotion of women's writing. See also Nancy K. Gish's discussions of Eliot, Marianne Moore, and Djuna Barnes, "T. S. Eliot," in *The Gender of Modernism*, ed. Bonnie Kime Scott (Bloomington: Indiana University Press, 1990), 139–43.
6. Marjorie Perloff, "Avant-Garde Eliot," in *21st Century Modernism: The "New" Poetics* (Malden: Blackwell, 2002), 10.
7. For Yeats, see Elizabeth Butler Cullingford's *Gender and History in Yeats's Love Poetry* (New York: Cambridge University Press, 1993). Important studies uncovering the sex/gender complexities of Joyce include Suzette Henke, *James Joyce and the Politics of Desire* (New York: Routledge, 1990); Colleen Lamos, *Deviant Modernism*; Christine Froula, *Modernism's Body: Sex, Culture and Joyce* (New York: Columbia University Press, 1996); and Lisa Rado, *The Modern Androgyne Imagination: A Failed Sublime* (Charlottesville: University of Virginia Press, 2000).
8. Michael North, *Reading 1922: A Return to the Scene of the Modern* (New York: Oxford University Press, 1999); hereafter abbreviated *RSM*; Janet Lyon, *Manifestoes: Provocations of the Modern* (Ithaca, N.Y.: Cornell University Press, 1999); hereafter abbreviated *M*; Lawrence Rainey, *Institutions of Modernism: Literary Elites and Popular Culture* (New Haven: Yale University Press, 1998); Rita Felski, *Doing Time: Feminist Theory and Postmodern Culture* (New York: New York University Press, 2000); hereafter abbreviated *DT*.
9. Rainey, *Institutions of Modernism*, 2.

10. Jeffrey M. Perl, *Skepticism and Modern Enmity: Before and after Eliot* (Baltimore: Johns Hopkins University Press, 1989), 10. While this anthology is not concerned with Eliot and philosophy, a number of studies have reclaimed Eliot for emancipatory, postmodern perceptions of metaphysics, history, and reality. These include Cleo McNelly Kearns, *T. S. Eliot and Indic Traditions* (New York: Cambridge University Press, 1987); Walter Benn Michaels, "Philosophy in Kinkanja: Eliot's Pragmatism," *Glyph* 8 (1981): 170–202; James Longenbach, *Modernist Poetics of History: Pound, Eliot, and the Sense of the Past* (Princeton, N.J.: Princeton University Press, 1987); Harriet Davidson, *T. S. Eliot and Hermeneutics: Absence and Interpretation in* The Waste Land (Baton Rouge: Louisiana State University Press, 1985); Richard Shusterman, *T. S. Eliot and the Philosophy of Criticism* (New York: Columbia University Press, 1988); and Michael Beehler, *T. S. Eliot, Wallace Stevens and the Discourses of Difference* (Baton Rouge: Louisiana State University Press, 1987).

11. See the two special sections, "T. S. Eliot and anti-Semitism: the Ongoing Debate" and "T. S. Eliot and anti-Semitism: the Ongoing Debate II" in *Modernism/Modernity* 10, no. 1 (January 2003) and 10, no. 3 (September 2003). David Chinitz, *T. S. Eliot and the Cultural Divide* (Chicago: University of Chicago Press, 2003).

12. Chinitz, *T. S. Eliot and the Cultural Divide*, 4.

13. For arguments concerning the contradictions implicit in Eliot's relation to Semitism, see Ronald Schuchard's "Burbank with a Baedeker, Eliot with a Cigar: American Intellectuals, Anti-Semitism, and the Idea of Culture," *Modernism/Modernity* (January 2003): 1–26; and Jonathan Freedman's "Lessons out of School: T. S. Eliot's Jewish Problem and the Making of Modernism," Bryan Cheyette's "Neither Excuse nor Accuse: T. S. Eliot's Semitic Discourse," Ranen Omer-Sherman's "Rethinking Eliot, Jewish Identity, and Cultural Pluralism," and Jeffrey Perl's "The Idea of a Jewish Society," all contained in *Modernism/Modernity* (September 2003): 1–47.

14. The most notable work arguing for a male-defined modernism remains Sandra Gilbert and Susan Gubar's three-volume study, *No Man's Land: The Place of the Woman Writer in the Twentieth Century* (New Haven: Yale University Press, 1988–94).

15. Gilbert and Gubar's first volume of *No Man's Land, The War of the Words* (New Haven: Yale University Press, 1988), dwelled on Eliot's violence toward women (31, 235–6). For studies treating the separate "male" and "female" traditions succeeding Gilbert and Gubar, see especially Suzanne Clark, *Sentimental Modernism: Women Writers and the Revolution of the Word* (Bloomington: Indiana University Press, 1992); Marianne DeKoven, *Rich and Strange: Gender, History, Modernism* (Princeton: Princeton University Press, 1991), which alludes to Eliot's aversion to "the maternal feminine" (190–3); Shari Benstock, *Women of the Left Bank: Paris, 1900–1940* (Austin: University of Texas Press, 1985); and Nancy K. Gish, "Eliot and Marianne Moore: Modernism and Difference," *Yeats-Eliot Review* 2, no. 2 (1991): 40–3. For other notable works treating Eliot's violence against women and aversion to the female body, see Tony Pinkney's

Women in the Poetry of T. S. Eliot: A Psychoanalytic Approach (London: Macmillan, 1984). Pinkney uses the work of Freud, D. W. Winnicott, and Melanie Klein to argue that Eliot's conflicted relation to the maternal body compels his textual violence toward women. See also Jacqueline Rose's *Sexuality in the Field of Vision* (London: Verso, 1986), in which Rose argues that Eliot's aversion to the Oedipal drama of Hamlet and particularly his disgust toward Gertrude in "Hamlet and His Problems" emerges from his perception of her as interfering with the Oedipal boy's transition from the mother into the symbolic order of the Law of the Father (123–36).

16. Lyndall Gordon, *Eliot's New Life* (New York: Farrar Straus Giroux, 1988), 3. See also Gordon's earlier biography *Eliot's Early Years* (New York: Oxford University Press, 1977). Gordon's most recent biography, *T. S. Eliot: An Imperfect Life* (New York: Norton, 1998), combines the two earlier biographies and revises some of her interpretations of and opinions about Eliot's attitudes (particularly toward women and Jews).

17. James E. Miller, Jr., *T. S. Eliot's Personal Waste Land: Exorcism of the Demons* (University Park: Pennsylvania State University Press, 1977). In an unpublished paper, "*T. S. Eliot's Personal Waste Land* Comes of Age," given at the December 1999 meeting of the Modern Language Association, Chicago, Ill., Miller describes the "indignation" aroused by his book appearing in reviews published in the *New York Review of Books*, the *New York Times Book Review*, the *Times Literary Supplement*, and elsewhere (2). Miller subsequently discussed the revival of interest in his book expressed in essays by queer theorists; see especially Merrill Cole's "Empire of the Closet," *Discourse* (Spring 1997): 67–91; and Wayne Koestenbaum's "The Waste Land: T. S. Eliot and Ezra Pound's Collaboration on Hysteria," in *Double Talk: The Erotics of Male Literary Collaboration* (New York: Routledge, 1999), 3. See Miller's more recent essay, "T. S. Eliot's 'Uranian Muse': The Verdenal Letters," *ANQ* (Fall 1998): 4–20. Carole Seymour-Jones, *Painted Shadow: The Life of Vivienne Eliot, First Wife of T. S. Eliot, and the Long-Suppressed Truth about Her Influence on His Genius* (New York: Doubleday, 2002).

18. Kenneth Asher describes Eliot as "the primary theoretical whipping boy of deconstruction" in *T. S. Eliot and Ideology* (New York: Cambridge University Press, 1995), 1. Asher's book is among those situating Eliot in the politics of his own milieu. His politicization of Eliot demonstrates the influence of Charles Maurras and the tradition of French reactionary thought from the beginning of his career.

19. Christine Froula, "Eliot's Grail Quest, or, the Lover, the Police and *The Waste Land*," *Yale Review* 78, no. 3 (1989): 235–53.

20. Maud Ellmann, *The Poetics of Impersonality: T. S. Eliot and Ezra Pound* (Cambridge, Mass.: Harvard University Press, 1987), 1–132. Andrew Ross, *The Failure of Modernism: Symptoms of American Poetry* (New York: Columbia University Press, 1986), 3–92.

21. Rainey, *Institutions of Modernism*, 2. See Rita Felski's discussion of how postmodernism was perceived as "coming after and redeeming the modern" in debates surrounding postmodernism in the 1970s and 1980s (*DT*, 60–1).

22. Ross argues in *The Failure of Modernism* that such a failure is exemplified by Eliot's *The Waste Land* and other works which, despite their struggle with issues of subjectivity, language, and desire, ultimately reassert "purification" through religious authority or authoritarianism (4–92).

23. For discussions of the movement from postmodernism to a more inclusive modernity-at-large with an emphasis on cultural studies (including gender studies), see also *Questions of Modernity*, ed. Timothy Mitchell (Minneapolis: University of Minnesota Press, 2000); Susan Stanford Friedman, *Mappings: Feminism and the Cultural Geographies of Encounter* (Princeton, N.J.: Princeton University Press, 1998); Rita Felski, *The Gender of Modernity* (Cambridge, Mass.: Harvard University Press, 1995) and *Doing Time*; Michael North, *The Dialect of Modernism: Race, Language and Twentieth-Century Literature* (New York: Oxford University Press, 1999) and *Reading 1922*; and Andreas Huyssen, "High/Low in an Expanded Field," *Modernism/Modernity* 9, no. 3 (2002): 363–74; hereafter abbreviated "HL." On the contradictory meanings of "modernity," see Susan Stanford Friedman, "Definitional Excursions: The Meanings of Modern/Modernity/Modernism," *Modernism/Modernity* 8, no. 3 (2001): 493–513.

24. Rainey, *Institutions of Modernism*, 3. See also Leonard Diepeveen, "'I Can Have More Than Enough Power to Satisfy Me': T. S. Eliot's Construction of His Audience," in *Marketing Modernisms: Self-Promotion, Canonization and Rereading*, ed. Kevin J. H. Dettmar and Stephen Watt (Ann Arbor: University of Michigan Press, 1996), 37–60.

25. For essays on Eliot and popular culture, see also Barry J. Faulk, "Modernism and the Popular: Eliot's Music Halls," *Modernism/Modernity* 8, no. 4 (2001): 603–21; Sebastian D. G. Knowles, "'Then You Wink the Other Eye': T. S. Eliot and the Music Hall," *ANQ* 11 (1998): 20–32; and Ronald Schuchard, *Eliot's Dark Angel: Intersections of Life and Art* (New York: Oxford University Press, 1999), 102–18.

26. Maud Ellmann, *The Poetics of Impersonality*, 93–109. Tim Armstrong, *Modernism, Technology and the Body: A Cultural Study* (New York: Cambridge University Press, 1998), 68–74.

27. *Behind the Lines: Gender and the Two World Wars*, ed. Margaret Higonnet (New Haven: Yale University Press, 1987), 3.

28. Elaine Scarry, *On Beauty and Being Just* (Princeton, NJ: Princeton University Press, 1999); Marjorie Perloff, "In Defense of Poetry," *Boston Review* (January 2000): 22–31; Rachel Blau DuPlessis, *Genders, Races, and Religious Cultures in Modern American Poetry, 1908–1934* (New York: Cambridge University Press, 2001); Andreas Huyssen, "High/Low in an Expanded Field"; and Jan Clausen, "The Speed of Poetry," *Nation* (July 2000): 38–42. Critics urging a return to the aesthetic frequently refer back to the leftist, modernist debates of the 1930s by Walter Benjamin, Ernst Bloch, Theodor Adorno, and others. These debates are outlined in Ernst Bloch et al., *Aesthetics and Politics* (London: Verso, 1977).

29. "PMLA Special Topic: On Poetry," *MLA Newsletter* 34, no. 3 (2002): 13.

30. Rachel Blau DuPlessis, "Propounding Modernist Maleness: How Pound Managed a Muse," *Modernism/Modernity* 9, no. 3 (2002): 388; hereafter

abbreviated "PMM." This essay is from material left over from DuPlessis's *Genders, Races, and Religious Cultures in Modern American Poetry, 1908–1934*, and it also propounds her theory of a "social philology of words."

31. Clausen, "The Speed of Poetry," 24; Perloff, "In Defense of Poetry," 25, 26.

32. Miller, *T. S. Eliot's Personal Waste Land*, 36.

33. Terry Eagleton, *Literary Theory: An Introduction* (Minneapolis: University of Minnesota Press, 1983), 39.

34. Ellmann, *The Poetics of Impersonality*, 198–9.

35. Edward Larissy, *Reading Twentieth-Century Poetry: The Language of Gender and Objects* (Cambridge, Mass.: Basil Blackwell, 1990), 33, 34. See also Andrew Ross's *The Failure of Modernism* for how the New Critics appropriated Eliot's comments on the primacy of the eye over the ear for their view of the text as "a fetishized object of cognition [from which] the subject becomes entirely disconnected" (29). In *Women of the Left Bank*, Shari Benstock observes that Pound's subject-object "equation" imposes a phallogocentric notion of language (327, 328)

36. Louis Menand, *Discovering Modernism: T. S. Eliot and His Context* (New York: Oxford University Press, 1987), 35.

37. Theoretically sophisticated critics calling for a return to the aesthetic may seem, ironically, to be echoing their New Critical counterparts who wished still to value Eliot's poetry despite their distaste for the turn that his religion and politics had taken. However, it must be stressed that recent cultural critics do not regard aesthetics as "transcending" social concerns.

38. Jennifer Wicke also stresses the importance of aesthetic appreciation and issues of value that do not depend on distinction or taste in "Appreciation, Depreciation: Modernism's Speculative Bubble," *Modernism/Modernity* 8, no. 3 (2001): 389–403. Wicke asserts that "enthusiastic appreciations of modernism can be (should be) rigorous, historical, aesthetically incisive, and politically aware all at once" (402).

39. DuPlessis, *Genders, Races, and Religious Cultures in Modern American Poetry, 1908–1934*, 1.

40. Ibid.

41. Anthony Julius, *T. S. Eliot, Anti-Semitism and Literary Form* (New York: Cambridge University Press, 1995).

42. Perloff, "Avant-Garde Eliot," in *21st Century Modernism*, 25, 26. Jeffrey Perl anticipated Perloff's resituating of Eliot in *Skepticism and Modern Enmity* where he observed that Eliot "was a skeptic, whose politics and baptism might be viewed, but are not, as the gestures of a dadaist against an avant-garde establishment" (xii).

43. Andreas Huyssen, *After the Great Divide: Modernism, Mass Culture, Postmodernism (Theories of Representation and Difference)* (Bloomington: Indiana University Press, 1986).

44. Leo Bersani, *Homos* (Cambridge, Mass.: Harvard University Press, 1995).

45. Gail McDonald, *Learning to be Modern: Pound, Eliot, and the American University* (London: Oxford University Press, 1993), 53.

46. For his discussions of film, poetry, and technological society, see Walter Benjamin, "On Some Motifs in Baudelaire," "The Image of Proust," and "The Work of Art in the Age of Mechanical Reproduction," in *Illuminations*, ed. Hannah Arendt (New York: Schocken, 1968). T. S. Eliot, "The Metaphysical Poets," in *Selected Essays, 1917–1932* (New York: Harcourt Brace, 1932), 248. For works considering the influence of Benjamin's thought on film, the arts, poetry, and modes of attention, see especially Jonathan Crary, *Suspensions of Perception: Attention, Spectacle, and Modern Culture* (Cambridge, Mass.: MIT Press, 2001); Miriam Hansen, "Benjamin, Cinema and Experience: The Blue Flower in the Land of Technology," *New German Critique* 40 (Winter 1987): 179–224; *Walter Benjamin*, ed. David S. Ferris (Stanford, Calif.: Stanford University Press, 1996); Alessia Ricciardi, "Cinema Regained: Godard between Proust and Benjamin," *Modernism/Modernity* 9, no. 3 (2001): 643–61; and Susan McCabe, "'Delight in Dislocation': The Cinematic Modernism of Stein, Chaplin, and Man Ray," *Modernism/Modernity* 8, no. 3 (2001): 429–52.

47. Clausen, "The Speed of Poetry," 38.

48. Bradbrook, *Women and Literature, 1779–1982,* 115.

49. Cynthia Ozick, "Eliot at 101," *New Yorker*, November 20, 1989, 120.

PART I

Homoeroticisms

CHAPTER I

The love song of T. S. Eliot: elegiac homoeroticism in the early poetry

Colleen Lamos

T. S. Eliot presents the dilemma of an avowedly heterosexual, homophobic writer whose work is obliquely yet significantly marked by homoerotic investments. How is one to understand such libidinal investments? Given the homophobic cultural climate of the twentieth century, what are the conditions under which a man's love for men could be articulated? Same-sex desires, like those for the other sex, are diverse phenomena; they do not spring from a fundamental essence, whose literary representations either obscure or reveal one's true self, but have multiple constituents and diverse manifestations. Moreover, same-sex desires are complexly interwoven with masculine and feminine identifications. Uncovering homoerotic impulses does not unlock the enigma of Eliot's personality, nor are they the hidden truth of his work. Instead of operating as the scandalous key to Eliot's writings, those desires are woven into its fabric and displayed on its most innocent surfaces. Paradoxically, I will argue, the conditions of possibility for Eliot's representation of homoeroticism are precisely the conditions for their disavowal.

The challenge of understanding the homoeroticism of Eliot's work is compounded by the fact that he actively suppressed public discussion of the issue. Although he almost never commented upon interpretations of his work, Eliot censored the only essay to appear in his lifetime that ventured a homosexual reading of *The Waste Land*. When John Peter published "A New Interpretation of *The Waste Land*" in 1952 – an essay in which the word "homosexual" is never mentioned – Eliot threatened a libel suit against him and demanded the destruction of all extant copies of the issue of *Essays in Criticism* in which the offending article appeared. Peter understands *The Waste Land* as an elegy whose subtext is as follows: "At some previous time the speaker has fallen completely – perhaps the right word is 'irretrievably' in love. The object of this love was a young man who soon afterwards met his death, it would seem by drowning."[1] In a 1969 "Postscript" to the essay, Peter is more explicit, asserting that "one can hardly avoid the conclusion that in his youth [Eliot] had a close romantic attachment to another young man, and that this far from uncommon type of friendship was rudely cut short when the other was drowned," adding that the young man was likely Jean Verdenal, Eliot's intimate friend during his years in Paris, who was killed in World War I (166). Although Peter does not pursue the psychological ramifications of same-sex mourning and employs only textual evidence to support a tentative biographical thesis, his claim that *The Waste Land* is an elegy on "the order of *In Memoriam*" was the impetus for the present study.[2] Unlike Peter, however, I argue that the elegiac mode was a means for Eliot *simultaneously* to affirm and to repudiate same-sex affection. In short, the literary register that enabled him to articulate homo-eroticism is the same that permitted his – and his critics' – denial of it. The intertwining of homophilia and homophobia in the same gesture attests to the productivity of the homosexual prohibition, which feeds upon the desire that it constrains.

Peter's 1952 essay was reprinted in *Essays in Criticism* in 1969, accompanied by a bizarre "Postscript" in which he volubly denies any knowledge of homosexuality and clears Eliot of any carnal knowledge of it as well. After mentioning how upset his wife was over his contretemps with Eliot, Peter says that he wrote him "a full apology for causing the poet pain and annoyance, offering . . . to withdraw my interpretation by publishing [a] . . . retraction" (165). He seems to have regarded the matter as "a breach of manners" by raising improper suggestions concerning Eliot's private life. "Discretion failed me," he confesses (169), but he nevertheless offers further evidence for his original thesis. Peter concludes his double-voiced defense, on the one hand, by asserting that Eliot's mask of impersonal classicism was "romanticism running scared," and, on the other hand, by repudiating his own argument. Maybe he leapt to conclusions and, besides, such a "recondite and labyrinthine modern poem" as *The Waste Land* cannot bear "pat answers" like his (172). Above all, Peter denies what he obscurely calls the "further meanings" that his un-named homosexual interpretation implied, claiming "incomprehension" of them (173). Citing Eliot's drama *The Elder Statesman*, Peter casts himself as Gomez, the false accuser of Lord Claverton, played by Eliot, who must "vindicate himself against the unfounded extensions" of Peter's essay. Eliot, like Claverton, is guilty of no "actual misconduct," his play "disavowing once and for all what my essay may have seemed to imply about the genesis of *The Waste Land*" (174–5). Peter's mea culpa, with its equivocations – I didn't know what I was doing; I'm sorry, but I was right anyway; it's only a private matter, although *The Waste Land* is a public poem; Eliot might have had a "romantic attachment," but he didn't commit sodomy – enacts the painful equivocations and denials that have marked discussions of the embarrassing problem of homoeroticism in Eliot's work. E. W. F. Tomlin is typical in his complaint against what he calls the "favourite charge" of homosexuality: "The difficulty with the present liberal attitude to homosexuality . . . is that all male friendships of sufficient closeness become automatically the subject of raised eyebrows."[3]

Eliot's denial of homosexuality and his suppression of queer readings of his work have been remarkably successful. Just as critics have been content for nearly a century to accept (or to reject, but often on the same grounds) the guidelines that Eliot laid out in his critical essays for the interpretation of his poetry, so, too, they have almost without exception followed his repudiation of homoeroticism. Critical obeisance to Eliot's dicta during the mid-years of the twentieth century was mirrored by the wholesale rejection of Eliot's authority in its closing decades, so that Cynthia Ozick, for instance, claimed in a 1989 essay that "*we no longer live in the literary shadow of T. S. Eliot* . . . The passion for inheritance is dead." No longer relevant for literary study, she claims, "now Eliot's elegiac fragments appear too arcane, too aristocratic, and too difficult."[4] In a sense, we as 21st-century readers of Eliot stand in a post-elegiac relationship to his texts.

Queer theorists have rarely taken a glance at Eliot, and what gay scholarship exists has been driven into the narrow channel of biographical speculation. Eliot's censorship of Peter's essay resulted in total silence on the subject for twenty-five years. James E. Miller's 1977 landmark study, *T. S. Eliot's Personal Waste Land*, takes up Peter's claim that *The Waste Land* was motivated by Eliot's grief over the death of Verdenal, supporting it by a detailed and insightful interpretation of the poem that links the latter with the figures of Phlebas the Phoenician and the "hyacinth girl" via the oft-quoted line from Ariel's song in *The Tempest* (1. 2. 398): "Those are pearls that were his eyes."[5] Miller's scholarship remains necessary for understanding the gay subtext of *The Waste Land*, but his work is limited by its biographical focus; lacking the tools of queer theory, Miller falls back on the Verdenal thesis to ground his argument.

Miller's book was largely ignored or dismissed. Scholars such as Ronald Bush and A. D. Moody simply disregarded it in their influential studies of Eliot.[6] Those more sensitive to the gender politics of Eliot's poetry and personal life have argued defensively that his misogyny does *not* imply a latent homosexuality. Peter Ackroyd, for example, claims that "it would be the tritest form of reductionism to assume that Eliot, because he could not adequately deal with female sexuality, was therefore homosexual . . . When

he allowed his sexuality free access, . . . it was of a heterosexual kind."
Ackroyd decries the search for a hidden scandal in Eliot's life: "The suggestions of homosexuality are . . . one aspect of the attempt to discover some
'mystery' which he wished to conceal."[7] What Ackroyd does not envision
is that homoeroticism, far from being a guilty secret, might be constitutive
of the *least* shameful aspects of Eliot's poetry. His defense of Eliot against
the imputation of homosexuality assumes that it is fundamentally incon-
gruent with heterosexual desires. Instead, one might argue that Eliot had
no "free access" to either same- or other-sex desires but that both impulses
were locked in conflict with his sense of masculinity and with his embattled
relation to femininity. To grasp the significance of the homoerotic energies
in Eliot's texts requires that we go beyond the limited homo/hetero binary
and examine the *productivity* of the homosexual prohibition upon his writings – that is, the ways in which that taboo, in conjunction with his sense
of masculine affiliation and his troubled relation to femininity, generated
the most remarkable poetry of the early twentieth century.

Until recently, critics have taken a hesitant, noncommittal attitude
toward the issue of Eliot's homoeroticism, which is typically framed in
terms of his friendship to Verdenal. In her 1998 biography, *T. S. Eliot: An
Imperfect Life*, Lyndall Gordon cautiously leaves the issue suspended in a
question: "Who can now determine the exact ways people of the past bent
their inclinations in order to construct gender according to absurd models of masculinity or femininity? Verdenal was easy with Eliot," helping
him to unbend his usually stiff personality. "The Frenchman's most important legacy for Eliot was to offer a blend of sensibility and intellect."[8] In
contrast to her detailed investigation of Eliot's relationships with women,
Gordon avoids any analysis of his relationships with men and fails to explore
the homoerotic aspects either of his friendship with Verdenal or of his
poetry, preferring to read the latter in terms of his spiritual vocation as a
Christian. She throws up her hands at the possibility of grasping the intricacies of same-sex affection, revealing a willful ignorance of gay historical
scholarship.

John T. Mayer offers a more ample account of what he calls Eliot's "very
special relationship" with Verdenal in his 1989 book, *T. S. Eliot's Silent
Voices*. Mayer places the love between Verdenal and Eliot in an obfuscating
and exculpatory foreign context: "The nature of this love is ambiguous, but
European traditions of male friendship recognized various kinds of male
bonding, as well as different ways of expressing affection between males
unknown to the inhibiting codes that governed male-to-male behavior in
the United States."[9] Mayer's sympathetic but confusing and unsupported

explanation of Eliot's relationship to Verdenal seems to be that, in France, anything goes. More persuasively, he argues that Eliot's unhappy marriage to Vivien Haigh-Wood "altered . . . his appreciation of his friendship with Verdenal . . . The relationship was transformed in Eliot's mind: a friendship that had died was resurrected in memory and charged with an imaginative power quite beyond the living experience."[10] Verdenal's death enabled Eliot, in his poems of the late 1910s and early 1920s, to transform him into an object of love. Despite the shortcomings of Mayer's argument, it frames Eliotic homoeroticism in an elegiac context. In contrast to the murderous aesthetic transfiguration performed in, for instance, "La Figlia" and the "marriage" monologues of this period, such as "Exequy," "Elegy," and "The Death of the Duchess," same-sex mourning in Eliot renders the lost object of desire beautiful after death.

Carole Seymour-Jones's *Painted Shadow*, a recently published, ground-breaking biography of Vivien, makes the strongest case to date for the significance and scope of Eliot's homoerotic experience. In addition to providing a detailed description of his friendship with Verdenal, she examines the erotic triangle between Eliot, his wife, and Bertrand Russell, arguing that "there was an element of homosexuality by proxy in the way in which Eliot offered Vivien to Russell."[11] Although Seymour-Jones neglects to explore the psychological ramifications of such triangulated desire, which fits the pattern first analyzed by Eve Kosofsky Sedgwick,[12] she offers a wealth of hitherto unknown information concerning Eliot's relationships with numerous young men throughout the 1920s and 30s, including Léonide Massine, a dancer with the Ballets Russes, and a German youth named Jack, who shared a cottage with the Eliots for six months. She concludes that "there is little doubt that [Jack] was, in fact, romantically and sexually involved with Tom" (368). Her extensive research turns up others, such as Philip Ritchie, a gay young man who occasionally stayed at Eliot's private rooms in Burleigh Mansions – a hideaway that enabled him to lead a double life. Eliot's obsessive interest in sodomy is evident in his pornographic verses, which shocked even Ezra Pound, who urged him to "try to normalfy your vices" (535). While some of Seymour-Jones's speculations are controversial, the breadth of her archival discoveries confirms the range and importance of both Eliot's homoeroticism and his homophobia.

In general, romantic love is represented as elegiac in Eliot's poetry. When the lost one is female, as in "Elegy," she is almost invariably execrated, but when the lost one is male, as in the "Death by Water" section of *The Waste Land*, he is venerated. As he wrote of John Webster in "Whispers of Immortality," Eliot was himself a man "much possessed by death." While nearly all forms of human passion – both hetero and homo – are represented in his early poems as in some sense morbid, that morbidity possesses distinctively different valences when the dead object is male rather than female. Only when the latter is male do Eliot's texts frame the loss in tender, memorial tones. By contrast, when the latter is female, his texts typically represent the departed in an aggressive or guilty manner. In both cases, death is the condition of the possibility for (or the outcome of) the expression of passion, whether affectionate or hostile.

Generically and emotionally, homoeroticism in Eliot's early poetry is elegiac inasmuch as it commemorates a love for the dead. Regardless of its biographical sources, the structure of this desire is indicative of the configuration of melancholic homoeroticism between men characteristic of the early twentieth century. Indeed, Eliotic melancholia seems expressive of a cast of mind characteristic of modern masculinity as a whole. With the advent of the sharp division between heterosexuality and homosexuality in this period, love between men was rendered pathological, resulting in the phenomenon that Sedgwick has called "homosexual panic." Eliot's disgust at and suppression of the Peter article is ample evidence of such a panic, yet his repudiation of homosexuality renders all the more compelling an examination of the conditions of an avowal of love between men in the early twentieth century. Eliot's strategy for affirming a denied or refused love appears to be one of displacement through the elegiac mode. More than an individual strategy, though, Eliot's poetry exemplifies what Judith Butler has described as a general "heterosexual melancholia" common to modern Western culture, in which normative gender and sexual identities are the products of the disavowal of homosexual attachments.

"Elegiac love" operates on several levels in Eliot's texts. The term, as I use it, embraces the many representations of love for dead men in his early poetry, so frequent as to constitute one of its most powerful themes. On the psychological level, these representations, taken together with the pervasive morbidity of his poetry, suggests that such love is structured as melancholic. This psychosexual dynamic is historically and culturally produced rather than a timeless truth of the unconscious or merely a peculiarity of Eliot's personal psyche. Finally, the homoerotic elegiacism of Eliot's poetry parallels the citational practice of his literary criticism, which memorializes a set of poetic forefathers with whom Eliot passionately identified and who, though dead, breathed life into his poetry. On each of these three levels – the thematic, the psychosexual, and the citational or intertextual – the elegiac mode enables the expression of affection but also permits the disavowal of a dangerous homosexuality. In short, in the elegy, the conditions of possibility for the expression of love are also the conditions for its denial. This is not to say that Eliot was latently homosexual but rather that he found a way of articulating same-gender desire that eluded the narrow terms of homosexual definition in his day and that affirmed his masculine identity. Such a strategy, which relies upon a poetic patrimony, was available to other male modernist writers but not to women. While the implications of Eliot's strategy for modernist literature call for further exploration, in the remainder of this essay I will examine the aforementioned aspects of elegiac love in Eliot's early poetry and offer readings of two poems, "The Love Song of St. Sebastian" and "The Death of Saint Narcissus," that exemplify such a love.

Eliot's mourning possesses the "emotional intensity and violence" that he sympathetically observed in Tennyson's lament for Arthur Hallam – in Eliot's words, an "emotion so deeply suppressed, even from himself, as to tend . . . toward the blackest melancholia" and reaching "no ultimate clear purgation."[13] In one sense, mourning the loss of a friend afforded Eliot, like Tennyson, freedom from homophobic self-censorship; death is the condition of possibility for giving breath to a love that, in life, has fatal consequences. The "pearls that were his eyes" of *The Waste Land* are beautiful only beneath the waves. In a more profound sense, Eliot constitutes himself, as an authorial subject, as already mortified. The personae in his early poetry typically speak as though they were entombed, and Eliot seems to have envisioned himself as enduring a living death. His "mortuary eroticism," in Frank Kermode's phrase, serves less as a legitimation for a denigrated homosexual passion than as a way of achieving imaginary union with the lost one.[14] Embracing in death like Dickens's mutual friends, Eliot's speakers identify with the deceased in a gesture that commingles desire and resemblance. Like Phlebas and the other drowned young men whom they tenderly describe, Eliot's speakers seem to wish to *become* them as well as to touch and possess them. Such an identificatory wish is characteristic of mourning.

An example of this recurrent pattern of postmortem love and an important intertextual site of homoeroticism in Eliot's early poetry is Statius's speech to Virgil in Dante's *Purgatorio*.[15] Addressing Virgil, his poetic mentor and dear friend, Statius says,

> So may you find
> the measure of the love that warms me to you
> when for it I lose all else from my mind,
> forgetting we are empty semblances
> and taking shadows to be substances.
>
> (Canto XXI, ll. 133–6)[16]

Eliot cited these lines as the epigraph to *Ara Vos Prec* (1920) and subsequently placed them at the head of the Prufrock section of *Poems: 1909–1925*. The shadowy voice of Statius in Purgatory resonated for Eliot with that of the late Verdenal. In the 1925 edition of *Poems* he brought together the earlier dedication to Verdenal of *Prufrock and Other Observations* (1917) with the quotation from Dante, affirming the posthumous significance of his friendship with Verdenal.[17] In subsequent editions, the Prufrock section ("Prufrock and Other Observations") remains headed by the double epigraph, "For Jean Verdenal, 1889–1915/mort aux Dardanelles," followed by Statius's speech, quoted in Italian.

Eliot's citation of Statius's speech, like his more frequent quotation of that of Arnaut Daniel, another penitent, is representative of a common rhetorical structure in his early poetry, what I call "the voice from the dead." The speaker of "Exequy," for example, addresses the reader from the grave and concludes by reciting Daniel's line "be mindful in due time of my pain" (*Purgatorio*, Canto XXVI, l. 147). The "dead jew eyes" of "Dirge," another unpublished poem from 1915, stare up luridly from under water. "Dirge" is a parodic version of Ariel's song, opening with the line "Full fathom five your Bleistein lies." Similarly, "Elegy" – a third unpublished poem that appeared in the *Facsimile* edition of *The Waste Land* – is, as Miller puts it, an "anti-elegy" in which the speaker, "as in a tale by Poe," tries to stifle the return of the ghost of his dead wife, the "wrong'd Aspatia," who refuses to remain in her "charnel vault."[18] Finally, one of the most interesting but overlooked poems of this period is "Ode," in which the author surrogate in the poem – a young bridegroom and failed poet – seems to write his own elegy from beneath the waves, his corpse a narcissistic reflection of his creator's morbid life. The motif of drowning is relentlessly reiterated in Eliot's texts, from "The Love Song of J. Alfred Prufrock," "Hysteria," and *The Waste Land* through *Four Quartets* and *The Family Reunion*. I have argued elsewhere that this motif of "death by water" reflects the rather obvious threat of female sexuality as well as Eliot's erotic idealization of the "Phlebas" figure.[19] The elegiac plangency and doomed narcissism of this figure is also reminiscent of Ezra Pound's self-memorialization in the first section of "Hugh Selwyn Mauberley."

The elegiac aspect of Eliot's poetry has been noted by a number of critics besides Peter, most recently by Jahan Ramazani, who, paraphrasing Eliot, observes that "his 'thought clings round dead limbs,' betraying a strong affinity for the elegy," and that "the elegy is one of the most important genres in [his] poetry."[20] Like Miller and Gregory Jay, Ramazani points out the presence of formal and stylistic elements of the genre of the elegy in

The Waste Land as well as the poem's well-known allusions to Whitman's "When Lilacs Last in the Dooryard Bloomed" and Milton's "Lycidas."[21] In keeping with the revisionist tendency of modern elegies, according to Ramazani, *The Waste Land* rejects the consolations of the traditional elegy in favor of an ironic and irredemptive stance toward death.

Most critics who regard *The Waste Land* as elegiac ask, understandably, for what or whom did Eliot mourn? What loss or whose death prompted Eliot's grief? The list of candidates is often rehearsed: Verdenal, in Eliot's words, "mixed with the mud of Gallipoli"[22]; Western literature, whose demise is recorded in the poem's allusive fragmentation; or, most broadly, Western civilization itself, ravaged by the Great War and modernity in general. Each of these candidates is in various ways an unsatisfactory answer to the question "Who died?" The poet's profound mourning seems motivated less by the death of someone or something than by an obscure yet pervasive sense of loss. Eliot would not and *could not* name his grief, I argue, because it is primarily not for a person or an object exterior to himself but is constitutive of himself as a subject. This is not to say that Eliot did not mourn the death of Verdenal or the decline of Western culture, but rather that the extent and structure of his melancholia suggests that it is fundamental to his subjective constitution and poetic practice. At bottom, Eliot's melancholia is not for a particular person but for a kind of love – that is, for an erotic aim, not an object.

In "Mourning and Melancholia," Freud argues that the melancholic responds to grief by incorporating the lost beloved within his ego.[23] Unwilling to give up his commitment to the beloved, he identifies with the latter in a regressively narcissistic move. The mingling of identification and desire in Eliot's elegiac references to dead young men, the mirroring relation between his speakers and those whom they mourn, and, finally, the echolalic effect of Eliot's poetic ventriloquism and his citational practice in general support a reading of homoeroticism in his texts as an imaginary incorporation of the dead. Such an identificatory union dissolves the distinction between mourner and corpse, thus threatening the dissolution of the elegist himself and the collapse of generic form, resulting in poems that, like Edgar Allan Poe's tales, feature a self-doubled, consciously dead speaker who gazes upon his own, ghostly self.[24]

The identificatory impulse in Eliot's early poems runs the risk of feminizing – and homosexualizing – their speakers. Rejecting the Victorian convention of sentimental, "womanly" grief (the Emmeline Grangerford tradition), modernist male elegists adopted a tough, satiric posture toward mourning that, while remasculinizing the genre, nonetheless betrayed the

homoeroticism that lurks within expressions of longing for and identification with dead friends or dead authors.[25] One recalls Eliot's essay on
In Memoriam and his 1919 article "Reflections on Contemporary Poetry,"
in which he discusses his "passionate" "feeling of profound kinship or . . .
peculiar personal intimacy with . . . a dead author."[26] Moreover, the remas-
culinization of the genre of the elegy points to the repudiation, by male
modernist writers, of feminine identifications, a repudiation that is a prerequisite of the heterosexualization of male desire, a process that is nonetheless
haunted by the residue of its forgotten losses.

According to Freud, the melancholic refuses to abandon his erotic
cathexis on a person whom he has loved and lost, unlike the mourner,
who eventually accepts his bereavement.[27] This refusal of abandonment
consists of two conflicting processes: first, the melancholic internalizes the
beloved within his ego, thus identifying with and preserving the lost person.
Second, he splits off a part of the ego (a part that Freud later calls the super-
ego), which, bearing his denied anger at his loss, torments the other part of
the ego that identifies with and preserves the beloved, thereby generating a
psychic battle that leads to an impasse. Freud assumed that melancholia is
an aberrant response to deprivation – an experience that befalls an already
constituted subject who refuses to come to grips with reality – but Judith
Butler argues that melancholia is the founding moment of subjectivation.

Butler's influential concept of "heterosexual melancholia" offers a useful conceptual paradigm for understanding the elegiac character of Eliot's
poetry, including his "elegiac" citational practice, and so warrants a cursory
account. In *The Psychic Life of Power*, she argues that, in a heteronormative society, subjects can achieve proper masculinity and femininity only
by abandoning early homosexual attachments. The child's renunciation
of the parent of the same sex as an object of love requires that both the
homosexual aim and the homosexual object be foreclosed, not transferred
onto a substitute. Instead of simply giving up one's love for the same-sex
parent, the very possibility of such a love must be forsworn and forgotten,
resulting in what Butler calls the "never-never" of homosexual disavowal:
for the heterosexualized subject, same-sex love never happened and was
never lost. That negated love is preserved through "melancholic incorporation" in the form of *identification* with the parent of the same sex. As a
consequence, "melancholic identification is central to the process whereby
the ego assumes a gendered character."[28]

Butler seizes upon Freud's concept of melancholia, first, because foreclosure, as she sees it, is an original, "preemptive loss" that precedes and forms
the self-reflexive subject and, second, because particular, socially regulated

foreclosures are constitutive of normal subjectivity. Specifically, the barring of homosexuality is "foundational" to what she terms "a certain heterosexual version of the subject" (23). Melancholia is the typical condition of heterosexual subjectivation in twentieth-century Western, heteronormative culture, while homosexual desire is the unconscious, disavowed abject of the normal, straight person's psychic constitution. Instead of an extreme version of mourning, as Freud saw it, melancholia is characteristic of the way in which subjects in general are formed. More than a psychological process of bereavement, melancholia, in Butler's final formulation in *The Psychic Life of Power*, is a decisive and apparently universal event in the prehistory of the ego, an originary moment that happens once and for all, and of which the subject is necessarily unaware. It is certainly not an affective state. For Butler, melancholia lies at the source of the psyche itself, denoting the primordial turn that "divide[s] . . . the ego and object" (170) and that generates the ego as its own, self-reflexive object. "The [melancholic] turn from the [lost] object to the ego produces the ego" as a *"psychic object"* (168; emphasis Butler's), so that "there can be no ego without melancholia" (171). In short, the ontological distinction between subject and object is the aftereffect of an "opaque" primal scene in which what will become the subject defends itself against the deprivation of the beloved, same-sex object by withdrawing the latter into itself. The ego "is the retroactive product" of this melancholic infolding (177). In Butler's scenario of the genesis of the reflexive subject, the object preexists the subject, which emerges as such only upon the withdrawal and subsequent incorporation of the lost object into itself, the subject thus becoming, in part, that object.

Among the problems and possibilities of Butler's scheme, it is noteworthy that, paradoxically, her attempt to denaturalize heterosexuality makes it difficult to understand how anyone could *not* become heterosexual. By situating homosexual foreclosure at the inaugural moment of the ego, Butler implies that the disavowal of same-sex love is structural to the very creation of the ego. In short, the ego is heterosexualized at birth. Although one might subsequently refuse heterosexual interpellation (as she argues), the process of subjectivation in a society such as ours is ineluctably heterosexual. As critics have observed, her model of subject formation requires a voluntaristic understanding of an human agent who is capable of bucking the very forces by which she has been constituted. Eliot was not such a resistant subject, however; indeed, he is a textbook illustration of her theory.

In Butler's terms, the elegiac mourning and the sadomasochistic violence of Eliot's early poetry are manifestations of heterosexual melancholia, in which disavowed same-sex love is partly incorporated within the self, and partly split off and debased through the torments of a sadistic conscience. Refusing to grieve his unacknowledged losses, Eliot wrote that disavowal into his texts. In a letter to Conrad Aiken in which he enclosed "The Love Song of St. Sebastian," Eliot wrote, "I have studied S. Sebastians – why would anyone paint a beautiful youth and stick him full of pins (or arrows) unless he felt a little as the hero of my verse? Only there's nothing homosexual about this."[29] Eliot continued to claim that there was "nothing homosexual" about his poetry, notably in his successful suppression of Peter's essay. His attack on Peter enacts the "never-never" of homosexual disavowal, as Butler describes it: I never loved a man, and I never lost him.

Eliot's remarks in the letter to Aiken reveal his identification with those who have painted Saint Sebastians and stuck him with arrows, murdering the beautiful youth who is also the object of their love, just as the speaker of "The Love Song of St. Sebastian" murders his female love object.[30] Confessing that "I would flog myself until I bled," the speaker revels in the "torture and delight" of self-flagellation. His nocturnal ritual is a form of religious devotion, performed in "hour on hour of prayer," strongly suggesting his deeper identification with Saint Sebastian himself, who was, according to legend, erotically tortured on account of his Christian faith. Moreover, his masochism acquires a certain beauty, as his blood "ring[s] the lamp / And glisten[s] in the light." As persecutor and persecuted, the speaker of Eliot's poem enacts the roles of *both* sadist and masochist or, in the imagery of arrows that is strikingly absent from the poem, the penetrator and the penetrated. At the psychic level, "The Love Song of St. Sebastian" stages the internal, homoerotic conflict of melancholia that Butler outlines while, at the textual level, it preserves the heterosexuality of its hero by rendering the object of desire female. As Richard A. Kaye observes, however, the only indication of the gender of the beloved is a single reference to her breasts.[31]

Kaye has provided an extensive and valuable survey of the literary sources and the historical context of Eliot's poem in the fin-de-siècle "homosexual cult" of Saint Sebastian. Building on the scholarship of Christopher Ricks and Harvey Gross, he reviews the numerous poems, novels, stories, mono-graphs, and plays produced on Saint Sebastian – "the suffering Bacchus of Christianity," as he is described in Anatole France's novel *The Red Lily* (1894) – in the period immediately preceding Eliot's composition of his poem in 1914.[32] Despite the ample evidence he adduces for the "homoerotic import" of the figure of Saint Sebastian in decadent literature, Kaye argues that Eliot "sought to erase St. Sebastian's implications as a feminized male" and to refashion him for "nonhomosexual ends," a gesture typical, he claims, of modernist poets who "mined material" from fin-de-siècle aestheticism yet cleansed it of its homosexuality.[33] In short, Kaye is faced with the dilemma of interpreting a poem that should be homoerotic yet which, on its face, is not. This dilemma arises, however, from Kaye's neglect of the psychosexual dynamics of the poem, in which melancholia, sadomasochism, and disavowed same-sex desire are potently conjoined.

This conjunction is spelled out in Freud's essay "A Child Is Being Beaten," which serves as a script for the first half of "The Love Song of St. Sebastian" and which clarifies the link between the theme of mourning in Eliot's poetry and the poem's sadomasochistic scene. According to Freud, the prototypical male masochistic fantasy is one of being beaten by the mother, yet behind it is another, displaced fantasy in which the son is beaten by the father. The mother is a stand-in, meant to screen the son from the ultimate wish expressed by the fantasy: that he is loved by the father.[34] The beating fantasy, in Freud's view, originates in the son's desire for the father and preserves that desire by disguising its object yet maintaining its aim, insofar as the son is in a "feminine" relation to him. In Eliot's poem, the speaker's self-flagellation is performed in subservience to a woman (Freud's mother figure) whom, in the second stanza, he proceeds to throttle. The climax of his devotion to her is her strangulation: "I should love you the more because I had mangled you." Far from being a "nonhomosexual" poem, "St. Sebastian" is charged with a veiled homoeroticism, while the switch from masochism to sadism in its second half may be driven by the speaker's (and Eliot's) disavowal that "there's [anything] homosexual about this." Moreover, Grover Smith observes that the poem features an "alter ego of the poet" much like the mad speaker of Poe's "For Annie," who, entombed alive, "speaks as one dead."[35]

"The Death of Saint Narcissus," a contemporary companion to "The Love Song of St. Sebastian," features a fiery rather than a watery death, for which Dante's *Purgatorio* is the primary locus. The chief difference between the voices from the flames and those from beneath the water is that the former are consumed by a refining fire seemingly intended to burn away the lusts of the flesh. Although some critics, notably Gordon,[36] interpret the former as admonitions to Eliot on his way to a Christian "new life," her redemptive reading fails to account for the pleasure with which these "singèd reveller[s] of the fire" ("The Burnt Dancer") indulge their passions. These two voices from the tomb – the voice from beneath the water and the sadomasochistic one from the fire – are complementary components of

Eliotic melancholia, self-elegies in which the speaker takes himself as the lost object of love.

Although no arrows appear in "The Love Song of St. Sebastian," there are plenty in "The Death of Saint Narcissus." The latter is absorbed in his bodily sensations, of the wind, of his own legs passing each other, and of his crossed arms. He becomes so enamored of his own beauty that "He could not live mens' ways, but became a dancer before God." The narcissistic saint indulges in a series of fantasies: that he was sure he had been a tree, that he knew he had been a fish held in his own fingers, and finally that he had been a young girl caught by a drunken old man. His visions entail the same sort of merging of the masculine subject and feminine object of desire that we have seen in Eliot's elegiac poems. Saint Narcissus is ultimately "struck down" by his "self-knowledge" in a death that enacts the martyrdom of St. Sebastian. Like the latter, "his flesh was in love with the burning arrows," and so he danced "Until the arrows came." The orgasmic "coming" of the arrows mimes his own orgasm in another intertwining of subject and object, sadist and masochist, or penetrator and penetrated. The phallic arrows (described as "penetrant" in the first draft of the poem) imply the homoeroticism that coincides with the autoeroticism of the text, confirming the link between male same-sex desire, self-love, and masochism that characterizes Eliot's elegiac poetry. Moreover, the opening lines of the poem, with the image of the shadow of a grey rock – recognizable from their subsequent insertion, in revised form, in the first part of *The Waste Land* – conclude with the speaker's direct address to the reader: "I will show you his bloody cloth and limbs / And the grey shadow on his lips." Displaying to us the livid corpse of Saint Narcissus, Eliot's speaker eulogizes not only a death that prefigures his own but also an affection that he can only affirm through the demise of its object.

We turn, finally and briefly, to the third aspect of Eliotic elegiacism, what I call his citational practice, by which I refer to the operation of quoting, alluding, borrowing, imitating, footnoting, and other forms of referring to other literary texts. Not only are Eliot's early poems preoccupied, thematically and psychologically, with men whose deaths they mourn and with whom the speakers of his poems identify, but Eliot's relation to the literary tradition in general is also melancholic. As I argue in *Deviant Modernism*, the profusion of allusions in his poetry constitutes an elegy for the literary tradition it evokes, which, in Eliot's case, refers to a distinctly paternal heritage.[37] Likewise, Ramazani notes that the fragmentary discourse employed by Eliot "implicitly functions as a mode of inscription – an epitaph," so that quotations, such as the repetition of Spenser's line

"Sweet Thames, run softly till I end my song" in *The Waste Land*, become "an elegiac device."[38] Eliot's citational practice manifests his identification with his self-designated literary forebears, concomitant with a guilty sense of failure at falling short of their standard and, more broadly, a feeling of loss. This is precisely the dilemma of the masochist hounded by his sadistic conscience. Indeed, Eliot's citational practice enacts an erotics of submission to the demands of paternal authority. The poet's "continual surrender of himself," as he writes in "Tradition and the Individual Talent," is a surrender to literary fathers.[39] The many allusions woven into the fabric of his poems point away from a Bloomian Oedipal scenario toward a masochistic one in which the father is the object of identification and, at bottom, of love. Eliot allied himself with his chosen literary patriarchs, internalized them as ideals, and wanted to accede to their ranks, yet suffered, in Bush's words, from "a perpetual feeling of unworthiness."[40] Eliot's citational practice placed him in a "feminine" position of subordination to literary authority, one in which his own mastery as a poet devolved from his devotion to his precursors – in a word, from the dead.

The cruelties of the conscience evident throughout Eliot's work attest to the internal aggression of melancholia, in which one part of the self makes war on the other, as well as, perhaps, to the self-annihilating desire for death. Freud observed that "in melancholia the super-ego . . . becomes a gathering place for the death instincts."[41] Should we thus understand the suppressed homoeroticism of Eliot's poetry as a manifestation of an impulse to die?

The drive toward death in Eliot's poems is indistinguishable from their disavowed homoeroticism inasmuch as, for Eliot, as for most heterosexual men of his time, the rectum is, so to speak, the grave. Leo Bersani describes "the jouissance of exploded limits, [and the] ecstacy of suffering" that comes from acquiescing to the "strong yet terrifying appeal of powerlessness."[42] Such a loss of control – or what Eliot describes in *The Waste Land* as "the awful daring of a moment's surrender" and, tellingly, in "Saint Narcissus," as becoming like "a young girl / Caught in the woods by a drunken old man" – was powerfully attractive to him. Eliot appears to have been drawn to self-abasement, even to the disintegration of the self. I disagree with Bersani that this "self-shattering" is "wholly alien" to "the melancholy of the post-Oedipal super-ego's moral masochism," yet his description of erotic ascesis in some respects aptly delineates Eliot's situation.[43] The punishments exacted by Eliot's conscience, and the annihilating pleasures of the escape that he envisioned from them, are continuous with what Freud called "erotogenic masochism," which he aligned with a fundamental striving toward organic equilibrium – in a word, with a yearning for death.[44] Bersani offers his theory as an account of male homosexual pleasure in which the latter, bound up with mastery and subordination, entails, in George Bataille's words, "a radical disintegration and humiliation of the self."[45] However, Bersani's theory expressly discounts the distinctly "moral" aspect of Eliot's self-torture, and what he calls "solipsistic jouissance" cannot be construed, as he claims, as "our primary hygienic practice of nonviolence."[46] While Eliot evidently imagined same-sex love as fatal – emotionally and socially, if not otherwise – that imagination does not necessitate positing an instinctual death drive; on the contrary, the powerful cultural prohibition against homosexuality amply accounts for his sense that to love another man was ruinous.

We may never know if Eliot loved Jean Verdenal, nor need we. It is clear, though, that most expressions of love in his early poetry are homo-elegiac. Not only are the gestures of affection in these poems phrased as grief over a "bewildering minute" of passion for a lost beloved, but they lament the deceased young men with whom the speakers of his poems identify, so that Eliotic melancholia embraces the narcissistic, masochistic death of the self together with the death of the beloved. Moreover, Eliot's oeuvre mourns a past masculine poetic tradition through his practice of citing. Despite his claim never to have loved, much less to have lost, a man, queer desires leak out of his poetry.

Eliot's elegies for drowned sailors, together with the perverse ecstasies of Saints Sebastian and Narcissus as well as his devotion to demanding literary fathers, portray a melancholia that has no discernable object, for Eliot's texts eloquently evoke the death of a love that they cannot affirm and thus cannot explicitly name. Indeed, the melancholia that pervades his early work need not and cannot be attributed to an individual bereavement but, given the general character of his homosexual disavowal, are better ascribed to a kind of love or erotic aim. Eliot's poetry demonstrates not simply his repression of homoerotic desire but the productivity of that repression in his profuse and moving expressions of fondness for dead men.

Inasmuch as the elegiac mode enabled Eliot to articulate an affection that he also denied, it is fitting to conclude by remarking on a handwritten scrap of verse that he left with the manuscript of *The Waste Land*. Beginning with the oft-quoted line from *The Tempest* referring to a drowned sailor ("Those are pearls that were his eyes. See!"), Eliot describes how "the crab clambers through his stomach, the eel grows big / And the torn algae drift above him," concluding with the tender words, "Still and quiet brother are you still and quiet."[47] Portions of this discarded scrap were subsequently incorporated into lines 48 and 401–4 of the published version of the poem. In the course of their transformation, these lines underwent a sea-change that silently buried their homoeroticism. Eliot's early draft of Part V of *The Waste Land* reads: "we brother, what have we given? / My friend, my blood, shaking my heart." The second line was revised to "My friend, my friend, beating in my heart," followed by the famous lines describing an instant of unforgettable passion: "The awful daring of a moment's surrender / Which an age of prudence can never retract."[48] Working on the draft, Eliot crossed out the Tennysonian reference to "brother" in the first line and further altered the second line, references that link the "brother" with "pearls that were his eyes" in the previous fragment. Instead, he prudently omitted any indication of a drowned blood-brother, retracting that expression of love while announcing his refusal to do so in ambiguous words cleansed of perversion. Edited out of *The Waste Land*, the "still and quiet brother" nevertheless haunts it as its disavowed ghost.

NOTES

1. John Peter, "A New Interpretation of *The Waste Land*," *Essays in Criticism* 19, no. 2 (1969): 143; further page references are included in the text.
2. A more distant but effectual inspiration for this essay is Christopher Craft's chapter on *In Memoriam*, "'Descend, Touch, and Enter': Tennyson's Strange Manner of Address," in *Another Kind of Love: Male Homosexual Desire in English Discourse, 1850–1920* (Berkeley: University of California Press, 1994), 44–70. Craft observes that Eliot, in his essay on *In Memoriam*, obliquely notices "the homoerotic basis of the elegy's extensive yearning" (53–4). Eliot "clearly recognizes that the elegy's desire for Christ is [in Eliot's words] 'at best but a continuance, or a substitute for the joys of friendship on earth,'" and "chastens" Tennyson for "the startling clarity of his longing" for Arthur Hallam (59). Craft claims that Eliot "inherits" Tennyson's "tactful" expression of homoeroticism but "reproves" his "passionate failure" to sublimate it sufficiently (59).
3. E. W. F. Tomlin, "T. S. Eliot: An Expostulation by Way of a Memoir," *Agenda* 23, nos. 1–2 (1985): 141.
4. Cynthia Ozick, "T. S. Eliot at 101," *New Yorker*, November 20, 1989, 152, 154 (emphasis Ozick's).
5. James E. Miller, Jr., *T. S. Eliot's Personal Waste Land: Exorcism of the Demons* (University Park: University of Pennsylvania Press, 1977). According to Miller, the line from Ariel's song is "a kind of refrain sounding throughout *The Waste Land*" (40) where it is associated with the Phoenician sailor (ll. 47–8). The latter, in turn, is linked to the hyacinth garden in the manuscript version of Part II of the poem. For the masculinity of the hyacinth "girl" see G. Wilson Knight, "Thoughts on *The Waste Land*," *Denver Quarterly* 7, no. 2 (Summer 1972): 1–13, whom Miller cites.

6. Ronald Bush, *T. S. Eliot: A Study in Character and Style* (New York: Oxford University Press, 1984), and A. David Moody, *Thomas Stearns Eliot: Poet* (Cambridge: Cambridge University Press, 1979).

7. Peter Ackroyd, *T. S. Eliot: A Life* (New York: Simon and Schuster, 1984), 310.

8. Lyndall Gordon, *T. S. Eliot: An Imperfect Life* (New York: Norton, 1998), 53. Gordon scarcely mentions Verdenal in her earlier biography, *Eliot's Early Years* (New York: Farrar Straus Giroux, 1977), and does not refer to the question of the homosexual valence of his friendship with Eliot.

9. John T. Mayer, *T. S. Eliot's Silent Voices* (New York: Oxford University Press, 1989), 199.

10. Mayer, *Eliot's Silent Voices*, 201.

11. Carole Seymour-Jones, *Painted Shadow: The Life of Vivienne Eliot, First Wife of T. S. Eliot, and the Long-Suppressed Truth about Her Influence on Eliot* (New York: Doubleday, 2002), 200; further page references are included in the text.

12. Eve Kosofsky Sedgwick, *Between Men: English Literature and Male Homosocial Desire* (New York: Columbia University Press, 1985).

13. T. S. Eliot, "*In Memoriam*," in *Selected Essays* (London: Faber and Faber, 1951; rpt. 1991), 332.

14. Frank Kermode, introduction to T. S. Eliot, *Selected Prose*, ed. Frank Kermode (New York: Harcourt Brace Jovanovich, 1975), 13.

15. The relevance to a queer reading of Eliot's poetry of his references to the *Purgatorio* and the *Inferno* calls for clarification. Although the sodomites in Hell (Canto XV) occupy the last ring and are compelled to tread on an arid and barren plain reminiscent of *The Waste Land*, Dante is surprised to discover there his beloved teacher, Brunetto Latini, in a recognition scene that Eliot openly imitates in the "dead patrol" section of *Little Gidding* (see Miller, *Eliot's Personal Waste Land*, 144–51). In the *Purgatorio*, sodomy is no longer a sin of violence against nature but one of excessive love. The circle of the lustful in Canto XXVI is occupied by both sodomites and *ermafrodito*, which is sometimes translated as *hermaphrodites* but which here is equivalent to "heterosexuals." (See Joseph Pequigney, "Sodomy in Dante's *Inferno* and *Purgatorio*," *Representations* 36 [Fall 1991]: 22–42). As one of the latter, Arnaut Daniel, like the sodomites, is guilty of sensual indulgence. Pequigney also points out that Virgil, Dante's guide and the dear friend whom Statius addresses in Canto XXV, was known to have been attracted to boys.

16. Dante Alighieri, *The Purgatorio*, trans. John Ciardi (New York: New American Library, 1957), 219–20.

17. See Mayer, *Eliot's Silent Voices*, 199–201, and Miller, *Eliot's Personal Waste Land*, 17–18, for the shifting position of this epigraph from Dante in the early editions of Eliot's poetry.

18. Miller, *Eliot's Personal Waste Land*, 83, 140.

19. See Colleen Lamos, *Deviant Modernism: Sexual and Textual Errancy in T. S. Eliot, James Joyce, and Marcel Proust* (Cambridge: Cambridge University Press, 1998), 108, 112–13.

20. Jahan Ramazani, *Poetry of Mourning: The Modern Elegy from Hardy to Heaney* (Chicago: University of Chicago Press, 1994), 25.

21. For Milton's and, especially, Whitman's presence in *The Waste Land*, see Gregory Jay, *T. S. Eliot and the Poetics of Literary History* (Baton Rouge: Louisiana State University Press, 1983), 170f. Jay observes the "recurrent fascination with watery death" in Eliot's poems from 1918 to 1921, which he understands in terms of Whitman's evocation of the ocean as a "Dark Mother." In a subsequent essay, Jay remarks briefly on *The Waste Land* as a homoerotic elegy and asks, suggestively, "What if, following Sedgwick, one reads the poem . . . as the internal crisis of the social construction of heterosexuality?" "Postmodernism in *The Waste Land*: Women, Mass Culture, and Others," in *Rereading the New: A Backward Glance at Modernism*, ed. Kevin Dettmar (Ann Arbor: University of Michigan Press, 1992), 236.

22. T. S. Eliot, "A Commentary," *Criterion* 13 (April 1934): 452. Peter Sacks argues that "Verdenal's death was certainly part of the private and public devastation mourned in *The Waste Land*." *The English Elegy: Studies in the Genre from Spenser to Yeats* (Baltimore: Johns Hopkins University Press, 1985), 261.

23. Sigmund Freud, "Mourning and Melancholia," in *General Psychological Theory*, ed. Philip Rieff (New York: Collier, 1963), 170.

24. See Grover Smith, "Eliot and the Ghost of Poe," in *T. S. Eliot: A Voice Descanting*, ed. Shyamal Bagchee (New York: St. Martin's Press, 1990), 149–63. Smith observes the similarity between Poe's "encoffined" speakers and Dante's damned.

25. Ramazani, *Poetry of Mourning*, 21. Ramazani neglects the homoerotic aspects of the elegy and deliberately conflates Freud's distinction between mourning and melancholia, which is crucial to understanding the link between desire and identification at work in the latter.

26. T. S. Eliot, "Reflections on Contemporary Poetry," *Egoist* 6, no. 3 (July 1919): 39.

27. Freud, "Mourning and Melancholia," 164–79.

28. Judith Butler, *The Psychic Life of Power: Theories in Subjection* (Stanford: Stanford University Press, 1997), 132–3; further page references are included in the text.

29. T. S. Eliot, *The Letters of T. S. Eliot*, vol. 1: 1898–1922, ed. Valerie Eliot (New York: Harcourt Brace Jovanovich, 1988), 44.

30. The Wildean echoes in "The Love Song of St. Sebastian" are noted by Christopher Ricks in T. S. Eliot, *Inventions of the March Hare: Poems 1909–1917*, ed. Christopher Ricks (New York: Harcourt Brace, 1996), 267–73.

31. Richard A. Kaye, "'A Splendid Readiness for Death': T. S. Eliot, the Homosexual Cult of St. Sebastian, and World War I," *Modernism/Modernity* 6, no. 2 (1999): 110.

32. Quoted in Kaye, "Splendid Readiness," 114; see Harvey Gross, "The Figure of Saint Sebastian," *Southern Review* 21, no. 4 (1985): 974–84, for an account of d'Annunzio's play "Le Martyre de Saint Sebastien," performed by Ida Rubinstein in Paris (1911), likely an influence on Eliot's poem.

33. Kaye, "Splendid Readiness," 109–10.

34. Sigmund Freud, "A Child Is Being Beaten," in *Sexuality and the Psychology of Love*, ed. Philip Rieff (New York: Collier, 1963), 126–7.

42 COLLEEN LAMOS

35. Smith, "Ghost of Poe," 153, 155.

36. Gordon, *Eliot's Early Years* (New York: Oxford University Press, 1977), 58–63.

37. Lamos, *Deviant Modernism*, 61–78.

38. Ramazani, *Poetry of Mourning*, 28.

39. Eliot, "Tradition and the Individual Talent," in *Selected Essays*, 17.

40. Bush, *Eliot*, 7.

41. Sigmund Freud, *The Ego and the Id*, ed. James Strachey (New York: Norton, 1962), 44.

42. Leo Bersani, "Is the Rectum a Grave?" in *AIDS: Cultural Analysis/Cultural Activism*, ed. Douglas Crimp (Cambridge, Mass.: MIT Press, 1988), 217.

43. Bersani, "Rectum," 217–18.

44. Sigmund Freud, "The Economic Problem of Masochism," in *General Psychological Theory*, ed. Philip Rieff (New York: Collier, 1963), 194. Without going into the details of Freud's or Bersani's theories of masochism and the death drive, it is worth noting the continuity (pace Bersani) between the death drive and erotogenic, feminine, and moral masochism in Freud's *The Ego and the Id*. Bersani's reasons for distinguishing among them as he does lie beyond the limits of this essay; however, in Eliot's case, these versions of masochism appear closely aligned.

45. Quoted in Bersani, "Rectum," 217.

46. Bersani, "Rectum," 222.

47. T. S. Eliot, *The Waste Land: A Facsimile and Transcript of the Original Drafts*, ed. Valerie Eliot (New York: Harcourt Brace Jovanovich, 1971), 123. The draft version contains some cross-outs and substitutions.

48. *Facsimile*, 77. Seymour-Jones also discusses Eliot's and Pound's revisions of this passage and their erasure of its homoerotic implications (304).

CHAPTER 2

T. S. Eliot, famous clairvoyante

Tim Dean

> Eliot, the smoothy whose whole career was an inside job, demands
> to be unmasked: his Englishness should be torn aside, his courtesy
> revealed as cowardice, and, above all, the coolness and distance of his
> verse reread as a front for emotional torment and the hiss of racial spite.
> Anyone who announces, as Eliot did, that poetry is an escape from
> personality can expect, now more than ever, to have his personality
> ripped open like a fox.[1]

Does modernist aesthetic theory amount to more than a set of masks that
criticism must tear away? Certainly it isn't hard to see how the doctrine of
impersonality bolsters claims for aesthetic disinterestedness – claims that
have been thoroughly demystified to reveal the self-interest and special
pleading that lie underneath. The modernist ideal of art's autonomy has
been regarded skeptically for several decades now, following the suspicion
that it rationalizes various forms of dissimulation. The critic's job is to
discover what, in any given case, this aesthetic ideology is being employed
to disguise. Since T. S. Eliot had so much to hide – a disastrous marriage,
his near-phobic hatred of women, the faint but unmistakable hint of sexual
deviancy, along with the expatriate's standard insecurities about fitting in,
not to mention his anti-Semitism and racialist bigotries – recent critics have
found plenty to expose.

Eliot's critical stock had declined precipitously even before Anthony
Julius delivered the coup de grâce in his 1995 indictment, *T. S. Eliot, Anti-
Semitism and Literary Form*, which argued that Eliot's noxious representations of Jews are not incidental but central to his poetics. Indeed, the
renewed critical interest in Eliot – sparked by Julius and inflamed by the
publication, one year later, of *Inventions of the March Hare* – has taken
almost invariably negative forms. After Julius, defenses of Eliot can seem
like apologies for anti-Semitism.[2] More broadly, defenses of his theory of
impersonality invite ridicule for their blindness to the cultural situatedness
of high modernist aesthetics, its entanglement with reactionary ideologies

of all stripes, most damningly fascism. Any literary critic with a modicum of political awareness knows that the only thing to do with impersonality is to demystify it, to strike through the mask.

The notion of impersonality as a mode of concealment has become so entrenched in modernist studies that it appears beyond question. I want to challenge this longstanding assumption, beginning from the simple hypothesis that impersonality represents a strategy of access, rather than a strategy of evasion. In the face of persistent critical stereotyping of this aesthetic mode, I think it's worth reexamining exactly what the modernists themselves said about impersonality and what they did with it. According to Eliot, the impersonalist poet becomes a medium for others' voices; in this way impersonality provides a means of access to others instead of a means of hiding oneself. To the extent that it clears a space for otherness at the expense of the poet's self, the impersonalist aesthetic should be considered ethically exemplary rather than politically suspect. Approaching impersonality from this different perspective allows us to grasp how Eliot's conception of the poet as a passive medium for alien utterances tacitly feminizes the poet's role. His feminizing poetic practice in this way suggests historically specific comparisons between the impersonalist poet and the figure of the medium as fortune-teller or clairvoyant. "Madame Sosostris, famous clairvoyante," in *The Waste Land*, represents not one of Eliot's demeaning portrayals of women, as is usually claimed, but his ideal poetic type.

Evoking occult practices in his impersonalist doctrine, Eliot requires me to differentiate two kinds of hiddenness: one associated with the impersonalist mask, which is generally thought to conceal the poet's true self and its interests; the other associated with the occult, which involves modes of being that are thoroughly alien to the self. The first kind of hiddenness – that of impersonality as an evasive tactic – partakes of what Eve Kosofsky Sedgwick calls the epistemology of the closet: a dynamic of concealment and revelation that makes sexuality central to modern ways of knowing. Building on Foucault's history of sexuality, Sedgwick argues that, around the turn of the century, an emergent opposition between heterosexuality and homosexuality installed itself at the center of the larger epistemological polarity of knowledge/ignorance – to the extent that homosexuality and its attendant mechanisms for escaping detection ("the closet") became inextricably associated with ignorance as such. Sedgwick maintains that ever since then social modes of secrecy, verbal strategies of indirection, and cultural techniques of concealment have all gestured toward sexual deviance.[3] As I indicate below, virtually every account of the function and significance of sexuality in Eliot's work operates within the terms of closet epistemology, even when no reference is made to Sedgwick's model or its philosophical antecedents. In other words, all previous discussions of Eliot and sexuality concern themselves with the dynamics of camouflage and exposure.

My account of impersonality shifts the critical debate away from closet logic toward a different way of conceptualizing sexuality's impact on Eliot's poetry. Sexuality in Eliot involves hiddenness not as a mode of concealment, but as an occult mode of access with erotic implications. His impersonalist theory of poetry compels Eliot – even in the face of his own conscious intentions – to embrace a passivity and openness that renders him vulnerable to what feels like bodily violation. Hence his propensity for embodying these qualities in women and sexually ambiguous youths such as Saint Sebastian and Narcissus. Eliot imagines figures for the ideal impersonalist poet as eminently rapable, and he conceives this violation as the paradoxical precondition for that "inviolable voice," which, in *The Waste Land*, he attempts not merely to represent but actually to approximate. The raped and wounded figures in his poetry do not represent abject bodies that Eliot repudiates as a means of shoring up his precarious masculine heterosexual identity, as recent critics have claimed. On the contrary, these violated figures represent Eliot's poetic ideal. Rejecting the terms of revelation and concealment that have dominated Eliot criticism, I shall argue that from his impersonalist practice something fundamental remains to be learned about the relation between transhistorical conceptions of poetic utterance and modern forms of sexuality.

ESCAPING PERSONALITY

The basic misunderstanding about impersonality may be traced to Eliot's own contradictory and ambivalent pronouncements on the subject – a subject that long preceded him, but which he made his own almost despite himself. In an irony of literary history that has not been fully appreciated, Eliot personalized impersonality to such a degree that the manifold shortcomings of his own personality have come to seem inseparable from a conception of poetic utterance that antedates modernism by many centuries. As a result, critical suspicion of impersonality is compounded by its association with Eliot and his noxious politics. Yet whatever Eliot's genius for maximally investing with cultural capital his own critical pronouncements, he cannot be accused of producing anything resembling a coherent theory of impersonality. In the process of formulating his first version of this theory, in "Tradition and the Individual Talent" (1919), Eliot has recourse to a series of metaphors that point in competing directions.

Demurring from Wordsworth's axiom that poetry "is the spontaneous overflow of powerful feelings: it takes its origin from emotion recollected in tranquillity," Eliot argues instead that "[p]oetry is not a turning loose of emotion, but an escape from emotion; it is not the expression of personality, but an escape from personality."[4] His rhetoric of escape has misled critics into speculating about exactly what Eliot wished to elude, as if literary commentary amounted to little more than an exercise in demystification. Hence Eliot criticism often takes the form of hunting for skeletons in the poet's closet – a project fueled by both Julius's critique and the subsequent appearance of previously unpublished poems in *Inventions of the March Hare*, a book whose interest lay partly in its drama of exposure and the voyeuristic thrill attendant upon a well-locked closet finally laid bare. The rhetoric of escape in Eliot's doctrine of impersonality intensifies our sense that his poetic theory simply rationalizes the concealment of certain secrets.

Eliot's secret is often assumed to be biographical in nature. James E. Miller, for instance, having quoted the sentences from "Tradition and the Individual Talent" about escaping personality, comments: "Such language seems not shaped by the 'impersonal theory' but by a personal anguish (and the possible need for concealment) that lies behind the theory itself."[5] Though somewhat atypical in its interpretation of the secret behind Eliot's poetry as that of homosexuality, Miller's approach is in fact wholly characteristic of the pervasive tendency to demystify impersonality as an evasion of personal conflicts and, more acutely, personal responsibility. This is where the critique of impersonality as a form of subterfuge gets its edge. In the benign version of this critique, Eliot's theory simply rationalizes his impulse to conceal personal problems: impersonality represents the poet's way of constructing for himself a carapace of privacy. But since his death, the reasoning goes, any claim to privacy is irrelevant, and critics are licensed to hunt for the secret that impelled his construction of privacy in the first place. This conception of impersonality spurs biographies of Eliot and authorizes the biographical orientation of much recent criticism, including ostensibly nonbiographical, poststructuralist commentary.

What I have characterized as the benign misconception of impersonality shades into a harsher critique when Eliot's rhetoric of escape is understood as rationalizing his evasion of not only personal problems, but also, more pointedly, personal responsibility. In this view, impersonality camouflages Eliot's responsibility for abandoning his first wife; it obscures his liability for producing offensive literary representations of women and minorities; and, by demoting the self, the doctrine of impersonality attempts to deflect attention from the various strategies of institutional self-advancement that

Eliot pursued so successfully. In other words, impersonality affords the poet a cloak of "deniability" with respect to his troubling personal and political activities: impersonality therefore should be considered a strategically self-serving form of disavowal. According to this perspective, impersonality dissimulates self-advancement and self-inflation by way of its theory of self-diminution.

A striking example of this mode of unmasking Eliot's aesthetic doctrine as an evasion of personal responsibility may be found in the film *Tom & Viv*, which, in a crucial scene, provides a voice-over of Eliot (Willem Dafoe) reading his sentence about poetry as "an escape from emotion" while his wife (Miranda Richardson) surreptitiously exits their home.[6] The film gains much of its poignance from focusing on the unjust treatment of Vivienne by her husband, in partial collusion with her family. We are led to believe that Eliot's theory of poetry as "an escape from emotion" was motivated by his inability to handle the emotional effects of his wife's hormonal imbalance. Yet rather than simply fleeing the challenge this presented, which would have made him a coward, Eliot had his wife institutionalized, which makes him worse. He escaped emotion through poetry and, less humanely, by having Vivienne locked up. *Tom & Viv* implicitly exposes the doctrine of impersonality as a rationale for moral cowardice and the unethical treatment of others.

Like much literary criticism, the movie attempts to demystify impersonality in biographical terms. However, nonbiographically oriented criticism follows a similar logic by treating Eliot's rhetoric of "escape" as a version of the modernist desire to escape history. According to Marxist and historicist critiques, it is not so much the contingencies of his personal history that Eliot is trying to elude as it is history *tout court*. Materialist critiques see in the doctrine of impersonality an argument for aesthetic autonomy – that is, a spurious rationale for art's transcendence of the historical conditions of its production. Eliot's infamous account of "an ideal order" of poetic monuments whose allegedly transhistorical existence remains independent of concrete social relations has led Marxist critics such as Terry Eagleton to regard impersonality as synonymous with the reactionary ideology of aesthetic autonomy.[7] Indeed, Eagleton's antipathy toward the claims made in "Tradition and the Individual Talent" is so fundamental to his own account of literature and literary criticism that he seems compelled to rehearse his critique of Eliot in book after book. Eagleton's misapprehension of the impersonalist doctrine is significant not simply because of this critic's stature, but also because his view of Eliot strongly influenced his student Maud Ellmann, whose book *The Poetics of Impersonality* consolidated negative critical opinion on modernist aesthetic theory. Since Ellmann's critique over a decade ago, the concept of impersonality has fallen into such disrepute as to be deemed unworthy of serious critical consideration.

Ellmann contextualizes the doctrine of impersonality as Eliot's response to Henri Bergson's theory of personality, which the poet heard when attending Bergson's lectures in Paris (1910–11). In a classic deconstructive move, Ellmann claims that Eliot's antisubjectivism, launched as an attack on Bergson, nevertheless remained complicit with the individualism he repudiated, and hence "the more the poet tries to hide himself the more he seems to have given himself away."[8] Arguing against scholars who "have used the doctrine of impersonality to rescue modernism from its racism and homophobia: to purify the poems of their authors' politics and hence to insulate aesthetics from history," Ellmann concludes that "the doctrine of impersonality was born conservative . . . [It] exemplifies the philosophical, aesthetic, and political assumptions which inspired the reactionary fervour of the modernists" (198–9).

The Poetics of Impersonality provides a powerful critique; its combination of archival research, poststructuralist sophistication, and leftist commitment has rendered Ellmann's verdict on impersonality practically unassailable. Her imputation that there has been dissimulation on the part of not only modernist poets but also their critics – who try to use impersonality "to insulate aesthetics from history" – has deterred any substantial investigation of her claims. To refute Ellmann's judgment on the politics of impersonality, it would be insufficient to point out how she inherits Eagleton's dubious political assumptions about the aesthetic without questioning them. Instead, refuting *The Poetics of Impersonality* requires me to historicize Eliot's aesthetic doctrine somewhat differently, by situating impersonality in the context of occult mediumship and the cultural fascination with clairvoyance that has been invoked to illuminate Yeats's and H. D.'s impersonalist poetic practices. But since Ellmann's account points to an issue in modernist literary studies of far wider scope than her own particular analysis, I would like to take this opportunity to delineate the full contours of the problem.

THE LIMITS OF DEMYSTIFICATION

Eliot's conception of poetry as something other than self-expression has become harder to grasp in the wake of an interpretive method – New Criticism – with which he remains closely associated. The following judgment still represents a critical consensus: "Eliot's notion of impersonal theory [was] elaborated by New Criticism, perhaps the most complete view that the work of art exists outside of, and should be treated outside of history, since art is self-contained and generates its own laws."[9] Critiques of New Critical formalism have tended to dispense with the doctrine of poetic impersonality alongside their dismantling of claims that literature be understood apart from its social contexts. Although over the past several decades literary studies has moved well beyond New Criticism's misguided assumptions, we have not yet relinquished completely the New Critics' view of Eliot and therefore have dismissed him with them.

Owing to New Criticism's appropriation of Eliot, the assumption persists that his definition of poetry as "an escape from emotion" remains central to a cultural project of disentangling the aesthetic from historical processes. According to Eagleton this cultural project ends in fascism: "Eliot's own solution is an extreme right-wing authoritarianism: men and women must sacrifice their petty 'personalities' and opinions to an impersonal order."[10] It would be hard to imagine a more damning criticism of impersonality than that it culminates in – or by virtue of its aestheticizing commitments is homologous with – fascist politics. In the specter of fascism we confront a threat that looms large over the academic study of high modernism. And we need not have recourse to Eagleton's coarse polemics – or the slightly less hasty condemnation in Paul Morrison's recent book on the subject – to witness this alignment of impersonality with right-wing politics.[11] In his fine study of Eliot and ideology, Kenneth Asher mounts a similar argument, contending that Eliot's entire career is unified by the indelible stamp upon it of the reactionary thinking of French proto-fascist Charles Maurras. Asher connects Maurras's ideas with Eliot's concept of an "ideal order" of poetic monuments, suggesting that "on the basis of Maurras's account, one can develop a theory of the relationship between the smallest component, the individual, and an Absolute that manifests itself as continuous cultural inheritance, and this is precisely what Eliot began to do in 'Tradition and the Individual Talent.'"[12] Asher's Marxist formalism is debatable, however, in that the individual's submission to an external authority greater than him- or herself need not translate into right-wing allegiances. Submission to an external authority could just as easily foster a left-wing commitment to elevating the well-being of the collective above that of the individual. It is certainly the case that locating authority outside the self – as the doctrine of impersonality advocates – *can* lead to fascism or, less dangerously, conservative Anglicanism. But the logic of impersonality can also lead to more progressive ways of imagining social relations.

The doctrine of impersonality tends as readily toward anti-authoritarian positions because it undermines, first and foremost, the authority of the self. And it is the notion of sovereign selfhood that, as Leo Bersani suggests in another context, "accounts for human beings' extraordinary willingness to kill in order to protect the seriousness of their statements."[13] My conception of impersonality as ethically admirable relies in part on a psychoanalytic critique of self-mastery and, in particular, on Bersani's thesis that a whole range of social and cultural ills are attributable to the ideal of authoritative selfhood.[14] What I find especially useful for understanding Eliot's impersonalist practice in *The Waste Land* is Bersani's describing the counterintuitive appeal of self-divestment in terms of homosexuality, since Eliot too has recourse to ambiguously sexualized figures in his experiments with the self-dissolution that impersonality entails.

The critical genealogy I have been tracing suggests just how hard it is, in the individualist societies of the West, to contemplate seriously the implications of divesting the self of its authority. These implications run counter to Enlightenment notions of individual sovereignty and self-possession, upon which rests a fundamental idea of political liberty. Any conception of selfhood that emphasizes self-dispossession – and hence challenges the sense of freedom consequent upon subjective autonomy – is bound to be regarded with suspicion. The basic incompatibility between Enlightenment and impersonalist models of the self helps explain critics' inability to view impersonality as anything but a politically dubious enterprise. More than other schools of thought, materialist literary criticism has been unable to see past the assumption that poets write always or ultimately in their own self-interest – and, by extension, in the interests of their class, race, or gender. When a poet appears to be writing not in his own interests, commentators assume that he must be dissimulating or otherwise "camouflaging" his own or his sociological group's agenda. While literary critics often concede that the poet may not be *consciously* pursuing his own interests at others' expense, their assumption of ultimate self-interest remains largely unquestioned.

This presupposition is tougher to circumvent than one might suppose, since the imperative to situate literary texts in their ideological context necessarily locates the critic on an epistemological terrain organized by metaphysical polarities of concealment and exposure. False-consciousness, dissimulation, and self-deception remain governing principles of ideological criticism; once having set foot on this terrain, it proves extremely hard to conceive of a poet as working directly against his own interests – that is, as pursuing an experience of self-dispossession rather than one of self-development (*Bildung*) – and equally hard to conceive of such poetic activity as anything but subterfuge or bad faith.[15] Implausible though it might sound to say so, I actually have little interest in shielding Eliot from Marxist critiques or in arguing that his work somehow remains immune from ideological pressures. Instead, I am interested in how Eliot's early poetics compelled him to write against self-interest – and how his impersonalist conception of poetry led to experiments with self-dispossession rather than self-advancement. The logic of demystification that propels materialist critiques prevents Eliot's experiments in self-dispossession from becoming visible, because the hermeneutics of suspicion considers impersonality as camouflage that must be stripped away to reveal the poet's true agenda. An equally disabling logic of demystification also motivates queer critiques of Eliot, which see in his theory of impersonality a strategy of concealment inseparable from the dialectic of the homosexual closet.

THE QUEER CRITIQUE OF IMPERSONALITY

Although queer theory is a new and still inchoate body of thought, the queer critique of impersonality stretches back half a century to John Peter's interpretation of *The Waste Land* in 1952. By this anachronistic claim I mean to indicate how substantial a pedigree the view of impersonality as a strategy of sexual subterfuge has in Eliot criticism. Peter described *The Waste Land* as essentially an elegy for the protagonist's drowned beloved, identified in the poem as Phlebas the Phoenician ("who was once handsome and tall as you"), and subsequently unmasked as Jean Verdenal, a young French medical student and aspiring poet whom Eliot befriended during his time in Paris. Two years after Verdenal's death in World War I, Eliot memorialized him by dedicating *Prufrock and Other Observations*, "For Jean Verdenal, 1889–1915 / *mort aux Dardanelles*." Although Peter's 1952 essay mentioned neither Verdenal's name nor the term *homosexuality*, Eliot reacted violently to his interpretation and had it legally suppressed. Only after Eliot's death, in 1965, was the essay republished, along with Peter's "Postscript" identifying Verdenal and relating the tale of how Eliot hushed up the original interpretation.[16]

Peter's essay reemerged in 1969 on the eve of Stonewall, the political rebellion that traditionally marks the birth of gay liberation. In retrospect, Peter appears to have brought Eliot out of the closet at exactly the historical moment that lesbians and gays throughout the United States became politically committed to mobilizing against the constraints that accompany enforced secrecy. There is a certain poetic justice in Eliot's being forced out of the closet along with everybody else. Yet, paradoxically, it was Eliot's censorship that drew attention to Peter's interpretation as an issue of the closet in the first place, since his legal suppression of an academic article that might well have languished in obscurity generated the impression that there was something to hide. (The official embargo on Eliot's letters to Emily Hale – which prevents scholars from examining the correspondence until 2019 – likewise contributes to this sense of a sexual secret.) It is almost impossible not to read Eliot's legal action against Peter as a desperate attempt to re-closet what Peter had un-closeted; but without the censorship we might not have considered *The Waste Land* a question of sexual concealment and exposure at all. If we were to acknowledge that Eliot produced this closet by acting as though he had something to hide, we might even suppose that his doing so represents a prescient strategy for confirming critics in their belief that a secret lurks behind his work, awaiting discovery and revelation. But actually all we need recognize is that, in an age when any secret seems to imply a sexual source, it was inevitable that Eliot's opacity would be interpreted as cloaking a specifically erotic mystery.

Peter's interpretation gained momentum in 1977, with James E. Miller's book-length treatment of *The Waste Land* as an elaborate dissimulation of the poet's homosexual secret. In demystifying this modernist monument by asserting it to be an intensely personal poem, Miller was obliged to deflate along with it the doctrine of impersonality that had protected Eliot's poetry from biographical readings. Although his account shows no evidence of a gay studies context to support it, Miller's reading certainly betrays signs of a Zeitgeist in which it became possible to characterize *The Waste Land* as "an act of therapy and exorcism" (42). Interpreting the poem biographically, as an exercise in personal catharsis, Miller reads *The Waste Land* almost as if it were a confessional poem in the mode of Robert Lowell, whose career, in 1977, had just ended. By 1977 the moment for conceptualizing poetry in anything other than lyric terms – that is, as either straightforward or disguised self-expression – appeared long since past.

Lesbian and gay critics have developed Miller's interpretation of *The Waste Land* beyond the biographical context of Eliot's own love-life. The broad significance of Wayne Koestenbaum's, Merrill Cole's, and Colleen Lamos's accounts of *The Waste Land* lies in their demonstration that, as Koestenbaum put it, there is "no sanctuary, not even iambic pentameter, from the pressure of sexuality."[17] These critics follow Freud and, somewhat differently, Foucault in viewing erotic dynamics not as confined to individual or private relationships but as permeating the whole social fabric, including the most rarefied zones of cultural production. It is not simply that libido manifests itself in socio-symbolic forms (per Freud), but also that sexuality can be understood as an effect of power dynamics that traverse and connect ostensibly unrelated cultural realms (per Foucault).

Queer critique aims to reveal how sexuality and erotic desire are implicated in multiple structures of power, all the better politically to resist their oppression. Koestenbaum reads collaborative authorship in this light, arguing that Pound's editing of *The Waste Land* embroils him and Eliot in a homoerotic exchange that leads to the birth of a poem rather than a baby. Associating his receptivity to Pound's aggressive editing with Eliot's mental exhaustion, passivity, and general neurasthenic debilitation around the time of *The Waste Land*'s composition, Koestenbaum contends that "this supposedly impersonal icon of New Criticism has profound connections with Eliot's own emotional disturbances" (112). Bringing out the poem's erotic dynamics seems to require dismissing its pretensions to impersonality – pretensions identified with the discredited methods of New Criticism.

Taking off from Miller's and Koestenbaum's readings, Merrill Cole makes good on queer theory's ambition to connect sexuality with more overtly public domains by arguing for *The Waste Land*'s "complicity . . . with a series of major cultural structures of power – the closet, the canon, and the empire."[18] He claims that uncovering the poem's homoerotic subtext remains insufficient unless we recognize how *The Waste Land* actively solicits homosexual meaning only to disavow it. Like all homophobic projects, argues Cole, the poem needs its queers in order to secure its own cultural authority; hence Eliot's practice of literary allusion may be read as a closet-making enterprise as well as the canon-building endeavor it has often been taken to exemplify. Yet while Cole's expert application of Sedgwick's theory of the closet generates an unusually insightful interpretation of *The Waste Land*, it does so at the expense of poetic impersonality: "Eliot's escape from personality dovetails neatly with the closet," he maintains (69). Cole understands the doctrine of impersonality as a strategy of dissimulation with ideological ramifications that encompass homophobic and imperial violence.

In *Deviant Modernism*, her rich study of high modernism's queer energies, Colleen Lamos also reads Eliot in terms of closet logic. I find myself in sympathy with her commitment to treating canonical modernism as less than monolithic by unraveling its claims to literary and cultural authority; yet I also find in Eliot's poetry stronger impulses toward the renunciation as well as the consolidation of authority. Lamos reads such impulses as merely camouflage, arguing that in his allusions to literary authorities "Eliot deftly veils his usurpation in elaborate displays of surrender."[19] His allusiveness

entails a specifically sexual dynamic, according to Lamos, because it "enacts
an erotics of domination and submission in relation to paternal authority"
(57). Although she sees in Eliot a masochistic attitude toward authority,
Lamos interprets his masochism – as Koestenbaum interpreted his passivity – as a ruse of power, a perverse strategy for securing greater dominance.
And, like Cole in his reading of *The Waste Land* as a poem that solicits
the homoerotic energies it phobically disavows, Lamos regards impersonality as just another strategy of dissimulation, referring to it as a "mask of
self-abnegation" (24).

A rather different way of reading Eliot's gestures of renunciation stems
from recognizing in the modernist use of masks a technique of self-
dispossession that entails a structural rather than a psychological form of
masochism. By this I mean that impersonal masking – the speaking in a
voice other than one's own – involves the poet in a suspension or diminu-
tion of self that tends to accompany the poetic medium itself, irrespective
of his or her own preferences. While modernist impersonality is readily
grasped as entailing the use of personae, we need not understand masking
as solely or even primarily a technique of concealment. *Persona* originally
referred to the mask worn by actors in Greek drama, but the word ety-
mologically derives from the Latin phrase *per sonare*, meaning "to sound
through." Rather than designating the visual form hiding the actor's face,
persona initially denoted the mask's mouthpiece or a reed device inserted
into it for amplifying the actor's voice.[20] Thus, in the first place, a persona
was less a means of visual concealment than of vocal channeling; it entailed
a form of speaking through rather than of speaking falsely. More than a
mode of camouflage, impersonation may represent a way to inhabit other
existences – a way to transform oneself by becoming possessed by others.
This distinction furnishes us with a rationale for approaching modernist
impersonality as a strategy not of dissimulation but of access to regions of
voice beyond the self's.

THE POETIC MEDIUM

It is exactly this structure of verbal utterance that Eliot attempts to describe
in "Tradition and the Individual Talent," his early impersonalist manifesto.
The essay proposes a paradoxical conception of poetic speaking in which
the poet's voice is most original when it is least his own: "not only the best,
but the most individual parts of his work," Eliot suggests, "may be those
in which the dead poets, his ancestors, assert their immortality most vigorously" (48). Self-dispossession is so much a precondition for poetic speaking

that it seems like an entailment of the medium itself. Eliot's atavistic emphasis on the dead ancestors' continuing life – the poet "is not likely to know what is to be done unless he lives in what is not merely the present, but the present moment of the past, unless he is conscious, not of what is dead, but of what is already living" (59) – makes his conception of poetry appear shamanistic or occult. Poetry is what you get when the ancestors become undead.

The idea that impersonality entails the poet's being *spoken through* gives rise to a disquieting sense of the uncanny, even as it raises questions about how this mode of speaking may be attained. Eliot equivocates over how the relationship between living and dead is to be established, disallowing both patrimony and research as means for securing the words of departed ancestors. "Tradition is a matter of much wider significance," he argues, "[i]t cannot be inherited, and if you want it you must obtain it by great labour" (49). His theory of tradition is not aristocratic or elitist in the way that is usually assumed; yet neither is it meritocratic in the sense of being a function of education or of studying. Eliot anticipates these criticisms when he remarks that, "I am alive to a usual objection to what is clearly part of my programme for the *métier* of poetry. The objection is that the doctrine requires a ridiculous amount of erudition (pedantry), a claim which can be rejected by appeal to the lives of poets in any pantheon. It will even be affirmed that much learning deadens or perverts poetic sensibility." He counters this objection by arguing that, "[w]hile, however, we persist in believing that a poet ought to know as much as will not encroach upon his necessary receptivity and necessary laziness, it is not desirable to confine knowledge to whatever can be put into a useful shape for examinations, drawing-rooms, or the still more pretentious modes of publicity. Some can absorb knowledge, the more tardy must sweat for it" (52). Though this sounds like Eliot at his most Olympian, his insistence that poetic knowledge is neither heritable nor accessible through study holds significant implications. The kind of knowledge Eliot recommends for the practice of poetry – knowledge derived from the dead ancestors' continuing life – appears decidedly esoteric, as if it required noncognitive techniques to access it. The alternatives of "absorb[ing]" or "sweat[ing] for" it both imply that poetic knowledge crystallizes as a consequence of corporeal as well as of mental experience. While in "Tradition and the Individual Talent" this experience requires the poet's "necessary receptivity," *The Waste Land* figures it as specifically sexual experience, a violation of bodily integrity that dramatizes the self-dispossession demanded by impersonalist poetry.

The peculiar status of poetic knowledge in Eliot's theory and the uncanny structure of impersonalist utterance help explain his repeated allusions to mediums – what, in the passage cited above, he refers to as "the *métier* of poetry." In "Tradition and the Individual Talent" the poetic medium designates not only the specific material of artistic practice, but also the special properties of a poet's mind. Eliot's comparing the impersonalist poet to a chemical catalyst represents nothing more than his fumbled attempt to veil an occultist theory in the garb of modern rationalism. As his critics have often noted, Eliot's scientific analogy is faulty because, having claimed that "[t]he mind of the poet is the shred of platinum" (54), he develops the comparison by arguing that "[t]he poet's mind is in fact a receptacle for seizing and storing up numberless feelings, phrases, images, which remain there until all the particles which can unite to form a new compound are present together" (55). Unable to decide whether a poet's mind should be understood as the receptacle that contains elements requiring catalysis or whether it represents the catalyst itself, Eliot also comes close to nullifying the distinction between a poet's mind and the medium of poetic practice.

Having invoked "the *métier* of poetry," Eliot develops his account of impersonality by defining poetic consciousness in terms of a medium: "the mind of the mature poet differs from that of the immature one not precisely in any valuation of 'personality,' not being necessarily more interesting, or having 'more to say,' but rather by being a more finely perfected medium in which special, or very varied, feelings are at liberty to enter into new combinations" (53–4). The *métier* of verse has been transposed into the catalytic mentation of the poet himself, as if impersonality entailed his becoming nothing more than an echo chamber through which the voices of others might be heard. Were this not strange enough, Eliot subsequently attempts to clarify his meaning in metaphysical terms by repudiating the notion of unified subjectivity – a claim that points to the philosophical continuity between modernist impersonality and postmodern critiques of the autonomous self.[21] "The point of view which I am struggling to attack," he maintains, "is perhaps related to the metaphysical theory of the substantial unity of the soul: for my meaning is, that the poet has, not a 'personality' to express, but a particular medium, which is only a medium and not a personality, in which impressions and experiences combine in peculiar and unexpected ways" (56).

In place of the modern rationalist understanding of individual personality, Eliot substitutes a premodern – or postmodern – notion of the self as disunified and unbounded, a self that functions as a conduit not only for voices of the dead but perhaps for others' experiences too. His understanding of poetic selfhood aligns Eliot with Yeats more closely than has been realized; and his explaining impersonality in terms of mediumship tries to dignify through a theory of high-cultural tradition what Yeats recognized as a popular, antimodern cultural practice, namely spiritualism. When Eliot disdainfully refers to "sweat[ing] for" poetic knowledge, he could be describing Yeats's lifelong experiments in the occult – experiments that, Yeats's prose works concede, almost always failed. The older poet's account of "frequent[ing] those mediums who in various poor parts of London instruct artisans or their wives for a few pence upon their relations to the dead" indicates an established folk version of the high-cultural function Eliot claimed for his poetry.[22] In his understanding of impersonality as a technique for establishing "relations to the dead," Eliot tacitly connected the modern poet with the medium or clairvoyant.

VOICES SINGING OUT OF EMPTY CISTERNS

Eliot's ideas about occult transmission are dramatized in *The Waste Land*. While Madame Sosostris stands as the poem's best-known medium, she is not the only figure associated with clairvoyance. Both the Sibyl, whose words compose the poem's epigraph, and Tiresias, who supposedly unites the poem, are second-sighted. Given that Eliot derived Madame Sosostris's name from a fortune-teller called Sesostris in Aldous Huxley's *Crome Yellow* (a novel published only in November 1921), biographer Lyndall Gordon is justified in claiming that the Sosostris scene must have been a significant late addition to the poem; her pack of cards "is a unifying device," Gordon suggests, "a late attempt to draw the fragments together with a parade of the poem's characters."[23] Madame Sosostris is thus in one respect a modern incarnation of Tiresias, himself "the most important personage in the poem, uniting all the rest," according to Eliot's note.[24] It is not only as mediums but also as ostensibly unifying consciousnesses that Tiresias and Sosostris represent surrogates for the impersonalist poet.

The similarities between Eliot's ideal poet and a working-class woman, on one hand, and a hermaphroditic seer, on the other, help explain his treating Sosostris with ironic distance:

> Madame Sosostris, famous clairvoyante,
> Had a bad cold, nevertheless
> Is known to be the wisest woman in Europe,
> With a wicked pack of cards   (*WL*, 136)[25]

The polyphony in the famous passage that follows these lines may suggest that Eliot's ventriloquism – his expertly manipulating a vast range of vocal tonality – is to some extent analogous to that of Sosostris, whose "bad cold" hardly impairs her capacity to "do the police in different voices." Like the poem's maker and the Dickens caricature Sloppy whose ventriloquistic talent inspired the poem's original title, Sosostris stands as a figure who has mastered the art of vocal imitation, even if only in a debased or fraudulent way. This cultural fact was not lost on Eliot. In order to differentiate his practice from hers – a differentiation motivated by considerations of both gender and class – Eliot must ironize Sosostris, even as he tacitly identifies with her techniques by giving her such a prominent place in the poem.

Having learned from Joyce more than from Dickens how to ironize characters by framing them in the idiom they might fondly use to describe themselves, Eliot inserts into his poem fragments from the discourse of Madame Sosostris's ideal self. The locution "famous clairvoyante" is clearly hers, not his, insofar as the Gallicism conveys her pretension to European mysteriousness and sophistication. Such irony cuts both ways, of course, since Eliot himself peppers the poem with French lines and terms. The passage following Sosostris's begins "Unreal City," a phrase that Eliot's note identifies as an allusion to Baudelaire's "Les Sept Vieillards," from which he quotes the lines *Fourmillante cité, cité pleine de rêves, / Où le spectre en plein jour raccroche le passant* ("Swarming city, city full of dreams, / Where the spectre in full daylight accosts the passer-by") (*WL*, 147). Eliot thus evokes the French of Baudelaire to conjure an image of the spirits of the dead mingling with the living in a rhetorical gesture that is not altogether different from Sosostris's motive for Gallicizing the name of her profession.

However, in the phrase "a wicked pack of cards" and her closing words ("One must be so careful these days"), Eliot captures the British working-class idiom that betrays Madame Sosostris's true origins. His reference, in "Tradition and the Individual Talent," to "the still more pretentious modes of publicity" offers additional context for the line "Is known to be the wisest woman in Europe," which echoes and thereby deflates the promotional discourse she has adopted. Although in his poetry Eliot uses the verbal form of the echo to achieve various effects, in this passage verbal mimicry functions primarily to ironize. Even the interpolated line from Shakespeare's ghostly Ariel – "Those are pearls that were his eyes" – is ironized by the imperative "Look!," as if to insist that these precious eyes cannot see. Since there is no real clairvoyance here, Eliot's mediumistic technique ostensibly remains uncontaminated by the popular-cultural variant of impersonalist utterance that he observed in London's fortune-tellers.

But the impersonalist poet's feminization is ineluctable. The association of physical blindness with spiritual vision connects the Sosostris passage to a more authentic clairvoyant, Tiresias, who, "though blind . . . can see" ("I Tiresias, old man with wrinkled dugs / Perceived the scene, and foretold the rest" [*WL*, 141]).[26] In the myth Tiresias, who has inhabited both male and female forms, is blinded by Juno for reporting that women enjoy sex more than men do. His blindness is inflicted for acknowledging the greater pleasure of being erotically penetrated over that of penetrating – a punishment, in other words, for admitting what Leo Bersani calls the "appeal of powerlessness."[27] By this Bersani means not impotence or disenfranchisement, but a *jouissance* achieved through renouncing the exercise of power in favor of an experience of self-dissolution. Following Jean Laplanche's reading of Freud, Bersani locates the origin of human sexuality in masochism, which makes the intensity of erotic pleasure a consequence of abandoning the self rather than of consolidating it through domination of others.[28]

Although associated with femininity and so-called passive homosexuality, the experience of self-dispossession cannot be understood as the prerogative of any psychological identity because it represents the loss of identity as such. Self-dispossession is rendered intelligible by psychoanalytic theories of masochism – or by cultural stereotypes about heterosexual women and effeminate homosexuals – but may in fact be a structural entailment of the poetic medium as much as a psychological impulse. "[T]he poet has . . . no identity . . . he has no self," argued Keats, in a formulation suggesting that the poet's identity consists in the loss of identity or, as he put it in the same letter, in self-annihilation.[29] In this transhistorical conception of poetic utterance, which stretches back to Plato's *Ion*, the suspension of individual identity, by whatever means, is deemed necessary for poetic making. With Bersani's account in mind, we could say that the "appeal of powerlessness" concerns aesthetic pleasure as much as it does erotic *jouissance*, because the medium requires a self-shattering or impersonalization that is synonymous with poetic practice itself.

By figuring this exigency in terms of sex and gender, Eliot's poetry makes clear that aesthetic impersonality threatens masculinity as we know it. Impersonality undermines masculinity because it enjoins the renunciation of self-possession and self-control. The freakish hybrid Tiresias – "throbbing between two lives, / Old man with wrinkled female breasts" (*WL*, 140) – represents a particularly disturbing outcome of the self-transformation that poetic utterance demands. When Tiresias is apprehended in this way, Eliot's comment about him – "What Tiresias *sees*, in fact, is the substance of the poem" (*WL*, 148) – achieves new significance. Tiresias's importance does not lie in his role as the poem's unifying device (per New Critical criteria), nor in his representing a type for other characters (such as Madame Sosostris). Instead, as a figure for gender-switching and self-transformation, Tiresias embodies the medium's entailments.

PLAGUED BY THE NIGHTINGALE

If classical myth pictures poetic self-transformation in corporeal terms, it does so not only as gender-switching but also, more drastically, as species-crossing. The myth of Philomel provides a story of attaining poetic voice through bodily violation (rape) and the denial of self-expression (her rapist cuts out Philomel's tongue), followed by metamorphosis into a nightingale. According to Allen Grossman, the Philomel story is Western poetry's oldest paradigm for poetic voice and designates a prototypically feminine origin for lyric utterance: "Philomela's song (the nightingale's song) is omnipresent in history in the same way that pain is omnipresent in history and therefore [is] mythographically older than Orpheus's narrative, because always already there, even as witness to Orpheus in his pain."[30] Grossman's claim that Philomel's narrative takes precedence over Orpheus' as a model for poetic production holds a number of implications. While both models predicate poetry upon violence, the Philomel story specifies a form of sexual violence that can be understood by male poets only as emasculation. "Rape founds poetry," Grossman insists, "because it is the radical challenge to the woman's self-characterization as human – as the Orphic bereavement is the man's" (34). Here rape is a paradigm for depersonalization, and Grossman thus suggests that the rapist robs his victim of personhood in the same way that the structures of representation deprive a poet of social personhood.[31]

While a lack of space prevents me from fully considering Grossman's account of poetry's "bitter logic," I would like to entertain his claim that postromantic Anglo-American poetry tends toward the Philomelan model, irrespective of the author's gender. Since bodily vulnerability and erotic self-dispossession are much harder for men to contemplate than they are for women – men are raped less easily and less frequently than are women – poetic voice can be accessed more readily via feminine than masculine modes of being. *The Waste Land* confirms this counterintuitive hypothesis in its representation of "[t]he change of Philomel, by the barbarous king / So rudely forced;" the heavy caesura that interrupts the latter line signals a volta or turn, from which issues transformation: "yet there the nightingale / Filled all the desert with inviolable voice" (*WL*, 137). This scene of Philomel's rape recurs throughout the poem in episodes of sexual aggression and degradation – such as that of the typist and "the young man carbuncular" – that end with images of music or song. The typist, having been sexually assaulted, "puts a record on the gramophone" (*WL*, 141). And it is this transaction – the exchange of corporeal integrity for song – that Tiresias "*sees*": "I Tiresias have foresuffered all / Enacted on this same divan or bed" (ibid.)

Like the gramophone record, the nightingale's song offers an image of disembodied voice: a voice whose inviolability stems precisely from corporeal alienation. Proverbially the nightingale has no body; if one were to capture and cut open this bird, one would find that it contains no flesh, only a voice. The nightingale is a figure for imperishable vocality – a voice whose incorruptibility is purchased at the expense of corporeal violence, erotic self-dispossession, and the denial of self-expression. Thus the dissociation of voice from body that is so central to Eliot's poetic ideal entails becoming a medium (and thereby being feminized) or suffering the fate of Philomel (and thereby enduring a double emasculation).

In *The Waste Land* Eliot represents this "inviolable voice" by more and less conventionalized forms of onomatopoeia, employing a whole range of verbal imitation in which sound mimics sense. The Philomel scene ends with the sixteenth-century's standard poetic representation of nightingale song: "And still she cried, and still the world pursues, / 'Jug Jug' to dirty ears." Later in the poem, "Jug Jug" becomes

> Twit twit twit
> Jug jug jug jug jug jug
> So rudely forc'd.
> Tereu   (*WL*, 140)

Manuscript drafts of the poem show that, in an earlier version, this approximation of the nightingale's song immediately followed the scene of Mr. Eugenides's homosexual proposition, as if to emphasize the idea that being penetrated by a man represents the precondition for poetic voice (*WL*, 31).[32] The violent scene of poetry's origins is invoked throughout the poem by Eliot's increasing recourse to onomatopoeic utterances. After repetition of the nightingale's song, "The Fire Sermon" quotes Wagner's Rhinemaidens singing "Weialala leia / Wallala leialala" (*WL*, 142), which becomes another onomatopoeic refrain fading to "la la" (*WL*, 143). In the poem's closing section the hermit-thrush takes over the nightingale's role, and Eliot's onomatopoeic depiction of its song – "Drip drop drip drop drop drop drop" (*WL*, 144) – is intensified by his presenting the hermit-thrush's negative double: "Only a cock stood on the rooftree / Co co rico co co rico" (*WL*, 145). Finally, the sound of thunder is condensed into the ontomatopoeic phoneme "DA," whose repetition through variation generates the poem's conclusion.

The Waste Land's commitment to onomatopoeia enacts on the linguistic level its search for a mode of speaking that would attain universal intelligibility by virtue of being completely desituated or context-independent. The nightingale's "inviolable voice" provides a model for this style of speaking; yet the poem is crammed with scenes of horror that suggest the personal forfeit entailed by impersonalist utterance. Far from a ruse of self-empowerment, aesthetic impersonality in *The Waste Land* is pictured as a virtually intolerable discipline of self-dispossession. The difficulty with which this poem confronts us is, finally, not epistemological but ontological: it solicits less our powers of demystification or interpretive mastery than a radical renunciation of mastery. It is therefore perhaps unsurprising that Eliot never repeated this experiment, choosing instead to sublimate his self-dispossession and its attendant spiritualism in the institutional structures of the Anglican church. His move toward orthodox religion and his shifting from poetry to drama testify to his conviction that the pleasures of self-dispossession were outweighed by their cost.[33]

NOTES

1. Anthony Lane, "Writing Wrongs," *New Yorker*, March 10, 1997, 91.
2. Anthony Julius, *T. S. Eliot, Anti-Semitism and Literary Form* (Cambridge: Cambridge University Press, 1995).
3. Eve Kosofsky Sedgwick, *Epistemology of the Closet* (Berkeley: University of California Press, 1990).
4. Wordsworth's preface to the 1802 edition of *Lyrical Ballads* (in William Wordsworth and Samuel Taylor Coleridge, *Lyrical Ballads*, ed. R. L. Brett and A. R. Jones [London: Routledge, 1991], 266); T. S. Eliot, "Tradition and the Individual Talent," in *The Sacred Wood: Essays on Poetry and Criticism* (1920; London: Methuen, 1980), 58; subsequent references provide pagination in main text.
5. James E. Miller, *T. S. Eliot's Personal Waste Land: Exorcism of the Demons* (University Park: Pennsylvania State University Press, 1977), 36; subsequent references provide pagination in main text.
6. *Tom & Viv*, dir. Brian Gilbert (Miramax, 1994). See also Carole Seymour-Jones, *Painted Shadow: The Life of Vivienne Eliot, First Wife of T. S. Eliot, and the Long-Suppressed Truth about Her Influence on His Genius* (New York: Doubleday, 2002).
7. Terry Eagleton, *Criticism and Ideology* (London: Verso, 1978), 147.

8. Maud Ellmann, *The Poetics of Impersonality: T. S. Eliot and Ezra Pound* (Brighton, Sussex: Harvester, 1987), 15; subsequent references provide pagination in main text.

9. Robert Onopa, "The End of Art as a Spiritual Project," *TriQuarterly* 26 (1973): 372.

10. Terry Eagleton, *Literary Theory: An Introduction* (Minneapolis: University of Minnesota Press, 1983), 39.

11. Paul Morrison, *The Poetics of Fascism: Ezra Pound, T. S. Eliot, Paul de Man* (New York: Oxford University Press, 1996).

12. Kenneth Asher, *T. S. Eliot and Ideology* (New York: Cambridge University Press, 1995), 62.

13. Leo Bersani, "Is the Rectum a Grave?" in *AIDS: Cultural Analysis/Cultural Activism*, ed. Douglas Crimp (Cambridge, Mass.: MIT Press, 1988), 222.

14. See Leo Bersani, *The Culture of Redemption* (Cambridge, Mass.: Harvard University Press, 1990).

15. For example, in a particularly bald judgment, Eagleton measures Eliot's poem against a criterion of political realism and finds it wanting: "In this sense *The Waste Land* is ideological: it shows a man making sense of his experience in ways that prohibit a true understanding of his society, ways that are consequently false." Terry Eagleton, *Marxism and Literary Criticism* (Berkeley: University of California Press, 1976), 17.

16. John Peter, "A New Interpretation of *The Waste Land,*" *Essays in Criticism* 2 (1952): 242–66; and Peter, "Postscript," *Essays in Criticism* 19, no. 2 (1969): 165–75.

17. Wayne Koestenbaum, *Double Talk: The Erotics of Male Literary Collaboration* (New York: Routledge, 1989), 71; subsequent references provide pagination in main text.

18. Merrill Cole, "Empire of the Closet," *Discourse* 19, no. 3 (1997): 71; subsequent references provide pagination in main text.

19. Colleen Lamos, *Deviant Modernism: Sexual and Textual Errancy in T. S. Eliot, James Joyce, and Marcel Proust* (New York: Cambridge University Press, 1998), 67; subsequent references provide pagination in main text.

20. The complex history and etymology of *persona* is charted usefully in Gordon W. Allport, *Personality: A Psychological Interpretation* (New York: Henry Holt, 1937), 26.

21. What I am calling a postmodern critique of the autonomous self is articulated in French literature by Georges Bataille and Maurice Blanchot, in French psychoanalysis by Jacques Lacan and Jean Laplanche, and in French philosophy by Jacques Derrida, Michel Foucault, and Emmanuel Levinas, to name only its most obvious proponents. The critique reaches back to Flaubert's ideas about impersonal authorship in his letters describing the composition of *Madame Bovary* – ideas that influenced Joyce's theory and practice of aesthetic impersonality. To compare Roland Barthes's critique of authorship with Eliot's version of the theory is to register the full force of a continuity between modernist aesthetics and postmodern theory. Barthes announces "the necessity

to substitute language [the medium] itself for the person who until then had been supposed to be its owner," and continues, "it is language which speaks, not the author; to write is, through a prerequisite impersonality (not at all to be confused with the castrating objectivity of the realist novelist), to reach that point where only language acts, 'performs,' and not 'me.'" Roland Barthes, "The Death of the Author," in *Image – Music – Text*, ed. and trans. Stephen Heath (London: Fontana, 1977), 143. On the continuity between modern and postmodern ideas of authorial selfhood, see Seán Burke, *The Death and Return of the Author: Criticism and Subjectivity in Barthes, Foucault, and Derrida*, 2nd edn. (Edinburgh: Edinburgh University Press, 1998). Although the terms of this continuity cannot be elaborated here, I want to note that by developing the postmodern critique of the autonomous self, queer theory can be understood as extending rather than repudiating the impersonalist principles Eliot lays out in "Tradition and the Individual Talent."

22. William Butler Yeats, "A General Introduction for My Work," in *Essays and Introductions* (New York: Macmillan, 1961), 517. Eliot's ambivalent relation to occultism is treated especially cogently in Donald J. Childs, "Fantastic Views: T. S. Eliot and the Occultation of Knowledge and Experience," *Texas Studies in Literature and Language* 39, no. 4 (1997): 357–74, whose effort to situate the poet's engagement with the occult in terms of his epistemological concerns anticipates the present essay's argument. For further discussion of Eliot's relation to occultism, see Leon Surette, *The Birth of Modernism: Ezra Pound, T. S. Eliot, W. B. Yeats, and the Occult* (Montreal and Kingston: McGill-Queen's University Press, 1993); Timothy Materer, *Modernist Alchemy: Poetry and the Occult* (Ithaca, N. Y.: Cornell University Press, 1995), 71–86; and, most interestingly, Helen Sword, *Ghostwriting Modernism* (Ithaca, N. Y.: Cornell University Press, 2002), which discusses *The Waste Land* in terms of mediumship. I regret that the appearance of *Ghostwriting Modernism* only after I'd completed this essay prevents my properly engaging with it here.

23. Lyndall Gordon, *T. S. Eliot: An Imperfect Life* (New York: Norton, 1999), 541.

24. T. S. Eliot, *The Waste Land: A Facsimile and Transcript of the Original Drafts Including the Annotations of Ezra Pound*, ed. Valerie Eliot (New York: Harcourt Brace Jovanovich, 1971), 148; subsequent references provide pagination in main text using the abbreviation *WL*.

25. Circumstances prevent my quoting the relevant passage in full; I hope readers will take this opportunity to consult their copies of *The Waste Land*, lines 43–59, at this point.

26. It is perhaps worth recalling that the speaker of "Gerontion," which Eliot intended as a prologue to *The Waste Land*, is also blind: "Here I am, an old man in a dry month, / Being read to by a boy."

27. Bersani, "Rectum," 217. This idea forms a central concern of Bersani's work; in *Homos* (Cambridge, Mass.: Harvard University Press, 1995) he discusses "the appeal of renunciation" most extensively in relation to homosexuality (95).

28. See Jean Laplanche, *Life and Death in Psychoanalysis*, trans. Jeffrey Mehlman (Baltimore: Johns Hopkins University Press, 1976).

29. Keats to Richard Woodhouse, October 27, 1818, *Letters of John Keats*, ed. Robert Gittings (Oxford: Oxford University Press, 1970), 157–8.

30. Allen Grossman, "Orpheus/Philomela: Subjection and Mastery in the Founding Stories of Poetic Production," in *The Long Schoolroom: Lessons in the Bitter Logic of the Poetic Principle* (Ann Arbor: University of Michigan Press, 1997), 21; subsequent references provide pagination in main text.

31. Grossman is adamant about the predatory, dehumanizing effects of the poetic principle: "the logic of representation is unendurable by the natural person. The function of poetic practice is to defer the implosion of the poetic principle into the actual world" ("Orpheus/Philomela," 35).

32. Manuscript drafts show that this idea of being penetrated is also an explicit preoccupation of what became "The Death of Saint Narcissus," a poem subsequently absorbed into *The Waste Land*. In the first, untitled version of "The Death of Saint Narcissus" the subject of the poem

> wished he had been a young girl
> Caught in the woods by a drunken old man
> To have known at the last moment, the full
>   taste of her own whiteness
> The horror of her own smoothness.
>
> (*WL*, 93)

The wish to experience forcible penetration motivates the saint's religious commitment, as the draft continues,

> So he devoted himself to God.
> Because his flesh was in love with the penetrant arrows
> He danced on the hot sand
> Until the arrows came.

In the subsequent version of this poem, "penetrant arrows" has been softened to "burning arrows" (*WL*, 97), though Eliot retains the theme of experiencing rape from the vantage of both aggressor and victim, in the mode of Tiresias.

33. For feedback on this essay and its critical issues, I would like to thank especially Jed Esty, Nancy Gish, Suvir Kaul, Cassandra Laity, Janet Lyon, Shannon McRae, Ramón Soto-Crespo, and Joseph Valente.

CHAPTER 3

"Cells in one body": nation and eros in the early work of T. S. Eliot

Michele Tepper

One of the most fascinating things about T. S. Eliot's "Tradition and the Individual Talent" is that its meaning is so often taken for granted.[1] Perhaps because of Eliot's tremendous influence as a critic, writers are often loath to take such an important work at anything other than its received meanings, and thus end up not really reading "Tradition and the Individual Talent" itself, but rather rereading its readings, resedimenting its sedimentations. Even the literary scholars who have been most influential in reshaping their field only seem able to view Eliot's criticism through the lenses Eliot himself crafted for them. To take one notable example, Edward Said's magisterial reconceptualization of the Western tradition, *Culture and Imperialism*, refers to "the occasion as well as the intention" of "Tradition and the Individual Talent" as "almost purely aesthetic," with only the "almost" to distinguish Said's professed materialism from the formalism of Eliot's New Critical acolytes.[2] This is a profoundly odd description; after all, Said's own work gives the lie to any claim for the autonomy of the aesthetic from the political. Yet Said's discussion of the essay offers only one sentence of quibble to two paragraphs of explanation, and presents itself not as an interpretation but as a *definitive* reading of the essay. Because "Tradition and the Individual Talent" is an essay whose meaning everybody already knows, Said can claim to understand Eliot's "intention" in writing it.

But what happens when we do take the work as a subject of inquiry? Tracing the essay's genealogy through Eliot's other 1919 formulations of the individual's relationship to tradition – "Reflections on Contemporary Poetry [IV]" and "Was There a Scottish Literature?" – demonstrates how Eliot's closely interrelated anxieties around sexuality and around his own self-perceived debased position as an American writer motivate the formulation of his earliest and most influential critical positions.[3] In the first essay, "Reflections on Contemporary Poetry [IV]," the individual's relationship to the literary tradition is an eroticized one, in which the poet is formed by a passionate love affair with a poet of the past. "Was There a Scottish

Literature?" and the two-part "Tradition and the Individual Talent" quickly move on to sublimate the desired body of the poet/lover into a fantasized male embodiment of the *corpus* of the national literary tradition, which becomes eroticized in turn. The first essay's codes of intimacy give way to the talk in "Was There a Scottish Literature?" of nation and national identity – a discussion that still speaks of affiliation to a literary tradition as a fulfillment of desire. But the register is a different one, and it is one that, by the time of "Tradition and the Individual Talent," will make room for an imagined literary community, understood as an expression of English national culture, in what had first been envisaged as a passionate dyad. In imagining that community, Eliot reshapes English literary identity from outside the existing English national culture of letters, and fashions a new center from which a modernist, and specifically Eliotic, literary culture could and did grow. Thus, an analysis of the circulation of bodies and desires in "Tradition and the Individual Talent" can allow us not only to see a crucial yet underappreciated aspect of an important critical text, but also to open up a space for a more fully embodied and historicized understanding of our own critical practices.

As early as June 1919, Eliot was beginning to formulate an eroticized theory of influence. In "The Education of Taste," he describes intellectual development in terms that suggest the process of physical maturation as well: referring to the poet's early apprenticeship as "our intellectual pubescence," Eliot speculates that "some one book or poem" which "first . . . revealed to us our capacities for enjoyment of literature" may cause "the mind of a boy of fourteen" to "burst into life."[4] The equivalence Eliot draws here between intellectual and physical pubescence is a provocative one, but it is no further developed in this essay. "Reflections on Contemporary Poetry [IV]," published a month later in the *Egoist*, is in fact the first essay in which Eliot advances a fully developed theory of poetic influence rather than assuming one in passing reference. "Reflections" begins its theorizing by returning to the earlier essay's analogy between intellectual and physical pubescence and reformulating it, observing that "it is not true that the development of a writer is a function of his development as a man, but it is possible to say there is a close analogy between the sort of experience which develops a man and the sort of experience which develops a writer" (39).

Where the earlier piece's brevity allowed for a shallow reading that directly equated a boy's intellectual and physical maturation, here Eliot takes the time to lay out his argument in detail. The earlier essay's reference to a fourteen-year-old boy's mind bursting into life, evocative though it may be of the symmetries between physical and poetic development that Eliot is drawing, is not the only possible image for the moment of readerly maturity; and Eliot is careful to point that out, noting that adulthood and literary maturity need not go hand in hand. But having once made the gesture of separating manliness from writerliness, he immediately moves to strengthen the link, claiming that "similar" types of experience nourish both masculine maturity and poetic talent (39). From this linkage, Eliot proceeds to develop his most eroticized theory of poetic influence, describing an unnamed "kind of stimulus" which is "more important than the stimulus of admiring another writer." This deep-seated intimacy is described as increasingly urgent, impassioned, and transformative: "a feeling of profound kinship," "a peculiar personal intimacy," an "imperative intimacy [that] arouses for the first time a real, an unshakeable confidence." The young writer is "seized with his first passion of this sort" so profoundly that "he may be changed, metamorphosed almost, within a few weeks even, from a bundle of second-hand sentiments into a real person." Describing this stimulus of influence as "a genuine affair," Eliot concludes that it changes the young writer as a person and a poet. If the affair has been with a "real poet," the experience will allow the young writer to recognize later "when we are not in love," and will reshape his work with the imprint of the poet with whom he has been intimate: "we have not borrowed, we have been quickened, and we become bearers of a tradition" (*RCP*, 39).

Critics have long stumbled over, or refused to see, the workings of desire in this essay.[5] Louis Menand, for example, uses love as an "analogy" for what Eliot is trying to argue rather than acknowledging it in the passage itself, allowing desire to be held at a remove and tied to the heterosexual respectability of marriage: "the writer's private affair has plugged him . . . into a public thing; the analogy might be that love seems private to each, but marriage, even in secret, is an institution."[6] Lucy McDiarmid acknowledges the passage's passion, but backs away from drawing any conclusions from it: "The notion is vivid . . . perhaps too vivid. Such a sexual understanding of literature was not an idea Eliot elaborated with any immediacy again."[7] In failing to address this essay fully, these critics cut themselves off from understanding the insistent physicality and sensuousness of even Eliot's most remote-seeming texts, and thus overlook a crucial aspect of Eliot's early criticism and self-fashioning.[8]

In many ways, this is a passage that it would be easier to overlook; its rhetorics are exceptionally slippery. It speaks of "we" and "you," but never of "I." It begins by speaking of "development as a man" and ends with an image of pregnancy: "we have been quickened, and we become bearers of a tradition." The terms that Eliot uses are often connotative of homosexual desire, and yet "desire" is never invoked by name. Primarily, the essay concerns itself with "intimacy." When intimacy is first mentioned, it is both tied to, and immediately distinguished from, familial feelings: one's feeling for the dead poet is "a feeling of profound kinship, *or rather* of a peculiar personal intimacy" (emphasis added). This intimacy is also immediately marked as "peculiar," something outside the norm. When it is next mentioned, it is an "imperative" intimacy; the adjective can be read as removing the intimacy from the agency of the intimate subject, in much the same way that physical maturation and the entry into adult sexuality happens to fourteen-year-old boys whether they will it to or not. ·

The word "intimacy" reappears almost immediately in the next sentence with the assertion "you possess this secret knowledge, this intimacy, with the dead man." Not only does the repetition of "this" bring emphasis to the passage, but the apposition of "intimacy" and "secret knowledge" is the clearest sign of what sort of intimacy we are supposed to understand this to be. As Eve Kosofsky Sedgwick has shown, "by the end of the nineteenth century, when it had become fully current . . . that knowledge meant sexual knowledge, and secrets sexual secrets, there had in fact developed one particular sexuality that was distinctively constituted *as* secrecy," and that was male homosexuality.[9] Even today, the cultural links between secrecy and male homosexuality have not yet been fully broken. By linking his "peculiar intimacy" with "secret knowledge" here, Eliot foregrounds the homoerotic content of his theorizing, but only within a psychological wilderness of mirrors in which not even the things that seem obvious can be known for certain.

This wilderness may, however, be a central part of the pose of secrecy. David Miller notes that in saying one has a secret – in referring, as Eliot does, to "a secret knowledge" – one ceases to maintain secrecy. "I have had to intimate my secret, if only *not to tell it*; and conversely, in theatrically continuing to keep my secret, I have already *given it away*."[10] To mention that one is keeping a secret is to have the privilege of being able to tell it. Similarly, for Eliot to speak so openly of a homoeroticized "secret knowledge" is for him to make fantasmatic contact with a closet door that he knows he can keep firmly shut – that in fact has to remain firmly shut if his "passion" for another man, even a safely dead one, is not to mark him as Other. It is not entirely coincidental that Sedgwick calls "The Love Song of J. Alfred Prufrock" a "manifesto of male homosexual panic," by which she means to denote "a panicky response to a blackmailability over homo/heterosexual definition that affects all *but* homosexual-identified men"[11] – but where the earlier poem reacts to that panic through stasis and fragmentation, the essay is set into motion by it.

Indeed, the link that the essay makes between male adulthood and writerly maturity almost guarantees that its understanding of poetic development will be shaped by male homosexual panic. As Sedgwick convincingly argues, all postromantic Anglo-American men are

force[d] into the arbitrarily mapped, self-contradictory, and anathema-riddled quicksands of the middle distance of male homosocial desire . . . [and] enter into adult masculine entitlement only through acceding to the threat that the small space they have cleared for themselves on this terrain may always . . . be foreclosed.[12]

It is the extraordinary achievement of this essay to turn those quicksands to its own advantage, to openly eroticize precisely the male bonds that are most threatened by male homosexual panic, but to do so in the service of patriarchal values: as Lee Edelman says about another modernist work, Wallace Stevens's poem "Life on a Battleship," "what distinguishes this enabling seizure . . . of one male by another is its determining *hetero*sexuality – its participation, that is, in a psychic economy that defines itself *against* the historically available category of the 'homosexual.'"[13] The passion in "Reflections on Contemporary Poetry [IV]" works for and within the strictures of a heterocentric and patriarchal Anglo-American literary tradition, and these strictures serve as guarantors that the terrain on which this passion is established will not be closed in upon by the unspeakable specter of male homosexual desire.

Within modern Anglo-American culture, "the stimulation and glamorization of the energies of male-male desire . . . is an incessant project that must, for the preservation of that self-contradictory tradition, coexist with an equally incessant project of denying, deferring, or silencing their satisfaction."[14] Eliot's keeping of a secret can be bruited about because all the forces working to maintain the tradition that he explicates ensure that were the secret to be revealed, its content would be illegible, untranslatable, or simply silent; the closet which is most available for spectacularization is the one which can be shown, at least in certain lights, to be empty. It is particularly telling in this context that the only essay on *The Waste Land* that Eliot ever actively worked to suppress hypothesized a narrator who mourned a dead homosexual lover.[15] I would argue that the reason Eliot could not allow that hypothesis to circulate, even as other debates about his works raged on, was that once homosexual desire entered into the discourse around the poem as a possible "answer" to the work's many ambiguities, the "quicksands of . . . male homosocial desire" could have begun to shift again and his access to the terrain he carved out early in his career might have been foreclosed.

The essay's "participation . . . in a psychic economy that defines itself *against* the historically available category of the 'homosexual'" is not only implicit but explicit in the text, most notably in its use of the word "friend." The first use of it comes in the same long sentence in which "secret knowledge" and "intimacy" are first linked: "That you possess this secret knowledge, this intimacy . . . [that you] can call yourself alone his friend." The phrase "can call yourself alone his friend" is the emphatic center of this sentence, the point it builds to and away from. "Friend," like "intimacy," is a loaded word; as George Mosse bluntly states, "the history of sexuality cannot be separated from . . . that of friendship."[16] This is an inseparability that Eliot flirts with and exploits. To place "friend" at the center of a discussion of intimacy, to call this friendship a "crisis" in which "a young writer is seized with his first passion," and to make the fulfillment of this friendship only possible through the young writer's ability to "penetrate" the truth about the dead writer, is to invite an explicitly homoerotic reading of this passage's secret knowledge. But the essay continues on an entirely different note. Eliot turns to talking about the "usefulness of such a passion," and we learn that its use is to teach the young writer how to know when he is in (presumably heterosexual) love in real life; the homoerotic energies of the friendship are again channeled into the maintenance of the heterocentric social order.

Once this passage broaches the possibility of the poet's entering into a relationship with someone who is not dead, the essay shifts gears again, and the text's "we" becomes feminized, as if to normalize the peculiarity of its intimacies: "we have been quickened, and we become bearers of a tradition" – even though "we" are bearing a tradition that the essay's linkage of poetry and masculinity insists is a male-only club. Yet it seems clear that the child of this metaphoric quickening will be none other than the poet himself, now "changed, metamorphosed almost . . . from a bundle of second-hand sentiments into a person," made into a different and better man for having loved his predecessor. The feminized bearer of tradition both brings forth and becomes the completed and masculine poet. This image of self-creation through the tradition allows Eliot to imagine himself as "metamorphosed," freed of the history embedded in his American-born physical body and reconstituted as a creature entirely of the English literary tradition.

The importance of where a poet is created (or creates himself) is fore-grounded in Eliot's next formulation of his theory of tradition, "Was There a Scottish Literature?" The tie between nation and eros that this essay exem-plifies has been a topic of scholarly inquiry at least since the publication of Foucault's *History of Sexuality*, which ties the rise of the modern nation-state to the rise of "an analytics of sexuality."[17] George Mosse's groundbreaking work on bourgeois morality and sexual norms in modern Europe has made it clear that "homoeroticism [is] always close to the surface of nationalism," yet the ways in which the "deep, horizontal comradeship" of nationalism of which Benedict Anderson speaks spills over into libidinal identifications have only recently begun to be understood in literary studies.[18] The project of understanding these linkages must be a part of the project of understand-ing Eliot's initial self-fashioning as a critic as well, not least because "Was There a Scottish Literature?" refigures the relationship of the individual to the tradition as a passionate merging of writers past and present into one, specifically English, body.

Wayne Koestenbaum has argued that Eliot's collaboration with Ezra Pound on *The Waste Land* "engage[s] in a symbolic scene of homosex-ual intercourse while freeing [the two men] from imputations of inverted style."[19] In much the same way, I have argued above, Eliot's first formula-tion of tradition uses homoeroticism to theorize the maturation of a poet into a proper bearer of a heterocentric literary tradition. Eliot's formulation of national identity follows a similar pattern by providing a space for the marginal subject but not for marginality per se. To take up the space of marginality here is to be conclusively excluded from the construction of the transcendental and ahistorical unity signified by the metaphor of the body, the literary *corpus* as flesh, through which the great writers of the English tradition (including those writers from the margins who have dis-avowed their marginality) are joined. What makes this essay particularly interesting is not only its genealogical position between "Reflections on Contemporary Poetry [IV]" and "Tradition and the Individual Talent," but also the way in which it does, in fact, work as a pause between these two essays in order to try to explicitly delineate who may join with this body of tradition and who may not.

Ironically enough, the book that Eliot reviews in this essay stands at the beginning of a revival of interest in a specifically Scottish literature in this century.[20] But the real question posed by this essay is not the one in its title but rather "What Makes English Literature Special?" The occasion of reviewing a book that attempts to provide a scholarly basis for the study of Scottish literature as a distinct tradition allows Eliot to make clear what does and does not count for him as "literature," and he makes it clear from the outset that Scottish literature could not possibly count. Eliot begins the essay with a set of suppositions that attempt to draw the reader into sympathy with his argument, beginning with the most basic opposition that "we suppose that there is an English literature, and Professor Gregory Smith supposes that there is a Scotch literature." Eliot continues to repeat the "we suppose" as he draws the reader into his argument, redefining a "literature" as "one of the five or six (at most) great organic formations of history." And not just any history, "for there might be a history of Tamil literature," but History itself, "which for us is the history of Europe." "We suppose" next that a literature "is part of a mind" that is both part of history and transhistorical, "a greater, finer, more positive, more comprehensive mind than the mind of any period." And finally, "we suppose" that a writer of this literature is important not just as an individual talent, but as "a constituent of this mind." As Eliot notes in the final line of this passage, when we suppose that there is a literature under this definition, "therefore, we suppose a great deal" (680). The repetition of "we suppose" serves to make each point more emphatic as he goes on, and recruits the reader for the "we" that cannot imagine both an English and a Scottish literature, let alone an English and a Tamil-language literature, as separate but interdependent entities.[21]

The "great organic formations of history" this "we" lauds could also not possibly include American literature, since American literature is at best only marginally part of the history of Europe. Eliot had argued in an essay published just a few months before that nineteenth-century American culture was secondhand goods, a shadow of English literature rather than an original cultural formation.[22] Similarly, in "Was There a Scottish Literature?" he claims that insofar as Scottish literature can be divided into periods, those periods are not so much related to one another as to the corresponding eras of English literature (680). American, Scottish, and Tamil literature are thus all in the same category: historically insignificant literatures of a colonized or dominated people. Indeed, within Eliot's definition of what counts as a literature, America is a threat to English literature's cohesion if its literature is *not* English literature's shadow, in that "the danger of disintegration of English language and literature would arise if the same language were employed by peoples too remote (for geographical or other reasons) to be able to pool their differences in a common metropolis" (681). Since Eliot has just noted that English, Scottish, and Irish literatures are similar enough for their union under the rubric of "English Literature" to be a meaningful one, the only other English-speaking nation that he and his readers would have thought had a literature that could stand independently of England's would be the United States. In order to position himself as a poet within the English literary tradition, within a literature that is a part of "History," Eliot has to discount and discredit the possibility of an independent American literature, which he does here and, more implicitly, in "Tradition and the Individual Talent."

"Was There a Scottish Literature?" also introduces the metaphor of literature as the creation of the "comprehensive mind" of England, which reappears in "Tradition and the Individual Talent" as the omnipotent "mind of Europe." This is as much an idealized image of communion with the dead as anything in the "Reflections on Contemporary Poetry" essay: even the string of adjectives describing it – "greater," "finer," "more positive," "more comprehensive" – gush. But here the eroticism of the first essay is sublimated into nationalist sentiment. What makes the tradition represented by this mind worth gushing over is its undilutable Englishness: while, as noted above, Eliot argues that the periods of Scottish literature are best explained through reference to the periods of English literature, he insists that even explanations of English literature that take into account its Continental influences must always return to England to be complete (680–1). Nationalist feelings do not completely replace erotic desire in this second formulation of the writer's relationship to tradition: rather, the locus of desire shifts from an external one – the dead poet – to an internal and nationalized one – the "comprehensive mind" of England – and an embodied vision of the entire national literary tradition.

Eliot argues that supposing the existence of a literature requires supposing an "organic formation" that is, quite literally, a body of work; not merely a "corpus of writings in one language, but writings and writers between whom there is a tradition." The tradition serves to connect them not just "in time," but in an ahistorical union that makes them "in the light of eternity contemporaneous," or even more tightly joined together as "cells in one body, Chaucer and Hardy" (WSL, 680). Here we see another version of the transhistorical union between writers that Eliot discusses as a love affair in "Reflections on Contemporary Poetry [IV]," but, where the earlier essay's union was between two distinct selves, here Eliot presents the reader with a union that creates one greater self: each writer is important not just as himself but because of his role as an element of this self. In "The Love Song of J. Alfred Prufrock," sexual anxiety reduces bodies, and in particular female and feminized bodies, to their parts: arms and legs and perfumed dresses; in this essay we see a male body *constructed* metonymically.[23] The image joins Chaucer and Hardy, and by implication all the canonical poets between them, into an organic whole, an unfragmented and unfragmentable body. It is not an image that the essay sustains – the next sentence turns to the equally idealizable but less fleshly "comprehensive mind" discussed above – but the possibility that the bonds that tie this body together are corporeal and erotic ones remains implicit within this essay and all of Eliot's early theorization of tradition.

Where his slightly senior contemporary Gertrude Stein could claim, in a very different mode and moment, that "it is a pleasure to know that there is so much English literature and that at any moment in one's life it is all inside you. At any rate it is all inside me," for Eliot the pleasure seems to be in an embodiment into which he can disappear rather than one he can encompass.[24] A writer who is willing to subsume himself within the tradition of a significant literature, to both submit to its dictates and make it his own, can be rewarded with his own place in this tradition: with stature equal to the other constituents of this mind as a poet of the metropolis, and with precisely the sort of intense and ahistorical connection to the past that the "Reflections on Contemporary Poetry" essay sought to describe. In the first essay, a submission to the "imperative intimacy" of his relationship with a poet of the past changes the young writer into a person worth considering; in this essay, submission to the dictates of the tradition gives the writer born outside of History a chance to enter into and become part of the core of Europe's historical narrative.

"Tradition and the Individual Talent" continues in this vein by presenting the relationship between the two terms in the title as one of complete obeisance on the latter's part: "The progress of an artist is a continual self-sacrifice" (40). The essay figures culture as imperial and the poet as a sort of colonial subject: "[The poet] must be aware [of] the mind of Europe – the mind of his own country – a mind which he learns in time to be much more important than his own private mind" (39).

The conflation of the "mind of Europe" and the "mind of his own country" here is crucial. In the summer of 1919, with World War I a very recent memory, it's unlikely that the Britons of that era, let alone the residents of the Continental nations that had suffered occupation and carnage at a previously unimaginable level, thought of themselves as part of a united "Europe." Indeed, a year earlier, in a tribute to Henry James, the man on whom his early career was most closely based, Eliot had claimed that "It is the final perfection, the consummation of an American to become, not an Englishman, but a European – something which no born European, no person of any European nationality, can become."[25] Chris Baldick argues that Eliot's deployment of his broad knowledge of European culture in his early criticism and poetry was successful because it was the moral literary strategy for the postwar world: "this was at the time the most appropriate response to the challenge of the war and its aftermath: a creative and critical vision which did not attempt to measure up to the international scale of the holocaust and its significance would not have been, in Arnold's terms, 'adequate.'"[26] This may offer a partial explanation for Eliot's success, but it is certainly not a complete one: what Baldick overlooks is how Eliot's formulations serve not only the purposes of an English literary culture seeking to bind up its wounds, but also Eliot's own purposes as well in fashioning a new literary culture with himself at both its center and its edges. For in conflating England – implicitly claiming it, in an English journal, as "his own country" some eight years before he applied for British citizenship – and Europe, presenting them as a unified whole, as literally of one mind, Eliot lays claim both to the privilege of the English metropolis and to the distance from and leverage on the various traditions of Western Europe provided by his status as an American.

Once we see this conflation, it may be less surprising than it appears at first glance that Eliot does not attempt to claim the central place in the comprehensive mind of Europe for the English literary tradition. In fact, "Tradition and the Individual Talent" begins by chiding the English for failing to honor the European tradition, and for failing in literary criticism. Since tradition is the crucial element in Eliot's literary theorizing, and criticism is, for Eliot, an inevitable part of the formation of traditions of taste, for the English to fail at criticism is also for them to fail at the larger project of maintaining a "great organic formation . . . of history." It might seem counterproductive for Eliot to so fault the very tradition whose body he wishes to be a cell of, but in doing so he is accomplishing something important in his project of assimilating himself to Englishness and making a new English literature in his own image. In the process of his own metamorphosis from a writer of the provinces to a citizen of the metropolis, he constructs the English as being at the cultural periphery of Europe. From there, he can replay his own process of assimilation, but this time it is the assimilation of the English back into the mainstream of European culture, as guided by T. S. Eliot. Eliot's own liminal status, as an American on the outside of the tradition seeking to work his way in, is transformed into the only position from which the tradition can be defended and revitalized. Yet it is worth stressing that Englishness remains the sine qua non of Eliot's theoretical model: a glance backwards at "Was There a Scottish Literature?" or at Eliot's openly anti-Semitic poems of this same time period should make it clear that those who will not submit to the dictates of the metropolitan culture will be anathematized by it.[27] The Englishness that prevails here is internationally minded but still undilutably English, an English literature that can easily absorb and even grant pride of place to the multilingual but still recognizably English unreal city of *The Waste Land*. I would argue that it is Eliot's claim to knowledge of how "the mind of Europe" works, as much as the "punctiliousness and erudition" that Louis Menand cites, that made Eliot's criticism so popular among English students and critics when it was first published in book form.[28] "*The Sacred Wood* was apparently regarded as a kind of holy text by literature-minded undergraduates at Oxford and Cambridge in the 1920s" not only because in following in Eliot's footsteps one could lay claim to a "scientific" study of literature, but also because it allowed literary studies to lay claim to all of European culture.[29]

What is it that will allow this access? And how does a literary tradition become the sort of cohesive, organic body that Eliot claims all great literatures are? Eliot makes his only claim for the agency of the poet, in the essays I consider here, in his suggestion that the cohesion is provided by the poet's laborious immersion in the European tradition, which, as he famously notes, "cannot be inherited, and if you want it you must obtain it by great labor." This labor serves primarily to develop the "historical sense" which "compels" the poet to write "not merely with his own generation in his bones," but from within a subsumation in the "whole of the literature of Europe from Homer and within it the literature of his own country," which he now can see has "a simultaneous existence and composes a simultaneous order" (*TT*, 38). Access to the tradition is thus not a birthright that the American Eliot might have been denied, but a privilege he can earn through the conscious development of a sensibility. It is through this tradition that England can be assimilated into Europe and that the poet can be assimilated into England, and it can only come to life in the "bones" of the writer who understands the "simultaneous existence" of the writers who make up the literary tradition.[30] "Reflections on Contemporary Poetry [IV]" shows the young poet becoming "quickened" by tradition; although the passion of that essay might seem far removed from the vatic pronouncements of "Tradition and the Individual Talent," we can see that essay's traces here in the poet's carrying of the tradition in his body. What is produced from the poet's labor in both these essays is not a new child, but the poet, reproducing himself as a "changed man" who can claim his place in a patriarchal literary and social order (*RCP*, 39). This reproductive process allows the success of Eliot's quest to become English, or rather to gain critical leverage on Englishness from within. In absorbing English and European culture into his bones, he can be absorbed into the body of the English literary tradition and into the history of Europe.

Eliot's theorization of poetry would go on, in 1921, to famously bemoan the "dissociation of sensibility," the lack of unity between ideas and deeds, between the mind and the body. He argues that, to Donne, thought was almost physical: "an experience" that could "modif[y] his sensibility." Like the dramatists of Shakespeare's time, the poets of the seventeenth century "possessed a mechanism of sensibility" so "perfectly equipped" to their purposes that it could "devour any kind of experience." But after their era, the dissociation of sensibility, from which Eliot claims "we have never recovered," set in.[31] This theorized dissociation may have, as Eliot would admit three decades later, some connection to the English Civil War, but I would argue that it also has something to do with the time in which the Metaphysicals lived.[32] They wrote at the end of a period of remarkable consolidation and definition of discursive formations of English identity, and at the beginning of an era of expansion and imperialism.[33] The imperial venture changes not only the colonized world but the colonizers as well: English and American literature after Donne has to come to terms with the "new-found land" as more than a metaphor. The colonial project may increase the audience and influence of English literature, but it can also threaten its very existence: "The danger of disintegration of English language and literature would arise if the same language were employed by peoples too remote . . . to be able to pool their differences in a common metropolis" (*WSL*, 681). To have written when this was not a threat, when English literature was still unitary, might in this theorization have allowed a writer to be unitary within himself as well, and, for Eliot, tying his own project to that idealized past time – insisting on his unmediated access to that past as part of the "simultaneous order" of the literary tradition – is a way of overcoming the history that might tear the organic body of English Literature apart.

In Eliot's descriptions, the bodies of the Metaphysicals are hardy ones, much like the body of the national tradition that can take him in. Donne is a valuable poet because he "devour[ed]" and digested the world, while Tennyson and Browning merely ruminated (*MP*, 64–5); he "amalgamated disparate experience" into "new wholes" (64). Again, Eliot's metaphors tie bodies and the physical world inextricably into poetry-making and literary tradition. In his May 1919 review of *The Education of Henry Adams*, on the brink of his career as a literary theorist, Eliot had ventured that "many men will admit that their keenest ideas have come to them with the quality of a sense-perception; and that their keenest sensuous experience has been 'as if the body thought.'"[34] The bodies of Eliot's Metaphysicals thought, and their thoughts were embodied; through the body and thoughts of the poet who works in the tradition of the Metaphysicals, the chaotic and fragmented modern world can be made into a harmoniously amalgamated whole, an organic formation (*MP*, 66). And, as we have already seen, the poet can only accomplish this reparation of history's wounds by stepping outside history, embracing and being embraced by the national tradition rooted in the Metaphysicals that will "devour" him and recreate him as he in turn devours the world and recreates it in poetry. In the words of a poet who Eliot always strenuously denied had influenced his work despite all evidence to the contrary, "The proof of a poet is that his country absorbs him as affectionately as he has absorbed it."[35]

This absorption is more than simply the absorption of Eliot's poetry into a new canon-formation. Within his invented England and Europe, the historical Eliot can be absorbed into Europe – can in fact vanish without a trace even as the name "Eliot" becomes affixed to the poetic works that are absorbed into the tradition. As in "Reflections on Contemporary Poetry [IV]," the poet's biological body is equated with an abstraction, a literary corpus, in the first section of "Tradition and the Individual Talent": by the second section, the poet's body is disappearing into that corpus, much as the individual cells disappear into the body of the literary tradition in "Was There a Scottish Literature?" The second section of "Tradition and the Individual Talent" compares the function of the poet within poetry to that of the catalyst in a chemical reaction: something which needs to be there for the reaction to occur but leaves no traces in the final product. Once again, the poet has no volition in the process, much as in the "imperative intimacy" of the first essay; any actions taken by the biographical Eliot can be so effaced in the process of his assimilation into the tradition that he disappears, leaving only the poetry (which his criticism ties to his own European-inflected version of the English literary tradition) to remain as a part of the ecstatic body of that tradition.

This is all, of course, as much of a performance as Eliot's performance of secrecy in the first essay under discussion here. In both cases, Eliot is attempting to theorize a marginal identity into the center. In the first essay, we see homoeroticism being used to bolster a heterosexist tradition, and here we see Americanness being used to bolster Englishness by bringing it into Europeanness. These two strategies converge – as we have seen in "Was There a Scottish Literature?" – in the figure of the national body of tradition.

But, as we have also seen in the history of critical silence surrounding "Reflections on Contemporary Poetry [IV]"'s eroticism, these are performances whose results criticism has been far more comfortable with than it has with their causes. They are not, however, performances from which we can afford to avert our eyes further. Eliot's formulation of tradition can deepen an ongoing conversation in queer theory, in that although his ideas may be readable through same-sex erotic desire, they are not always reducible to it. His works also speak of nonnormative forms of carnality and eroticism that are not reducible to genital sexuality: the desire to consume and be consumed, the desire to lose oneself in something greater, and the desire to encompass that greater thing within one's own body – to have it in one's bones and blood. Eliot's Metaphysical models lived in an era in which desire was not as easily reduced to homo- and heterosexual as it is (even, too often, by queer theory) in the twenty-first century, and it may be that we can read in his desire for a transhistorical union with them a desire as well for a cultural dispensation under which desire need not take sexuality so literally.[36]

Conversely, to acknowledge that "Tradition and the Individual Talent" grew out of Eliot's eroticized formulation of the poet's relationship to the past, that this formulation remains in traces in the poet's absorption into the body of tradition, which in turn interacts with the other great "organic formations" of European literature, is to understand that a drive toward sensual connection underlies even criticism's most emphatic statements of disinterested impersonality. It is to acknowledge the libidinal energies of our own work, and the erotic as well as intellectual discipline necessary to maintain ideological structures such as community and tradition. It is, if not to see our critical heritage from Eliot as steadily and whole as he would have the critic do, then at least, in that modernist cliché, to make it new.

NOTES

1. T. S. Eliot, "Tradition and the Individual Talent," in *Selected Essays*, ed. Frank Kermode (New York: Harcourt Brace Jovanovich and Farrar Straus Giroux, 1975). First published in *Egoist* 6, nos. 4–5 (August and November/December 1919); hereafter cited in the text as *TT*.
2. Edward Said, *Culture and Imperialism* (New York: Knopf, 1993), 4.
3. T. S. Eliot, "Reflections on Contemporary Poetry [IV]," *Egoist* 6, no. 3 (July 1919): 39–40; hereafter cited in the text as *RCP*; and T. S. Eliot, "Was There a Scottish Literature?," review of *Scottish Literature: Character and Influence*, by G. Gregory Smith, *Athenaeum* (August 1, 1919): 680–1; hereafter cited in the text as *WSL*.

4. T. S. Eliot, "The Education of Taste," *Athenaeum* (June 27, 1919): 521.
5. See also Colleen Lamos's *Deviant Modernism: Sexual and Textual Errancy in T. S. Eliot, James Joyce, and Marcel Proust* (Cambridge: Cambridge University Press, 1999) which deals with this essay in particular and Eliot and sexuality in general; Cassandra Laity's *H.D. and the Victorian Fin de Siècle: Gender, Modernism, Decadence* (Cambridge: Cambridge University Press, 1996) briefly discusses the workings of desire in this essay as well (8–10).
6. Louis Menand, *Discovering Modernism: T. S. Eliot and His Context* (Oxford: Oxford University Press, 1987), 71.
7. Lucy McDiarmid, "Eliot: The Dead, the Living, and the End of Poetry," *Yale Review* 78, no. 2 (Winter 1989): 267.
8. I do not mean to suggest that these particular critics are shortsighted in ways that their colleagues are not: rather, I take them as individual cases of a more general syndrome.
9. Eve Kosofsky Sedgwick, *Epistemology of the Closet* (Berkeley: University of California Press, 1990), 73.
10. D. A. Miller, *The Novel and the Police* (Berkeley: University of California Press, 1988), 194.
11. Sedgwick, *Epistemology*, 240, 240n.25.
12. Ibid., 186.
13. Lee Edelman, "Redeeming the Phallus: Wallace Stevens, Frank Lentricchia, and the Politics of (Hetero)Sexuality," in *Homographesis: Essays in Gay Literary and Cultural Theory* (New York: Routledge, 1994), 39.
14. Sedgwick, *Epistemology*, 56.
15. John Peter, "A New Interpretation of *The Waste Land*," *Essays in Criticism* 2, no. 3 (July 1952): 242–66. Eliot's solicitor threatened to sue the journal for libel but dropped the suit after receiving an apology from Peter and a promise that undistributed copies of the journal would be destroyed. See James E. Miller, Jr., "T. S. Eliot's 'Uranian Muse': The Verdenal Letters," *ANQ* 11 (September 1998): 4.
16. George Mosse, *Nationalism and Sexuality* (Madison: University of Wisconsin Press, 1985), 66.
17. Michel Foucault, *The History of Sexuality: An Introduction*, trans. Robert Hurley (New York: Vintage Books, 1990), 135–50.
18. Mosse, *Nationalism*, 67; Benedict Anderson, *Imagined Communities*, rev. edn. (London: Verso, 1991), 16.
19. Wayne Koestenbaum, *Double Talk: The Erotics of Male Literary Collaboration* (New York: Routledge, 1989), 139.
20. Douglas Dunn builds his introduction to *The Faber Book of Twentieth-Century Scottish Poetry* (London: Faber and Faber, 1991) on a refutation of Faber's most celebrated editor's death-warrant for an independent Scottish literature. For recent literary, cultural studies, and linguistic approaches to specifically Scottish modern literature, see, for example, Robert Crawford, *Devolving English Literature* (Oxford: Oxford University Press, 1992); Ray Ryan, *Ireland and Scotland: Literature and Culture, State and Nation, 1966–2000* (Oxford: Oxford University

Press, 2002); and Jeffrey Skoblow, *Dooble Tongue: Scots, Burns, Contradiction* (Newark: University of Delaware Press, 2001). There have also been several critical studies of poet Hugh MacDiarmid, for example, *The Age of MacDiarmid*, ed. P. H. Scott and A. C. David (Edinburgh: Mainstream, 1980); and Nancy K. Gish, *Hugh MacDiarmid: The Man and His Work* (London: Macmillan, 1984) and *Hugh MacDiarmid: Man and Poet* (Orono, Maine: National Poetry Foundation, 1992).

21. See Leonard Diepeveen, "'I Can Have More than Enough Power to Satisfy Me': T. S. Eliot's Construction of His Audience," in *Marketing Modernisms: Self-Promotion, Canonization, and Rereading*, ed. Kevin J. H. Dettmar and Stephen Watt (Ann Arbor: University of Michigan Press, 1996), for a more detailed discussion of Eliot's use of "we" as a rhetorical strategy in his early criticism.

22. T. S. Eliot, "American Literature," *Athenaeum* (April 25, 1919): 237.

23. See Michael North, *The Political Aesthetic of Yeats, Eliot, and Pound* (Cambridge: Cambridge University Press, 1991), 75–81, on metonymy in "Prufrock."

24. Gertrude Stein, "What is English Literature?" in *Lectures in America* (1935; reprint, Boston: Beacon Press, 1957), 12.

25. T. S. Eliot, "In Memory of Henry James," *Egoist* 6, no. 1 (January 1918): 1.

26. Chris Baldick, *The Social Mission of English Criticism* (Oxford: Oxford University Press, 1983), 111–12.

27. Similarly, the misogynist portrait of a female poet in *The Waste Land* manuscripts makes it clear that, even within the metropolis, access to poetic authority remains for Eliot almost always a male privilege.

28. Louis Menand, *Discovering Modernism*, 154.

29. Ibid.

30. Tim Dean, in this volume, has a compelling reading of this passage which differs from my own, but on the central point that for Eliot "poetic knowledge crystallizes as a consequence of corporeal as well as mental experience," our arguments concur (see p. 55).

31. T. S. Eliot, "The Metaphysical Poets," *Times Literary Supplement*, October 20, 1921; repr. *Selected Essays*, 64; hereafter cited in the text as *MP*.

32. T. S. Eliot, *On Poetry and Poets* (London: Faber & Faber, 1957), 153.

33. Richard Helgerson, *Forms of Nationhood: The Elizabethan Writing of England* (Chicago: University of Chicago Press, 1992).

34. T. S. Eliot, "A Sceptical Patrician," *Athenaeum* (May 23, 1919): 362.

35. Walt Whitman, introduction to *Leaves of Grass*, 1855 edition (reprint, Harmondsworth: Penguin, 1986), 24.

36. My thinking on this topic has been greatly sharpened through conversation with Dana Luciano; see her "'Perverse Nature': *Edgar Huntly* and the Novel's Reproductive Disorders," *American Literature* 70, no. 1 (March 1998): 1–27.

CHAPTER 4

The masculinity behind the ghosts of modernism in Eliot's Four Quartets

Peter Middleton

There are two *Burnt Norton*s: one was published as a single, freestanding poem in 1936 as the closing work in *Collected Poems 1909–1935*; the other was published eight years later at the beginning of a wartime serial poem, *Four Quartets* (1944). The first appeared at a time when there was no world war, and its author's avowed "anti-secularism" was at odds with the dominant literary-political ideologies of the day. The second was much more consonant with the new public mood, and would make its author the most influential living English writer for at least the next decade. Republication of the same text as the opening scene of a new poem created an internal division between two moments of historically situated writing and reading that effected far more of a transformation than mere repackaging might have done. This was not done without some confusion for readers, since by then it had also appeared as a pamphlet in the same year as *The Dry Salvages*, making some, like Kathleen Raine, think *Burnt Norton* was the *second* poem in the sequence.[1] The publication of all four poems as a continuous series opening with *Burnt Norton* finally established its position in 1944. I will argue here that, on its reappearance, *Burnt Norton* is made to stand for a modernist temporal poetics which *Four Quartets* decisively brings to an end, with far-reaching effects on the subsequent history of British poetry. The new positioning of *Burnt Norton* transformed it: the three serial poems that now followed it incrementally erased its meaning, calling forth melancholic ghosts of gender and desire in the process.

The first *Burnt Norton* appeared in the same year as *Murder in the Cathedral* (1936), during a time of great personal stress and uncertainty in T. S. Eliot's relations with both Vivienne Eliot and Emily Hale. Lyndall Gordon speculates that it had its immediate personal source in a romantic episode whose only trace is a sketch Eliot mailed to his brother in 1935, in which "a man experiences 'leaping pleasures' that release him from a mood of futility and reach a 'matchless' moment; then fade all too fast, 'impaired by impotence.'"[2] Its complex mood of regret, renunciation, and longing was briefly anticipated in an apparently hastily written commentary for the *Criterion* a year earlier, in 1934, where he alludes to Jean Verdenal with a constellation of images of sun, flowers, gardens, and mud that is repeated more elaborately in *Burnt Norton*: "I am willing to admit that my own retrospect is touched by a sentimental sunset, the memory of a friend coming across the Luxembourg Gardens in the late afternoon, waving a branch of lilac, a friend who was later (so far as I could find out) to be mixed with the mud of Gallipoli."[3] It is an odd, poignant, if not angry way of describing his male friend's wartime death, and suggests that the "garlic and sapphires in the mud" of *Burnt Norton* might be allusions to Verdenal (the association of sapphire with hope and garlic with both exorcism and lust adds to the force of this connection).

Personal history was not the only prompt to the poem. Eliot was also responding directly to his own signature poem, *The Waste Land*, which loomed so largely in public perceptions of his work. The unfolding structure of *Burnt Norton* can be read as a close counterpoint to almost all the main thematic passages in the earlier poem, and even presents a fourth section with the same number of lines as "Death by Water" and a similar *memento mori*. We are still in London, the "unreal city," there is still a sense of death in life offset by random moments of desire and longing, the Word is still in the desert, love remains a hope. Yet *Burnt Norton* is abstract where *The Waste Land* is specific, generalized instead of citational, anonymous instead of populous with idiosyncratic characters, and this gives it a leverage over the earlier poem because its judgments and categories always subsume those earlier particularities. It effects an attempted closure. This was recognized by contemporary reviewers whether they approved it ("It seems that the pilgrimage is ended, and there is peace") or dismissed its relevance ("diffidently inserted at the end, Mr. Eliot's new long poem *Burnt Norton*, [is] rather a dull meditation on time and God and love, which breaks only a few times from a thin monotony into richness").[4] *Burnt Norton*'s pessimistic judgment that words "strain / Crack and sometimes break, under the burden" of expression, reads more readily as a diagnosis of the disjunctive language of *The Waste Land* (which has a number of broken words) than as a comment on its own highly fluent and unbroken articulation. This *Burnt Norton* doesn't refute its predecessor so much as control it from the rear of the book, notably by its judgments on the salience of desire in the earlier poem, a desire which is constantly switching gender and subject position, and is mobile, abject, and confessional.

The significance of this construction of the *Collected Poems* was noticed at the time. R. P. Blackmur was especially explicit in his review: "It is the more astonishing, specifically, how much the latest poem in the book, *Burnt Norton*, both depends on all the earlier poems as their inalienable product and adds to them critically and emphatically. *Burnt Norton* makes the earlier poems grow and diminish, as it illuminates them or shows them up."[5] Blackmur even speculates on the reception of the poem, worrying that the lack of "a driving or dramatic form" might lead the poem to "fail": "*Burnt Norton* will seem successful, perhaps, if the earlier poems supply the lack; it will fail if it remains a mere appended commentary upon the material of the other poems" (51). Blackmur and others may have had in mind one tantalizingly suggestive allusion back to the poem that had already made Eliot famous: "Ridiculous the waste sad time / Stretching before and after."[6] These lines almost suggest that *The Waste Land* is sad and therefore ridiculous because of its handling of history (seeing land where it should have seen time), and this mode of almost, but not quite, saying what relation the poem possesses, variously, to its authorial antecedents, poetic tradition, the poetry of contemporaries, and contemporary politics, leaves a wake of uncertain propositions behind it. Eliot's indistinct but slighting allusion to the earlier poem emphasizes both connection and disconnection between the two poems, the sense of being after that modernist work, and also the sense that modernism still stretches out before and after.

In making this gesture at the very end of *Collected Poems 1909–1935*, the first *Burnt Norton* remains modernist in the sense controversially proposed by T. J. Clark in his recent major study of modern art:

Not being able to make a previous moment of high achievement part of the past – not to lose it and mourn it and, if necessary, revile it – is, for art in modernist circumstances, more or less synonymous with not being able to make art at all. Because ever since Hegel put the basic proposition of modernism into words in the 1820s – that "art considered in its highest vocation, is and remains for us a thing of the past" – art's being able to continue has depended on its success in making that dictum specific and punctual. That is to say, on fixing the moment of art's last flowering at some point in the comparatively recent past, and discovering that enough remains from this finale for a work of ironic or melancholy or decadent continuation to seem possible nonetheless.[7]

Clark's paradigm of a repeated failure of modernist attempts to represent the strangeness of onrushing modernity is brilliantly worked out for individual artists, and also recognizes the half-life of art works to a degree that is often unacknowledged by academic criticism. Although he doesn't claim his account can be extended to writing, the emphasis on the ending of art – and its return in melancholy forms as a function of social, technological, and cultural change – makes it useful for thinking about Eliot's difficult relation to modernism. How was it he could be the most famous modernist poet in English and later be one of the architects of the anti-modernist reaction of the 1950s through his editorial role at Faber and Faber? Part of the explanation can be found in this history of *Four Quartets*.

Here in the first *Burnt Norton* are many signs of the "ironic or melancholy or decadent continuation" that Clark believes are ubiquitous in modernist art. Section four of *Burnt Norton* offers all three kinds of continuation from Part IV of *The Waste Land*. The Fisher King who was the point around which the desolation revolved returns as the kingfisher, now the "still point of the turning world." Phlebas was buried by the sea; now it seems as if it might be writer and reader who are buried by the "spray" of overgrowth in the whirlpool of the entire "turning world." The sea picked the Phoenician's bones; now it is "Chill / Fingers of yew" (the cemetery tree) that do the work, and the pun on yew/you suggests ambivalent desire. The word "yew" is at once ironic pun, melancholic evocation of the graveyard, and decadent intimation of a sinister seduction of straying, bending, spraying, clinging fingers and their bodies. To read like this, of course, is to strain against the controlling surface of *Burnt Norton*, which, unlike *The Waste Land*, resists such explicit polysemy and open expression of desire.

There is a widespread view that gender and sexuality have no place at all in *Burnt Norton* or the remainder of *Four Quartets*. Carol Christ speaks for this assessment of Eliot's later poetics, observing that the language of *Four Quartets*, "in its abstraction, in its predominantly natural and religious imagery, avoids the issues of gender and body that dominate Eliot's early poetry."[8] *Burnt Norton* avoids the issues, but it is pervaded by a subdued eroticism and awareness of the body, as in the fourth section already discussed briefly. Love is repeatedly mentioned. The floral array of the rose garden enacts fantasies of phallic mastery, most suggestively in the observation that "the lotos rose, quietly, quietly," forming a wonderful conflation of symbols of fulfillment, beauty, and erotic desire, with a whole history of poetic usage behind it. Rose and lotos function at once as heterosexual male potency (the appearance of the lotos is followed by the sound of children), flirtation ("the unseen eyebeam crossed"), and the masculine gaze ("the roses / Had the look of flowers that are looked at"). In addition to its association with children, the phallic pun on the traditional symbol of romantic passion ("the lotos rose"), with the upthrust Freudian signifier of sexual difference, marks the poem's eroticism as heterosexual desire. Further, the lotos that is both there and not there proffers an almost perfect ghost-image of the phallus, an ideal that can never be possessed and therefore never quite seen, while it functions as the mnemonic of a moment of plenitude which the poem affirms as a lasting guide to action. The poem thus offers a glimpse of hegemonic masculinity which, in Thomas DiPiero's words, "is irreducibly phallic in its construction of a unified and complete subjectivity, and . . . works to conceal any deficiencies or discontinuities in its ideal subject."[9] Accordingly, *Burnt Norton* simultaneously offers an incipient critique of the ideological fiction of masculinity figured by the lotos, a fiction that works to conceal the processes by which men are engendered, revealing its "deficiencies" and "discontinuities" in several ways: the moment when the "lotos rose" is just a hallucinatory trick of the light; the entire episode is an alternative history that probably never happened; the root of the lotos is in a "drained pool" (for which we might read exhaustion and impotence); and the concealment of engendering is manifest (children are hidden in the leaves as if emerging from a part of nature that requires no human intervention) but "hidden excitedly," their presence revealed by the excitation of desire.

Desire made intense by lack continues to reappear in different forms throughout the succeeding sections of *Burnt Norton*. Memories of moments of intense feeling reemerge in section two as the "moment in the rose-garden" picks up an echo of the past tense of the rising lotos, and the remembered "moment in the arbour where the rain beat" gains force from the near homonym of "arbour" with "ardour." Section three begins by stigmatizing the present as a "place of disaffection," the prefix "dis" indicating an absence of affection and sexual love, which is reinforced by the way the "sensual" is emptied by "deprivation." And section five begins with an echo of the Shakespearean idea that writing about love can transcend history and the loss of desire ("only by the form, the pattern, / Can words or music reach / The stillness" [17]). Even the attempt to describe the still point as "neither flesh *nor fleshless*" creates a similar atmosphere – the phrase I have italicized working to remind readers of the similarities between the "partial ecstasy" of sexuality and the *ecstases* of time recommended by the poem. From beginning to end, desire produces ghosts, but because the poem calls them "guests" (characteristically allowing near homonymic associations to hover nearby), and they take form as almost everything but the traditional ghost (a partial list would include words, footfalls, they, lotos, water, children, laughter), this haunting is subdued. And because the poem is so closely tied to its predecessor, *The Waste Land*, references all appear to hark back to that poem's many dramatic figures who suffer various indignities of desire. The first *Burnt Norton* thus depicts a psychic landscape in which male heterosexual and homoerotic desire is counterpoised with a place of complete passivity, the static center of the whirlpool of the turning world.

Blackmur and his contemporaries may have believed that *Burnt Norton* was an inalienable part of *Collected Poems 1909–1935*, but Eliot was about to prove otherwise, and "alienate" the poem almost entirely from this setting. In its second manifestation as part of a wartime poem, gender and desire will be constrained to play the role of "dignified, invisible, moving" presences – ghosts representing a melancholic longing for lost male sexualities, ghosts of what has not been adequately mourned.[10] When George Orwell reviewed what in 1942 appeared to be a sequence of three poems, this melancholy made him think of *Burnt Norton* as distinct from the other poems in *Collected Poems 1909–1935*: the "later poems express a melancholy faith and the earlier ones a glowing despair."[11] He is insistent on the break, adding that this newer poetry "does not *contain* the earlier, even if it is claimed as an improvement upon it" (56). Orwell's italicization of this slightly odd verb, "contain," emphasizes his conviction that the later poetry is trying to transform the poetry prior to the new sequence, and failing to do so. Orwell's response to the poem suggests that contemporary readers were likely to be at least partly aware that the emerging sequence of *Four Quartets* was a failed attempt at mourning the past.

We usually think that a sequence of poems or art works accumulates meaning along its path, each unit extending, clarifying, or reaching closer to the possibly unattainable goal of expression. In the case of *Four Quartets* a subtraction occurs. The second *Burnt Norton* undergoes a poetic conflagration oddly congruent with its title, so that by the end of *Little Gidding*, when the poem concludes that "the fire and the rose are one," the earlier poem has fully earned its name. Its prewar affirmations of time and love are consumed to ashes by the sequential revisions and reinterpretations to the point where all modernist articulation of simultaneity is burnt to nothing and there is no pastness of art to overcome, leaving a spectral textual double "caught in the form of limitation / Between un-being and being." Eliot was successful at "unwriting" *Burnt Norton*, leaving it apparently untouched (not a word changed) while publishing it in a form that radically altered its potential meanings for readers. He accomplished this "unwriting" by encouraging readers to think of *Burnt Norton* as the first chapter of a new poetic narrative, *Four Quartets*, rather than as a culmination of his modernist poetry epitomized by *The Waste Land*, and by using its Janus-faced relation to modernism as a sign of what was to be overcome. He also retained *Burnt Norton*'s structural format in the subsequent poems so that they could be read as cumulative transformations of its forms and themes. The additional poems therefore enact the truth of George Bataille's dictum: "among various sacrifices, poetry is the only one whose fire we can maintain, renew."[12] A refining fire sacrifices the earlier poem's masculine ideals and desires. Fighting men use the most modern techniques – dive-bombers and incendiaries – to create a material waste land in which men are destroyed and only compound ghosts are left from the auto-da-fé of this poetry of war.

Why do this? What are the specters in the first *Burnt Norton* that must be dispelled? Most obviously, the contrast of erotic longing and con-temporary vacuity had become an embarrassment by the onset of World War II – there must be no more birds and lotos-eating. Now masculine virtues are needed, and the metaphorical death of the urban culture is all too real. Other forces are at work too. The pervasive homage of poetic imitation points to one salient problem for Eliot as he continued work on *Four Quartets* during the opening phases of World War II. *The Waste Land* had become an icon of high-modernist poetics, and so *Burnt Norton* as con-ceived in 1935–6 remained a high-modernist poem. By the 1940s, Eliot had become deeply ambivalent about what such modernist poetics represented and entailed, and not only in terms of sexual identity (Dallas Kenmare voices Eliot's fear when he observes that Eliot is "imitated with disastrous results by his followers").[13] Eliot's uneasiness shows through even when he is ostensibly making a case for modernist poetry. In his preface to Anne Ridler's collection *A Little Book of Modern Verse* (1941), written as he was working toward a draft of the *Four Quartets*, he struggles to define what makes poetry "modern" in terms that reveal considerable ambivalence.[14] The acceleration of change in modernist writing is due to "the history of a changing and bewildered world, the mutations of which have given it a different appearance to poets no more than ten years apart in age."[15] Instead of just a praiseworthy modernization leading toward a better world, recent history has also brought much ugliness and confusion, and therefore, by implication, modernist poetry has also been contaminated. He avoids direct judgments on contemporary poetry, however, by appearing to reflect objectively on current discourses of literary value. These he delineates in the gendered terms of strong and weak masculinity. The usual terms of modernist praise for a new poetry, he explains, are that the poet is "the voice of his time," whereas the usual terms of condemnation are that his work manifests "perversity, affectation, or incompetence" – the manly poet, Eliot implies, speaks for modernity, while the weak poet who speaks only for his own personal concerns displays a diminished masculinity depicted in blatantly homophobic terms. "Perversity, affectation, or incompetence": these adjectives could describe many of Eliot's own earlier poems and por-traits, from Prufrock through the many decadent figures in *The Waste Land* to the speaker in "Ash Wednesday" and the anonymous observer in the opening of *Burnt Norton*. As so often in Eliot's work, we are left uncertain where he stands in relation to these judgments. Is he amused and detached from such gestures, and inviting us to ask more questions about these ghosts of masculinity behind the celebrations of modernism, or are these his own forms of judgment projected onto the consensus he had helped to create? We are given no way of deciding. Instead, after approaching the problem of defining modernism through negations, he concludes: "for an explanation of what makes modern poetry would have to be an explanation of the whole modern world; to understand the poet we should have to understand ourselves – we should have, in fact, to reach a degree of self-consciousness of which mankind has never been capable, and of which, if attained, it might perish." Not only are we left with our question deliberately unanswered, we are also left with an implied threat. Modernism's fulfillment would be a general destruction already perhaps initiated by the encompassing war, and therefore to be resisted all the more. Eliot's preface might have been a celebration of the achievements of modernist poetry; instead it reads much more like a troubled farewell to his own earlier poetic commitments.[16]

Also consumed, in this symbolic erasure of modernism, are the earlier poem's hopes for the productivity of a masculine desire manifest in both scenes of romance and scenes of male identification. The temporal dislocation internal to *Burnt Norton* stirs up surprisingly dissonant masculinities. During the wartime writing of the longer sequence, the peacetime moment when the "lotos rose" must have seemed – by contrast with the new urgencies of war – indulgent, narcissistic, and preoccupied with desires that would threaten male autonomy. The wartime *Burnt Norton* now stages phallic display not as a poetic image for the necessary recognition of the impossibility of possessing the phallus, but as a scene of melancholy-inducing loss in which manhood will be valued as an essential component of the war effort. As David Morgan notes, "It could be argued that war and the military represent one of the major sites where direct links between hegemonic masculinities and men's bodies are forged."[17] Now the fiction that is the phallus cannot be acknowledged. The lotos male will be replaced by the ghosts of warrior males, whose homoerotic desire emerges to defend the social order best represented by the image of the patriarch beyond, the father who was killed by his sons in Freud's allegory of civilization, *Totem and Taboo*. Instead of recognizing the impossibility of phallic plenitude, the poems will opt for melancholic masculinity in a refusal of the mourning that also made possible a nascent sexual desire, so tentatively adumbrated in the structure of *Burnt Norton*. The result is a transformation of the first *Burnt Norton* and the generation of ghosts: ghosts of gender, sexuality, and the body that haunt it and constantly recall the text to absent ideals of desire.

To trace how this happened, we need to follow in detail the masterful metapoetic control of the cycle of erasure. Aligning the poems in this way will show that each subsequent poem in *Four Quartets* bleaches out more of the significance from the starting text so that by the final poem we are left with a position beyond which this textual form of modernism cannot proceed. *Four Quartets* also forestalls resistance to this process; it tries to anticipate all the moves which interpretation could possibly make, all its possible textual futures, revisions, regrets, and makings new, by a repetition which gradually negates what has been said, refining it to the simplicity of tautology.

This "refining" begins with *East Coker*, which is often said to be a little too close to its predecessor for even the metapoetic claim to intentional doubling – "you say I am repeating / Something I have said before" – to dispel sufficiently the suspicion of a lack of invention. From its opening material images of the temporal decay entailed by the determinism that finds ends in beginnings – "houses rise and fall, crumble, are extended, / Are removed, destroyed, restored, or in their place / Is an open field," and so on – this second poem appears to reprise the first very closely. We have a glimpse of unattainable sexual fulfillment in the vision of a medieval marriage celebration; a lyric is dismissed as "a periphrastic study in a worn-out poetical fashion" (although there is a slight shift away from the earlier pattern here – in *Burnt Norton* the contrasting style of disenchantment did not directly deconstruct its lyric partner); men are again glimpsed commuting between work and home in a state of momentary loss of identity that signifies moral emptiness; we are again offered a metaphysical lyric about the mortal condition now represented as a hospital; and a final section outlining the impossibility of referential determinacy leads to images of possibility, probably derived from sources like Tennyson's "Ulysses," which hint that only the man who adventures out beyond all domesticity can hope to achieve fulfillment. The masculinity of these themes rerun from *Burnt Norton* is now greatly intensified; this is a world of men who are men. They own or command the public world (as company directors); they fight for noble causes (either in "undisciplined squads" awaiting forceful, authoritative officers of reason, or are set to "conquer / By strength and submission"). Further, they issue their editorial commentaries from positions of strong masculine authority (reinforced by the surety implied by the repetition of phrases such as "if you do not come too close," or the certainty of expression in a sentence such as "we are only undeceived / Of that which, deceiving, could no longer harm," and the monitory tone of phrases such as "you must go"). The poem's masculine authority is given additional force by the patriarchal authority of the institutions of Christianity implicit in allusions to doctrine. Even the seemingly abstract metaphysical statement appropriated from Mary Queen of Scots's epigram – "In my end is my beginning" – might be read as an affirmation of male self-sufficiency. The male narrator has mastered the entire cycle of creation or reproduction from beginning to end of subjectivity; female reproduction is rendered otiose for this enwombed male ego.

The Dry Salvages finds a new origin for the timeless moments: "a strong brown god" represented as a river whose "rhythm" plays through these memories (the racism implicit in the equation of African Americans with rhythm and primitivism now sounds harshly dissonant to 21st-century ears). Presumably, the river's presence in the timeless moments was meant to indicate the continuance of a "natural" physical substratum in experience. If so, this further etiolates Burnt Norton's tentative dance of love and desire with asceticism and transcendence, by downgrading it from divine music to a persistent drone of primitivism beneath the harmonies of high culture. The poem then contrasts this minor riverine deity and its reminders of the nature at the heart of culture with the bordering, unbounded ocean signifying the adventurous journey of life into the unknowability of the future. This use of a temporal discourse to articulate a politics is endemic to Four Quartets, evident even in the typically Eliotic counter-hermeneutic strategy of the final section, where he ridicules most forms of interpretation, notably psychoanalysis, which might be brought to bear on his politics of "timeless moments" by mocking their temporal pretensions. In dismissing the anamnesis of "pre-conscious terrors" it also closes off many of the symbolic implications of fecundity, femininity, and regeneration borne by those invisible children in Burnt Norton.

Little Gidding completes the work of these two poems, further unsaying the same things again in forms that thin their meaning even more. By the end of this final poem in the series, instead of Burnt Norton's rejection of past artistic work and anticipation of a new aesthetic signaled by the line "quick now, here, now, always," Little Gidding offers only an untransformable totality reiterated with absolute finality: it follows a repetition of this earlier appearance of the line by a description of what is now to come instead, "a condition of complete simplicity." A fire and a rose that are one leave only ashes behind. Thanks to these ashes the poetic sequence now has its symbol of transcendence, the unrepresentable complementarity of fire and rose, but symbolic closure depends on the pyrotechnic kenosis of modernist poetry. *Burnt Norton* looked into the rose leaves and saw another world; the last poem sees the final closure of what it now retroactively judges a promiscuous modernist evocation of further possible worlds. It is tempting therefore to say that *Burnt Norton* has become a textual ghost of its former self. But this would be to dignify the most salient trope in *Four Quartets* to a degree that would both attribute too much authority to the poem's own rhetoric and underestimate the textual condition – all rereading renders any fixed idea of a text spectral on closer examination.[18] The poem's handling of the process of rereading is what needs investigation if we are to trace the largely unadmitted gendering of the textual ghosts, and trace how the doubling of *Burnt Norton* works with the time and gender of modernism.[19] To find out more about these ghosts, we begin by listening to what the last ghost in the sequence has to say about himself in section two of *Little Gidding*.

The passage itself is ghostly in its very form, comprising a modernized pastiche of Dante's *terza rima*, poetic landscape, and the typical plot of encounter with a denizen of a circle of hell (perhaps Brunetto Latini). Whereas Dante's narrator has Virgil as his guide in the face of danger, Eliot's narrator encounters the ghost alone. Nevertheless, commentators on Eliot's poem are usually reassured by the adjective "familiar" that the "compound ghost" means no harm, and concentrate on eliciting the bodies of literary work which it shadows, knowing that Eliot initially identified the ghost with Yeats. Eliot had good reasons for dropping this explicit identification, however. The poem is wary of making too glaringly obvious its already questionably arrogant identification with Dante by then claiming to have a street séance with the recently dead Yeats (notorious for his interest in the astral plane and the means of transport to it). Bad enough to be so identified with one dead male author; to claim to be two at once might raise eyebrows. More seriously, by effacing specific features, Eliot makes the ghost's generic qualities clearer; its representation of tradition, and even the masculinity of the ghost, become more salient than the fate and astral wisdom of a single author.

Apparently convinced that this scene was among the most important passages of the entire sequence, Eliot remarked in a public lecture that "this section of a poem – not the length of one canto of the Divine Comedy – cost me far more time and trouble and vexation than any passage of the same length that I have ever written."[20] Perhaps, but this section might also be regarded as a wonderfully comic demonstration of the impossibility of writing great poetry in such an age. In terms of an architectural analogy, it is not even Gothic revival, but cinema frontage, an attempt to impress the mass audience with all possible signs of artistic greatness: Virgil, Dante, Shakespeare, Shelley, Mallarmé, and Yeats. Writing in this way might exhibit a melancholic refusal to admit the pastness of the past, a refusal surpassing either the celebration of European tradition, or the creation of a valid and compelling poetic form revitalized for a historical moment in which the circles of Hell and Purgatory were appearing in war-torn Europe. The placement of the passage in section two reinforces this melancholic refusal. Structural expectations established by the previous poems invite readers to anticipate a passage in which the poet sets aside lyric intensity for a prosy expository tone made possible by the free-verse line. The expected authentic, world-weary voice of the poet, which appeared in the two previous poems, insisting on its truer register of contemporary sentiment than the lyric voice, fails to materialize. In its place is this anachronistic high style of verse. Previously, in each of the three preceding poems, section two has been divided between a rhyming lyric and a free-verse meditation; traditional lyric and modernist anti-lyric are sharply juxtaposed. Indeed, *East Coker* contains one of the most powerful moments in the entire poem when it exploits this contrast, one which has made some postmodernist poetic careers possible: "That was a way of putting it – not very satisfactory: / A periphrastic study in a worn-out poetical fashion." The line retracts what has just preceded these judgments, openly admitting its failure to become authentic lyric poetry; it was only a study, insincere, a pastiche of poetry (the ghost of a poem). To put it more strongly, the previous prose sections have burned or unwritten the accompanying lyric sections. Similarly, the pastiche of Dante reenacts this disenchantment with traditional poetry's capacity to write about the modern predicament of suffering and strife, but finds no "modern" style in which to say it. Instead of mourning the loss of poetry, it incorporates the lost object in a melancholy act of denial. The poetic pastiche's significance therefore lies in its failure to "emulate" as poetry. Readers are expected to have strong feelings about this failure, since they are being told that parts of the poem in which they have invested cognitive and emotional energy are worthless. *Little Gidding* gives voice to these reactions through the figure of the ghost interlocutor, as if the ghost of the failed high-poetic tradition itself were able to speak. In doing so the poem also brings to the fore the entire issue of masculinity.

Before we can learn more about the ghost, we need to recall how the poet is able to meet him. Eliot was a fire-watcher, posted at night to look out for fires caused by bombs and other incendiary devices in a London where, by the end of the Blitz in June 1941, over a million houses in the city had been destroyed or damaged. The damage was so extensive in some areas that Angus Calder describes West Ham as "a borough of ghosts," the landscape so ruined that the army used it for training in street combat.[21] One person who lived in St. John's Wood remembers only one other inhabited house in the "eerie street" full of ruins.[22] London was a landscape for meeting ghosts, making Eliot's choice of the setting appropriate for a Dantean dream encounter with a ghost of poetry past that will effectively exclude women and femininity. Here a man can meet lost figures of his own history, figures of spectral manhood. This is a landscape of risk where a man may be tested against a largely invisible enemy in the skies overhead, and he must exercise manly virtues of courage, vigilance, initiative, and fortitude.

In the ghost passage, it is easy to regard the ghost's words as benign wisdom. But here guns, bombs, and fire are not the only risks to the early-morning wanderer; ghosts themselves are often dangerous, associated with murder, revenge, and unmourned loss.[23] Hamlet's father's ghost speaks of his own poisoning in the ear (a symbolic warning of dangers that can enter the ear to which his son fatally does not listen), and, with tragic consequences for both Hamlet and the state, places his son under the obligation to revenge his death and usurpation.

Ghosts were regular performers in modernist war writing. In D. H. Lawrence's awkward, sadomasochistic fable "The Border," a representative of manhood sacrificed in World War I returns as an angry, murderous ghost bent on destroying Philip, the new husband of his widow, Katherine. Her first husband, Alan Anstruther, a captain in a Scottish regiment, was a very masculine figure who "even stark-naked and without any trimmings . . . had a bony, dauntless, overbearing manliness of his own," and Philip still thinks of Alan as the "only real man" that he has ever met. The homoerotic struggle between the two husbands is articulated in terms of weak and strong masculinities depicted in primary colors. In contrast to Alan, Katherine's new husband is a weak specimen, whose bodily strength ebbs in the presence of the ghost of masculine vigor. He dies while she mysteriously makes love to the specter, and she wakes up to find Philip dead "in a pool of blood."[24]

An equally dangerous ghost of a former comrade and lost masculinity appears to Septimus Smith, war hero and victim of war trauma, in *Mrs Dalloway*. His wife Rezia's comment, "It is time," triggers a hallucinatory vision of this noun and its referents which will be echoed by *Four Quartets*:

The word "time" split its husk; poured its riches over him; and from his lips fell like shells, like shavings from a plane, without his making them, hard, white, imperishable, words, and flew to attach themselves to their places in an ode to Time. He sang. Evans answered from behind the tree. The dead were in Thessaly, Evans sang, among the orchids. There they waited till the War was over.[25]

Four Quartets echoes this passage in several ways, including the unseen voices in the garden, the entire poem's preoccupation with time, and the final section of *Little Gidding* in which Eliot imagines a text "where every word is at home / Taking its place to support the others." Even more resonant is the passage shortly before Septimus's suicide when, after reading Dante's *Inferno*, he reflects that "Shakespeare loathed humanity . . . This was now revealed to Septimus; the message hidden in the beauty of words. The secret signal which one generation passes, under disguise, to the next is loathing, hatred, despair. Dante the same" (115). Septimus offers an alarming precedent for Eliot, since his meditations on time as a poetic theme, the perfect placement of words, ghosts of the dead, unseen voices, Dante, and despair for humanity, issue from a man so traumatized that he has psychotic episodes and kills himself.[26] This instance of intertextuality between *Mrs Dalloway* and *Four Quartets* appears to point to the past that Eliot's poem wishes to disavow, and specifically to the difference between Septimus's war and that of *Little Gidding*. Eliot's Dantean ghost may spend most of his time apparently passing on the secret despair, but, unlike Septimus, the ghost concludes by introducing the redemptive possibility of restoration in a "refining fire" associated with dance and measure, and, by implication, poetry itself. Ironically, it is this fire that the fire-watcher guards against, suggesting that Septimus's negations are here answered with a new form of martial spirit.

Of all the many tributary ghosts to Eliot's compound invention one stands out: the dead soldier in Wilfred Owen's dream poem in which the soldier-narrator meets the man he killed in an otherworldly landscape. As in the ghost passage of *Four Quartets*, the narrator begins by trying to remove all pain and danger from the situation. Indicating that the male competition to kill or be killed is over and done with, he complacently assures the ghost "here is no cause to mourn."[27] Yes there is, replies the ghost, and sets out what might have been possible if he had lived, projecting an alternate history (an idea that might have influenced Eliot's own thinking about alternate worlds) in a gloomy tone not dissimilar from that of Eliot's ghost. Owen's ghost's disenchanted vision has the power to drive the narrator into nihilism about the irredeemable loss of the war and the disastrous fate of their masculine values and desires. It is against such visions of the future that we should read the compound ghost's possibly poisonous advice and predictions for the poet-narrator in Eliot's poem.

Eliot had employed ghosts before. His narrator had met one in the streets of *The Waste Land*. As I argued in an earlier essay, the specter, the "third who walks always beside you," was an "uncanny" figure representing the unmournably vast number of male deaths during World War I.[28]

What is the psychic economy that produces such a ghost, and what is its relation to gender and desire? Ghosts are commonly associated with absent or failed rituals of mourning, and therefore Freud's speculative account of melancholia coupled with his late theory of the ego offer a theoretical framework for the gendered dynamics informing these ghosts of modernism. In *The Ego and the Id* (1923), he argues that the adult ego is the accretive outcome of melancholic refusals to admit the loss of sexual objects. Each loss is succeeded by the introjection of the lost object, an identification which means that the ego "is a precipitate of abandoned object-cathexes and that it contains the history of those object-choices."[29] Character is formed by the unmourned relationships and libidinal orientations making the ego a "compound ghost" of former loves. Freud understands this as the necessary foundation of sublimation on which the creativity and sociality which help constitute civilization actually rest, because the ego desexualises libidinal energy by making itself "the sole love-object." The result is "an abandonment of sexual aims."[30] Thus, incremental desexualization of *Four Quartets*, by which the erotic borders of experience in *Burnt Norton* are progressively erased, could be read as a symptom of the formation of a new ego identity based on narcissistic, intra-masculine desire called forth by a world at war. In *East Coker*, for example, the ghosts of medieval peasantry "daunsinge" around a bonfire of some long-ago marriage celebration offer a glimpse, soon dispelled, of lost heterosexual fulfillment. The language of the passage progressively downgrades their affects to the bestial and excremental, and finally buries them in the earth of death. Elsewhere, desire is either allegorized to the point where it becomes a disembodied dream (the rose garden) or expelled from the human altogether into the mechanisms of technological modernity (the highways and automobiles of "appetency" in *The Dry Salvages*). So the final ghost to appear may be seen as a compound of all these earlier ghosts, a compound of identifications both heterosexual and homoerotic, including warrior masculinity, from Jean Verdenal to the soldiers and fire-watchers of World War II, and figures of poetic creation.

Furthermore, according to Freud in his essay "The Uncanny" (1919), in addition to narcissism, the image of the double in supernatural fictions projects an "energetic denial of the power of death," a primitive way of understanding death related to fears about the unwanted return of the dead. And as a mode of the repetition compulsion, this denial figured by the double also signifies a desire for annihilation of the ego.[31] As many commentators have recognized, Freud's account of depression or melancholy draws on the same speculative framework he used to describe the uncanny. Because memories and identifications can play the same role as the ghost figures do, melancholy could be the equivalent of living with a ghost. For Freud, melancholy results from a failure to mourn a specific lost object of love, but what if this lost object were less a specific person than a gender?

This question forms the starting point of Judith Butler's syncretic theory of homophobia. Butler's skill at recombining elements of different philosophical, psychological, and political theories enables her to argue that Freud's model of ego-development could account for the construction of a heterosexual gendered subject that arises from the progressive rejection of homosexual object-choices, loves, and identifications subsumed under a social ban forbidding mourning. The ghosts of Lawrence's, Owen's, and Woolf's World War I narratives are all formed by unadmitted homoerotic desires, and equally murderous. The significance of the ghost of *Little Gidding* should therefore be searched for in the constituents of its compound nature. Butler explains the process of becoming gendered within a heterosexual structure as the adoption of a melancholic position, haunted by unwanted introjections. The heterosexual man's ego is a precipitate of lost male object-choices, and therefore "the straight man *becomes* (mimes, cites, appropriates, assumes the status of) the man he 'never' loved and 'never' grieved."[32] Even gay men and women may be subject to this sacrificial logic of sexual identity in relation to heterosexuality. Butler's theory implies wide social and historical consequences: "This raises the political question of the cost of articulating a coherent identity position by producing, excluding, and repudiating a domain of abject spectres that threaten the arbitrarily closed domain of subject positions. Perhaps only by risking the incoherence of identity is connection possible."[33] For Eliot the cost would be repudiation of modernist poetics as well as his own complex identity and desires.

Eliot's ghosts could be said to belong to this domain and show the cost of maintaining a coherent identity based on exclusion of same-sex identifications, both in the symbolic terms of the ontologically impossible ghost, and in disordered textualities where what is represented is neither real nor unreal, and words "decay with imprecision" (17). Unmourned homoerotic objects are undoubtedly a constituent of the ghost of *Little Gidding*; the subject-position of masculine authority developed by the poem's narrative stance disavows same-sex affects, especially "feminized" feelings, while repeatedly idealizing various male figures. This psychoanalytic account, however, leaves out the persisting influence of war and its mass slaughter of men in combat on the construction of masculine selves. Although Freud does not make reflections on the war an explicit element in his theorizing of ego-formation, he could not have developed a theory of the formation of consciousness based on continual mourning without such a recent history. We should say, therefore, that the melancholy of gender that we have found in *Four Quartets* is formed from disavowed identifications with the "strong passion [which] is only interesting or significant in strong men," as Eliot explained, with a certain prescience of his own later poetics, in *After Strange Gods*.[34] Back in the 1930s he had believed that only these exceptional individuals were capable of the kind of "violent physical passions" which would not reduce them to conformity, but now he discerned such capacity as a general virtue in the warrior male, whether soldier or poet. From *East Coker* onwards, to be a poet means to be a man capable of military action: ready to go on "a raid on the inarticulate," to "fight to recover what has been lost," to go into battle alongside Arjuna, or find love in the flame from the dive-bomber. In each case, the figure of the poet incorporates the identity of the male fighter who is defined by his relation to death, and therefore encumbers the poetry with melancholy.

During the revision stages described in Helen Gardner's account of the poem's composition, Eliot deliberately intensified the melancholic refusal to mourn that characterizes the encounter with the ghost in *Little Gidding*. In his first draft, the ghost tells the narrator that he sees no point in repeating his poetic theories now that they are out of date, and then goes on to be explicit about what does most matter, "essential moments": memories of crucial passages in one's life; memories of intense negative emotion; sensory memories from specific instants. The draft ghost's injunction to "remember," a word which is repeated twice, at the start of successive tercets, resembles the admonition to mourn properly in Freudian terms whereby "each single one of the memories and expectations in which the libido is bound to the object is brought up and hypercathected, and detachment of the libido is accomplished in respect of it."[35] Remembering what he has tried to repress would enable the narrator to be free of his inner burdens and be "united to another past, another future." One can only conjecture why Eliot dropped these lines: perhaps because they evoke a return to the world of the first *Burnt Norton* and its continual reawakening of memories of lost love. Perhaps because of the contradiction that would ensue from recommending the recall of timeless moments as a guard against spectrality itself. In such a case, the ghost's assumption of the narrator's position would only underline how much the ghost is a projection of the narrator's unavowed masculine poetic identity. Finally, Eliot may have excised the ghost's therapeutic advice because it is an ambivalent, potentially deadly figure whose advice concerning the way to return to a world of the living might be a delusion, and the outcome instead be a world of "the dead and the unborn," where there is a deeply ambiguous "final gift" of "one soil, one past, one future, in one place."[36]

What I called earlier the progressive unwriting of *Burnt Norton* articulates the unfinished process of melancholic introjection of the love represented in the first poem. It is therefore fitting that the lugubrious revenant out in the dawn at the end of another demonstration of the alliance between modernity and destruction should say that writing poetry leads only to bodily decay. The ghost is dangerous not because of what it is but because of the writing in which it appears; the arbitrariness and anachronism of its own decaying artifice threaten to poison the ears of readers with the realization that none of what has been said, shown, and argued is true or real – nor, what is worse, is it untrue or unreal. The compound ghost is the poet's ego, compounded of a heterogeneous series of identifications with lost loves that have not been mourned. The ego sometimes identifies with Yeats or Dante, and sometimes shows traits of other male figures with which it has identified – the broken king, the peasant dancer, the brown god – and these give the ghost its complex character. Perhaps this is why the ghost is "intimate and unidentifiable."

The progressive erasure of *Burnt Norton* transforms its "guests" into the ghosts of *Little Gidding*. In section five of *Burnt Norton* the narrative perspective is first that of an aesthetic philosopher speaking, then a religious hermit, then love, then an observer of the guests in the rose garden. Similarly, in section five of *Little Gidding*, which shadows *Burnt Norton* with uncanny repetitions, the first position is again that of an aesthetician, the second that of a zombie ("We are born with the dead: / See, they return, and bring us with them"), the third an angelic perspective, the fourth a spectral observer of the entire world, and the fifth a mystic's assurance of an ineffable harmony. Each perspective from the first poem is carefully neutralized in the later one. The philosophical/poetic reasoning of *Burnt Norton* is replaced by an aesthetics grounded in a vision of social hierarchy, as critics have noted, and the effect is to eliminate the possibility that language might be capable of transcendence. The Word in the desert, an image of the prophet undergoing ascesis, is replaced by the strange image of becoming a ghost, as if language can no longer sustain subjectivity. The remaining narrative positions in *Burnt Norton*, of love and the observer in the garden, are transmuted from local observations of love to omniscient and disembodied perspectives. Another way of describing these transitions is to say that mobile desiring identifications with figures whose gender and sexuality cannot be named are carefully bound into ghostly introjects such as the compound ghost that can no longer be located in the cycles of modernist art or in gendered, desiring relations.

The result was a poetic manifesto of great power for its time. In his study of the political climate in which *Four Quartets* achieved ascendancy, John Xiros Cooper argues that the poem helped formerly oppositional intellectuals reinsert themselves into dominant positions in the cultural and political hierarchies of the postwar world:

But as the most authoritative work of literary art written by the most celebrated author-sage in the 1940s, *Four Quartets* helped to re-orient subjectivity and to establish, despite Eliot's explicit doctrinal purposes, the new ideological conditions for what was to come in North Atlantic culture for the next three decades.[37]

The poem offered a recipe for internal exile from the socio-political commitments of the institutions for which intellectuals worked, in an "aesthetic refuge," or "a benign and voluntary programme of re-education for lost souls."[38] The key to this aesthetic retreat was the forgetting of history in "a culture of persistent and well-policed amnesia."[39] The ghosts of history are reeducated to forget history and remember only personal, individual moments – of an almost divine sense of harmony according to Eliot but more often as moments of individual desire by his readers, for, as Cooper points out, most of his readers detached the Christian message from what was more important to them: the reconfiguration of the social and political subject. Finally, a further reduction also took place. Part of this reeducation was sexual, leading to the present political conjunction which makes possible a collection of essays on gender and sexuality in Eliot's poetry, and simultaneously rendering his own resolution – the melancholic identifications of warrior masculinity – unreadable except as symptoms of a largely vanished sensibility.

NOTES

1. "*Burnt Norton*, the second of the three, is a less somber poem." As far as she was concerned in this review replying to George Orwell (see below), the sequence ran *East Coker, Burnt Norton, The Dry Salvages.* Kathleen Raine, "Another Reading," *Poetry* (London) 7 (October–November 1942): 59–62, 62.

2. Lyndall Gordon, *T. S. Eliot: An Imperfect Life*, rev. edn. (London: Vintage, 1998), 261. The MS she cites is in the Houghton library.

3. T. S. Eliot, "A Commentary," *Criterion* 52 (April 1934): 451–4, 452.

4. Dallas Kenmare, "Story of a Pilgrimage," *Poetry Review* 18 (January–February 1937): 23–7, 27; Editorial, "New Books," *New Verse* 21 (June–July 1936): 19.

5. R. P. Blackmur, "The Whole Poet" [Review of *Collected Poems 1909–1935*], *Poetry* 50 (1937): 48–51, 49.

6. T. S. Eliot, *Four Quartets* (1944; London: Faber and Faber, 1959), 18. This edition, which is still in print, gives a better sense of how this poem works than the version in the *Collected Poems*. Subsequent page references in the main text are to this edition.

7. T. J. Clark, *Farewell to an Idea: Episodes from a History of Modernism* (New Haven: Yale University Press, 1999), 371. Quotation from G. W. F. Hegel, *Aesthetics: Lectures on Fine Art*, 2 vols., trans. Malcolm Knox (Oxford: Oxford University Press, 1975), vol. 1: 11.

8. Carol Christ, "Gender, Voice, and Figuration in Eliot's Early Poetry," in *T. S. Eliot: The Modernist in History*, ed. Ron Bush (Cambridge: Cambridge University Press, 1991), 23–37, 36.

9. Thomas DiPiero, "The Patriarch is Not (Just) a Man," *Camera Obscura* 25–6 (1991): 101–24, 104.

10. "The appearance of the phantom always originates in a gesture of mourning that cannot be performed." Jean-Michel Rabaté, *The Ghosts of Modernity* (Gainesville: University of Florida Press, 1996), 229. Rabaté argues that the temporal logic and the secularization of modernity produce spectral effects, ranging from *Geist* to Beckett's discursive phantoms.

11. George Orwell, "T. S. Eliot," *Poetry* (London) 7 (October–November 1942): 56–9, 57.

12. Georges Bataille, *Inner Experience*, trans. Leslie Anne Boldt (1954; Albany: State University of New York Press, 1988), 149.

13. Kenmare, "Story of a Pilgrimage," 27.

14. His argument largely fits the pattern outlined by T. J. Clark.

15. T. S. Eliot, "Preface," in *A Little Book of Modern Verse*, ed. Anne Ridler (London: Faber and Faber, 1941), 7.

16. Michael Levenson also notes Eliot's persistent rejection or distancing from earlier writings, especially in the 1940s, and argues that this constant abandonment of previous positions is manifest in *Four Quartets*. My own view, however, is that the process was more contradictory and the results more troubled. Michael Levenson, "The End of Tradition and the Beginning of History," in *Words in Time: New Essays on Eliot's* Four Quartets, ed. Edward Lobb (London: Athlone Press, 1993), 158–78, 177.

17. David H. J. Morgan, "Theater of War: Combat, the Military, and Masculinities," in *Theorizing Masculinities*, ed. Harry Brod and Michael Kaufman (London: Sage, 1994), 165–82.

18. John Bowen claims that "spectrality" is also integral to *The Waste Land*: it is "not just another 'aspect' or 'theme' of the poem, but an effect of its entire formal composition." John Bowen, "'To Learn to Live with Ghosts': Teaching

The Waste Land," *CIEFL Bulletin* ii, nos. 1–2: special issue, *Da/Datta: Teaching* The Waste Land (2001): 185–95, 192.

19. In an earlier essay on *The Waste Land*, I argued that the poem deliberately set up interpretative paths for readers, both through the obvious device of the notes, and through other more implicit packaged tours dependent on a range of references from Jesse Weston to Dada. See Peter Middleton, "The Academic Development of *The Waste Land*," *Glyph Textual Studies* I: special issue, *Demarcating the Disciplines* (1986) : 153–80.

20. T. S. Eliot, "What Dante Means to Me," in *To Criticize the Critic and Other Writings* (London: Faber and Faber, 1965), 129.

21. Angus Calder, *The People's War: Britain 1939–1945* (London: Panther Books, 1971), 255.

22. Calder, *The People's War*, 256.

23. F. H. Bradley cites one of his own journal entries from the period of *Appearance and Reality* that uses the classical lore of specters to evoke the dangers of metaphysics: "The shades nowhere speak without blood, and the ghosts of Metaphysic accept no substitute. They reveal themselves only to that victim whose life they have drained, and, to converse with shadows, he himself must become a shade." F. H. Bradley, *Essays in Truth and Reality* (Oxford: Oxford University Press, 1914), 14. Eliot may have seen this text given his doctoral interest in Bradley, but, regardless, Bradley's rhetoric is further evidence of the willingness of intellectuals to conceptualize issues in terms of the folklore of ghosts.

24. D. H. Lawrence, "The Border-Line," in *The Woman Who Rode Away and Other Stories*, ed. Dieter Mehl and Christa Jansohn (Cambridge: Cambridge University Press, 1995), 78–9, 95.

25. Virginia Woolf, *Mrs Dalloway*, ed. Claire Tomalin (Oxford: Oxford University Press, 1992), 91.

26. Sue Thomas argues that the entire portrait derives from Woolf's reading of the Report of the War Office Committee of Enquiry into "Shell-shock" (1922). Sue Thomas, "Virginia Woolf's Septimus Smith and Contemporary Perceptions of Shell Shock," *English Language Notes* 25, no. 2 (1987): 49–57, 56.

27. Wilfred Owen, "Strange Meeting," in *The Collected Poems of Wilfred Owen*, ed. C. Day Lewis (London: Chatto and Windus, 1963), 35.

28. Middleton, "The Academic Development of *The Waste Land*," 172. The line comes from T. S. Eliot, *The Waste Land*, in *Collected Poems 1909–1962* (London: Faber and Faber, 1963), 77, line 359.

29. Sigmund Freud, *The Standard Edition of the Complete Psychological Works of Sigmund Freud*, trans. James Strachey et al. (London: Hogarth Press, 1955), vol. XIX: 29.

30. Ibid., 30.

31. Sigmund Freud, "The Uncanny," in *Works*, vol. XVII: 234. Freud cites the phrase in quotation marks from Otto Rank.

32. Judith Butler, *The Psychic Life of Power: Theories in Subjection* (Stanford: Stanford University Press, 1997), 147.

33. Ibid., 149.

34. T. S. Eliot, *After Strange Gods: A Primer of Modern Heresy* (London: Faber and Faber, 1934), 5.
35. Sigmund Freud, "Mourning and Melancholia," in *Works*, vol. XIV: 245.
36. Helen Gardner, *The Composition of Four Quartets* (London: Faber and Faber, 1978), 183.
37. John Xiros Cooper, *T. S. Eliot and the Ideology of* Four Quartets (Cambridge: Cambridge University Press, 1995), 181.
38. Ibid., 136, 188.
39. Ibid., 195.

PART II
Desire

CHAPTER 5

Discarnate desire: T. S. Eliot and the poetics of dissociation

Nancy K. Gish

A blind, dirty, senile old man haunts the margins of Eliot's 1910 poem "First Debate between the Body and Soul."[1] Along with a cast of characters in *Inventions of the March Hare* – clowns, actors, marionettes – he inserts himself in the consciousness of Eliot's narrators as both self and other, a voice at once within and without the "I" who ostensibly speaks. Unlike Eliot's theatrical personae, this often vile, chattering, drunken, or mad old man carries with him a horror of self-representation little mediated by a stage setting or controlled script. Similar figures appear in other poems, notably "Dans le Restaurant" and "Hysteria." Yet he plays one role among many; in other forms, alien and intimate figures serve, in Eliot's work, both to claim and to disavow desire. For example, the marionettes – "my marionettes" – of "Convictions (Curtain Raiser)" are filled with naive and exaggerated desires carefully detached from the narrator who also claims them: they "Await an audience open-mouthed / At climax and suspense" and have "keen moments every day." The narrator of "The Little Passion from 'An Agony in the Garret'" observes himself walking and notes, sardonically, his own "withered face" as if in a mirror behind a bar: speaker and other are strangely indistinguishable.

That Eliot's poetry, especially the early work, depicts states of internal division, disorder, doubling, or multiple voices is well known. Especially in regard to "The Love Song of J. Alfred Prufrock" and *The Waste Land*, these inner states have been defined in relation to Matthew Arnold's "buried life," Bergson's distinction between *durée* and external social life, F. H. Bradley's closed selves, and Freud's notion of the uncanny.[2] Yet such divisions of voice, personae, sensibility, even personality had long been recorded in pre-Freudian theories well known to Eliot, whose figures of modern unease depict recognizable forms of psychological distress – notably what was clinically defined as hysteria – and whose famous concept of the "dissociation of sensibility" can be traced directly to their language. Although this source remains almost wholly unrecognized, it offers both a new understanding of Eliot's elusive term and a new way of seeing his poetic forms.

Eliot affirmed in "The Music of Poetry" that poets, in their critical writings, are always defending the kind of poetry they are writing.[3] "The dissociation of sensibility" framed a definition of consciousness the sources of which – and therefore the specific meaning and significance of which – illuminate his claims about poetry and his own poetics. In psychological theories of dissociation Eliot found, first, a way of understanding the seemingly fragmented modern self and, second, a way of depicting "modern" states of consciousness in which desire is simultaneously present and absent, in which sensual and abstract converge. This poetic strategy helps explain the continuing fascination of readers with a poetry obsessed with death and etherized numbness, yet powerfully evocative in its sensation and emotion. In *Inventions of the March Hare* these starkly conflicting inner states appear overtly as forms of psychological disorder that return, in coded forms, throughout the poetry.

The dominant trope of *Inventions of the March Hare* is madness: "mad as a March Hare," "a Mad Tea Party," "the Mad Hatter." But "madness," in this text, is manyness, the failure of unity and control attributed to a traditional notion of unity and consciousness. In modernist literature multiplicity of voice is an acknowledged mode. *The Waste Land*'s many voices, for example, are understood as representations of plural discourses, experiences, emotions, desires. Yet a voice assumes also a body, a material site. While multiplicity in texts is generally read in an idealist mode such that dispersal of self, voice, identity, remains textual only, psychological theories of dissociation – both pre-Freudian and recent – acknowledge the internal splits, divisions, *dédoublements* represented in Eliot's early characters. Eliot had read key accounts of dissociation theory, notably by Pierre Janet and William James, but before turning to his immediate sources it is perhaps easier to clarify their explanatory power by considering a current theoretical model. "In its broadest sense," according to Etzel Cardeña in "The Domain of Dissociation" (1994), "'dissociation' (Janet's *désagrégation*) simply means that two or more mental processes or contents are not associated or integrated."[4] A more specific meaning still includes a range of psychological experience: "'dissociation' applies to mental processes, such as sensations, thoughts, emotions, volition, memories, and identities, that we would ordinarily expect to be integrated within the individual's stream of consciousness and the historically extended self, but which are not."[5] The form of dissociation called "depersonalization," for example, "refers to a wide range of chronic phenomena, in which the self experiences itself as detached or at an unbridgeable distance from ongoing perceptions, actions, emotions, or thoughts."[6] Or the person may feel as if he or she is dead.[7] Forms of this include sensations of numbness, distancing of bodily sensations from the self, and experiencing the self as outside the physical body, including the experience of the "double," in which "a person may actually 'perceive' and even interact with an external double of him- or herself."[8] "Doubling," in French *dédoublement*, is also applied to dual personality, a condition discussed in Janet.[9]

Like Janet's, most current theories of dissociation define internal splits or divisions as symptoms of pathology. For Eliot, drawing largely on Janet and similar theorists, no other conclusion was readily available, and his assumptions parallel those of Janet for whom, according to recent theorists, "dissociation – the splitting off of various mental contents from consciousness – was something that occurred under stress, particularly to individuals who were congenitally predisposed to dissociate. The implication was that there was some particular kind of mental deficit or biological weak-mindedness in people disposed to dissociation."[10] More recently neodissociation theory starts from a different position; rather than assuming the norm of original unity, it begins, according to Erik Z. Woody and Kenneth S. Bowers, "with the assumption that some multiplicity of mental process is typical and normal, in the sense of coexisting levels of control that are usually well-coordinated by higher conscious functioning." They take as their initial model Robert Louis Stevenson's statement, placed in the voice of Dr. Jekyll, "Man is not truly one, but truly two . . . I hazard the guess that man will be ultimately known for a mere polity of multifarious, incongruous, and independent denizens."[11] They further note an extension of this idea on the analogy of a computer:

Pursuing this computer metaphor, it is an intriguing fact that nothing can prevent the possibility of two operating systems coexisting on the same hardware – for example, Windows and OS/2, either of which could be "brought up" during a particular session . . . Returning to people, normally one good supervisory or operating system is all that is needed; but perhaps in rare cases, two alternative, coexisting executive control systems, each with its own memory-management processes and access to unique records, may develop.[12]

According to neodissociation theory, then, "dissociated" experiences need not be pathological, though of course they may be. But if pathology is presumed as a characteristic of such experiences, they will almost inevitably be disturbing, denied, and disavowed.

Such disturbed and disturbing states are repeatedly enacted in *Inventions of the March Hare*. Considering these representations together with Eliot's early prose reveals specific new ways of understanding both his theory of the "dissociation of sensibility" and the more coded versions of identity and desire in later published work. In these early poems desire is inseparable from the very conditions of existence and identity; it defines, by its exclusions, the limits of Eliot's ostensible "I," a speaking voice dissociated from the sensation and emotion it articulates. And its significance is inseparable from a theory of personality, identity, self, and sensibility developed in Eliot's critical commentary, particularly the Clark and Turnbull Lectures. By examining the relations among Eliot's sources, theories, and early poetry, I wish to make three key points: that Eliot knew and drew on pre-Freudian theories of dissociation when he began writing his poetry and his aesthetic theories of dissociation, that he developed – beginning with the *March Hare* poems – a distinctive poetics of dissociation, and that he found in the double as vile or dirty or mad old man a pervasive image of modern consciousness.

In the earliest poems, forms of consciousness represent complex and varied versions of the "dissociation" Eliot so elusively asserts in "The Metaphysical Poets." For example, "Convictions (Curtain Raiser)," the opening poem of the notebooks, enacts one end of the spectrum of Eliot's strategies of dissociation: "Among my marionettes I find / The enthusiasm is intense!" This depiction of poseurs who elaborately stage emotion in an era long past such awed belief is itself a pose of distanced superiority or knowledge: the director's encompassing vision. The poem serves, like the Madame Sosostris card scene, to introduce types of emotional resonance – the moment in the garden, the canting chat of pseudo-philosophers, the extravagant and pathetic romanticizing of single ladies whose portraits are yet to be drawn – all reduced to conventions of puppetry and treated with bemused and superior, if half-affectionate, mockery: "My marionettes (or so they say) / Have these keen moments every day." For these are, notably, *my* marionettes, types of figures who both act out convention and do so at the will of the puppeteer. Like the actors, clowns, dancers, opera singers, and comedians who populate many of the poems, they play roles only partially distinct from those of the speaker's imagined internal world. These figures are, in Arthur Symons's words, "by a further illusion, . . . marionettes who are living people; living people pretending to be those wooden images of life which pretend to be living people."[13] My point is that the marionettes become the embodiment of emotions and feelings detached from but nonetheless claimed by the speaker. Such detachment and fusion appear repeatedly in *Inventions of the March Hare*. In another early poem, "Opera," the narrator first describes extremes of sensation in *Tristan and Isolde*, only to pronounce on his ultimate indifference and the failure of emotional experience. Yet the experiences are depicted in extreme language: the music is "fatalistic," "passionate," and "ominous," and "love" is "torturing itself . . . Writhing in and out / Contorted in paroxysms, / Flinging itself." But despite the narrator's dismissal of such overwrought expression ("We have the tragic? oh no!"), his closing lines suggest, not knowing judgment, but absence and loss: "And I feel like the ghost of youth / At the undertakers' ball." Here the capacity to experience the senses is cut off in a narrator experiencing himself as dead, a ghostly presence, yet a watcher of life that can only be known from outside. In poem after poem, we find extreme sensation or passion disavowed by an "I" who expresses despair or cynicism or ennui. Yet the emotions remain on the page, for Eliot's poetry persistently states an emptiness or weariness its images of intensity persistently override. In much of his work, the most distinctive effects are created by strategies of dissociation in which what is denied intellectually is most present emotionally.

DISSOCIATION

In 1906, the year Eliot entered Harvard as an undergraduate, Pierre Janet delivered a series of lectures at Harvard Medical School entitled *The Major Symptoms of Hysteria*.[14] For Janet, although hysteria "incorporates a wide range of neurotic symptoms sharing specific characteristics, it is fundamentally "a malady of the *personal synthesis*." "*Hysteria*," he claims, "*is a form of mental depression characterized by the retraction of the field of personal consciousness and a tendency to the dissociation and emancipation of the systems of ideas and functions that constitute personality*."[15] For Janet, as later for Eliot, "dissociation" is a failure of unified consciousness. The term "dissociation," central to Eliot's early definition of metaphysical poetry,[16] is a primary concept throughout the Clark Lectures and Turnbull Lectures published in 1993 as *The Varieties of Metaphysical Poetry*.[17] This term, according to Ian Hacking, was invented by Janet and brought into English by William James, who was then in the philosophy department at Harvard; it was, he claims, "cemented . . . into English" by Morton Prince in *The Dissociation of a Personality*,[18] a now classic text well known to both Janet and William James. Though Hacking adds that Janet dropped the term after 1889, it was, in fact, retained in Janet's 1906 definition of hysteria. In the first two decades of the twentieth century, Eliot's Boston was a site of considerable study and discussion about related concepts developed in France in the nineteenth century: hysteria, dissociation, and dual or multiple personality. Moreover, Eliot read and took notes on both Janet and James – especially James's *The*

Varieties of Religious Experience, which includes a chapter on the "Divided Self" and attributes mysticism in part to the unifying of dissociated selves.

In both France and America in the late nineteenth and early twentieth centuries, a complex psychological conceptualization framed discussions of depression, dual and sometimes multiple personality, various states of amnesia, somatic reactions, and fragmented consciousness – categorizing them as aspects of the broader term "hysteria." In the first 1906 Harvard lecture, Janet claimed that "what has been most characteristic in France for a score of years in the study of nervous diseases is the development of pathological psychology," and that, to understand them, it is with "Hysteria . . . that one should begin."[19] Naming a long list of prominent early researchers including Charcot, Breuer, Freud, and Prince, he offers a comprehensive definition:

No doubt they seemed, like Professor Ribot, to speak of all possible mental diseases and to seek for mental disturbances in all the forms in which they present themselves. Now and then, it is true, they devoted a few lines to idiocy or insanity; but if you read their books again, you will see that, whatever the matter is, "Maladies de la mémoire," "Maladies de la Volonté," "Maladies de la Personnalité," they always speak of localized amnesias, of alternating memories, which in reality are only met with among hysterical somnambulisms; of irresistible suggestions, hypnotic catalepsias, which are, as I will try to prove to you, nothing but hysterical phenomena; of total modifications of the personality divided into two successive or simultaneous persons, which is again the dissociation of consciousness in the hysteria.[20]

Janet thus defines the primary new science of his time as the study of forms of personality, consciousness, and "sensibility" as a particular way of understanding "dissociation": "In a word, if any interest is given to the development of that pathological psychology which has been growing these twenty years, it ought to be recognized that this interest has for its object a special disease: Hysteria."[21] And hysteria is characterized, as his definition makes clear, by "dissociation and emancipation of the systems of ideas and functions that constitute personality." Discussion of hysteria was, moreover, intensified in Britain during World War I as "shell-shocked" soldiers came home exhibiting symptoms traditionally attributed to "hysterical" women, and doctors frequently focused on ways of curing "dissociative" disorders.[22]

With the rise of Freud's later theories in the 1920s, "dissociation" lost ground; interest in these early studies revived in the 1980s and 1990s with the developing study of multiple personality, and pre-Freudian models have recently been revived in neodissociation theories. But when Eliot famously wrote of the "dissociation of sensibility" in "The Metaphysical

Poets" and traced the disintegration of intellect from Dante through the Metaphysicals to the divided self of Laforgue and Corbière in *The Varieties of Metaphysical Poetry*, he was drawing on a widely held and pervasive theory of consciousness, the original texts for which he had read[23] and two of whose authors – William James and Morton Prince – were well known in the Boston of his college years.

The "dissociation of sensibility" has generally been read as a division between emotion and intellect. In "The Metaphysical Poets" this apparent meaning can be drawn from the very vagueness of definition. Yet in Eliot's 1926 Clark Lectures it is far more complex, and it refers to an ongoing "disintegration" from Dante to Laforgue. What disintegrates is not limited to the immediacy of thought and emotion, and "sensibility" does not refer simply to the common meaning of emotional responsiveness. Rather, it includes but goes beyond sensation itself – "sight, smell, hearing, taste and touch." Eliot's definition of "sensibility" in the Clark Lectures begins with a reference to Sappho's "Second Ode": "You will see that Sappho's great ode, for instance, is a real advance, a development, in human consciousness; it sets down, within its verse, the unity of an experience which had previously only existed unconsciously; in recording the physical concomitants of an emotion it modifies the emotion."[24] "Metaphysical periods," he claims, are those "moments of history when human sensibility is momentarily *enlarged in certain directions.*"[25] This occurs when a type of poetry is written in which an "idea, or what is only ordinarily apprehensible as an intellectual statement, is translated in sensible form; so that the world of sense is actually enlarged."[26] And "the characteristic of the type of poetry I am trying to define is that it elevates sense for a moment to regions ordinarily attainable only to abstract thought, or on the other hand clothes the abstract, for a moment, with all the painful delight of flesh."[27] "Metaphysical" poetry thus reverses the action of dissociation – enlarging rather than retracting the field of consciousness and unifying what has been split apart. Eliot finds this kind of poetry in three historical "moments": Dante, the seventeenth-century Metaphysicals, and the French Symbolists, chiefly Laforgue and Corbière. What these poets all share is a fusion of thought and feeling or sense; what they do not share is a system of thought that is an exact equivalent of feeling. For Dante this existed; for Donne there were fragments of a system that he was able to fuse with feeling. For Laforgue there was already a disintegration of intellect that he could only address by "the intellectualizing of the feeling and the emotionalizing of the idea."[28] In each case it is the fusion or integration of sense and idea or thought and emotion that is "metaphysical."

These ideas are worked out in great detail in the Clark Lectures, and any summary necessarily simplifies. Yet if we examine Eliot's key terms, we find that his idea of "metaphysical" poetry, which in Laforgue, he claimed, made possible his own early poetic voice, is a unity of consciousness achieved by bringing what has been unconscious into consciousness. Moreover, this involves not only emotion but sensation or the capacity to experience the senses, which become, through poetry, elevated to a level above flesh itself. He uses the word "beatitude" to describe this "intellectual completion."[29] In the lectures Eliot primarily uses the term "disintegration," a more common translation of Janet's "*désagrégation.*" Although the Janet texts Lyndall Gordon lists as read by Eliot are in French, the French term is translated both ways, and Janet himself used "dissociation" in his 1906 lectures in English. Eliot uses the terms almost, but not quite, interchangeably: "not quite" because – although both refer to internal division of consciousness – by 1926 "disintegrate" dominates, tracing a historical process from the Middle Ages to the present. This translation suggests a more total breakdown of self and consciousness than "dissociation," which refers to a separation of parts or "units" of self coexisting or existing in succession but not accessible to each other.[30] The term he chose for the 1921 essay "The Metaphysical Poets" more closely describes the characters represented in *Inventions of the March Hare*; that is, they frequently display what Janet calls symptoms of "hysteria" in the forms of dissociation.

That Eliot knew and represented the characteristics of "dissociation" in his early poems is apparent from his reading and his use of the term (along with the alternative translation of "disintegration") and from his specific attributions of what he saw as disorder and "hysteria," but he saw these in opposition to a capacity for re-associating through poetry, for achieving "beatitude," for an intellectual completion in spite of psychological fragmentation. Dissociation, in Eliot's prose, is "modernist," a psychological characteristic suffered in intensifying degrees from the Metaphysicals to the present but capable – in poetry – of being transformed by the poet's associations and, in Laforgue and Corbière, a source of poetic form he could use. Moreover, the mind of the poet could provide a counter to this inevitable "*maladie.*" Having claimed that the function of the metaphysical poet (that is, in the general sense that comprises the poets of his three "moments") is to "transform thought into feeling and feeling into thought," he offers an astonishingly sweeping claim: "What I am insisting on is the role of the artist in the development and maintenance of the mind."[31] Thus the "dissociation of sensibility" is not only an aesthetic style but also a psychological condition to be resolved in part through poetic means.

In 1921, the year of "The Metaphysical Poets," Eliot contrasted James Joyce and Virginia Woolf in their "craving" for the fantastic and strange, a "feeling" which Joyce, he claimed, made "into an articulate external world." Woolf's writing, on the other hand, in "what might more crudely be called a feminine type, when it is also a very sophisticated type, makes its art by feeling and by contemplating the feeling, rather than the object into which the feeling can be made." The result he calls an example of "a process of dissociation."[32] While he calls her writing both "sophisticated" and "remarkable," it is also crude, a distinction reiteratively made between what produces order or unity in aspects of consciousness and what leaves them apart or dissociated. Considering this commentary on the division in the artist in terms of the Clark and Turnbull Lectures, we see a pattern of language and conceptualization that places his own poetry in relation to the "process of dissociation," with its accompanying "moments" of re-association.

For example, Eliot takes over the term *dédoublement* in a different context to articulate again what is fundamentally "modernist"; the internal division modernists sought to reconcile is described as a central characteristic of Laforgue and his work. Laforgue's use of irony – a style Eliot appropriated – reveals this particular disturbance of the subject: "What we rebel against is neither the use of irony against definite men, institutions or abuses, nor is it the use (as by Jules Laforgue) to express a *dédoublement* of the personality against which the subject struggles."[33] Eliot wrote this in 1933, the year of the Turnbull Lectures that revised, shortened, and focused the argument of the Clark Lectures. In the later version, he tells us that "Laforgue is surprisingly modern," that he "is certainly in revolt against something, a revolt which, as with D. H. Lawrence, is enacted on a deeper level of consciousness than that which deals with political and social notions."[34] In this same lecture he acknowledges his own debt to the French Symbolists without whom he doubts whether he "should have been able to write poetry at all." In emphasizing their importance for the present," he admits that he "may only be defending [himself]."[35]

Reading these excerpts in relation to one another reveals a pattern of related ideas and poetic strategies that are, as so often in Eliot's prose, about Eliot himself as poet. How far this psychological framework might describe Eliot as a person is not my focus, not least because it would require biographical material beyond what is available. That it was familiar terminology in relation to his own early breakdown, however, is almost certain, given that Eliot's self-diagnosis of a form of "aboulia," and his trust in Dr. Roger Vittoz, who treated him at Lauzanne, both point toward theories of dissociation. Janet lists "aboulia" as one of the "hysterical stigmata," and Vittoz attributes this loss of will to dissociation of the conscious and unconscious.³⁶ Eliot's familiarity with the pre-Freudian analysis of a particularly "modern" unease or dis-ease as dissociation thus derives from his Harvard reading, his personal experience, and his extended thinking about the poetic revelations of the French Symbolists. In *Inventions of the March Hare* it allows for distinctive structures of identity and desire.

DISCARNATE DESIRE

In *Modernisms: A Literary Guide*, Peter Nicholls, who aptly notes the role of the double in modernism, comments on Eliot's "curiously empty poetic voice for which irony is a constant reminder of the self's instability, not to say intermittence." Yet he attributes this absence in "Prufrock" to a lack of different *personae* or masks and to Eliot's lack of interest in psychology. Eliot, he claims, "shows no nostalgia for the lost self . . . nor does he regard the resulting multiplicity of selves as anything more than the detritus of social role-play."³⁷ But this "empty voice" can be read as an acutely accurate description for different reasons: the "selves" in "Prufrock" are represented not as masks or *personae* but as dissociated doubles; there need be no nostalgia because the "self" is not lost. Moreover, Eliot's terms and references as well as his poetic voices show an intense interest in the psychology of doubling and depersonalization, which he denigrates and reframes as philosophy, not internal division as an individual condition but the absence of a unified philosophy (such as Dante could assume) that explains the "disintegration" of intellect in a time of fragmented ideas. I will come back to "Prufrock," specifically in the light of "Prufrock's Pervigilium," but first I wish to define the forms of desire consequent upon such an intellectual basis. "'The Love Song,'" in Nicholls's formulation, "is like a thin skein stretched across a chaos of inchoate romantic desire." Again, this is a precise description, but the desire is in fact located in an alter "self" (or selves) who could or would or might choose, or act, while it is distanced and detached from any speaking subject.

Desire, in Eliot's early poems, is discarnate: both disembodied and removed from the voice that speaks it, yet intensely realized in altered selves or states of consciousness from whom the speaker withdraws and in whom intensities of sensation and emotion exist apart from the ostensible "I" who speaks. Along with the many objectified personae of marionettes, clowns, and actors, in whom desire is contained and mocked, Eliot depicts states of depersonalization and *dédoublement* as representations of desire that it would seem madness to retain and also a kind of madness to detach, for dissociation was understood as hysteria, disorder, *maladie*, and yet a definitively "modernist" form of consciousness. In accounts of dissociation, Eliot would have found a way of understanding and portraying such inner division or "disintegration"; in Laforgue, on whom he drew for images of puppets, clowns, and poseurs, he saw precisely such doubling. Desire, which disturbs, is detached and relocated in these objectified personae or in the external world, or in a double perceived as outside the self.

If we return, for example, to "Convictions" and "Opera," we see an excess of sensation and emotion vividly realized in images of anticipation or theatrical performance. The mocking and empty voice of an undefined narrator presumes to diminish and exclude as ludicrous such "keen" moments, but only after they have been articulated, even indulged. And yet what is left is not philosophic insight, still less "beatitude," but a "ghostly" presence from whom any feeling is apparently evacuated. However sentimental or clichéd, the feelings and emotions of "Convictions" are presented only by report, and yet presented as deeply experienced for the marionettes. The voice of "Opera," left in indifference, "feels" like one who is dead or, in Cardeña's definition, "at an unbridgeable distance from ongoing perceptions, actions, emotions, or thoughts"; the players on the stage, if overwrought, are still intensely sentient. The effect of the poems is not to leave one sharing the mockery or deadness but to experience the "keen" intellectual awareness of sensation. The speakers themselves are unconvincing. Though "Opera" is adolescent in its contrived ennui (as Eliot later found Laforgue adolescent), what remains striking is the portrait of depersonalization, the sensation of being detached or dead, not the speaker's self-conscious and pseudo-weary denial.

As in "Convictions" and "Opera," the speakers in poem after poem both offer and withdraw desire, reiteratively voicing and projecting it outside the speaker. Desire is thus figured as undesirable, the excessive or banal or disgusting or mad longing after what does not or cannot satisfy. It can be acknowledged only in the "other." It is dealt with by a particular form of "disavowal" in S. Hall's terms, "the strategy by means of which a powerful fascination or desire is both *indulged* and at the same time *denied*."[38] For Eliot's early poems "disavowal" reveals the simultaneous possession and dispossession of desire by asserting while disclaiming it or by displacing it onto a persona or double. In actors, clowns, puppets, and doubles, the "I" of each poem both experiences and places outside the self what evokes longing and anxiety. If the voices are empty, it is because all feeling and emotions have been displaced. Yet desire is not erased or transcended or denied; rather it is evoked and placed where the "I" may observe, comment, or philosophize about it, or become absorbed in horrified identification with its "mad" manifestations. Rather than consider and reject desire, the narrators of these poems, for the most part, detach and multiply it; they attend to, mock, brood over, or agonize about it, but they simultaneously indulge in the possibilities of experiencing it. The "I" is thus reduced and abstracted – dissociated from both thought and feeling – while the potential sphere of sensibility is "enlarged" to include what the "I" finds intolerable to think or feel, even violence or degradation.

While many poems thus emphasize, even exaggerate, the "keen moments" they repel or mock, others place at the center the empty-voiced "self" who, having disavowed such sensation, is left with deadness or disgust. *Inventions of the March Hare* includes representations of much more disturbing, even terrifying emotions. If we read these poems in terms of dissociation, and particularly Eliot's own language about it, we find voices disavowing desire and personae or doubles overwhelmed by desire. Most frequently we find forms of "depersonalization" in which the "I" either experiences [him]self as unreal or dead, or encounters a strange and repellent other such as the mad and chattering old man, who is both outside and disturbingly within, one who is both self and not self. Identity is thus unstable and multiple, and personality is defined by disintegration, a sense of unreality, numbness, or doubling. What is desired is mocked or excluded but *in the poem* both real and intense. The poems, in Eliot's terms, "express a *dédoublement* of the personality against which the subject struggles." Desire tests the limits of self because it must remain outside the self, and identity is multiplied to contain what the emptied voice disavows.

Disavowal through dissociation appears in many forms. The "Burnt Dancer," for example, dances in a "circle of desire," warns of "agony nearest to delight," fills the room with tropic "odours" from "Mozambique or Nicobar." Yet the watcher/narrator internalizes the dance: "Within the circle of my brain / The twisted dance continues"; the waltzes of August afternoons in "Goldfish (Essence of Summer Magazines)" return "like the cigarettes / Of our marionettes"; the narrator of "Mandarins" notes "How very few there are, I think / Who see their outlines on the screen. / And so, I say, I find it good / (Even if misunderstood) / That demoiselles and gentlemen / Walk out beneath the cherry trees"; in "Humoresque" the narrator confesses to having liked "one of my marionettes" – now dead – and imagines him as a "mask." In such poems what is split off and disavowed is the clichéd and gauche "inchoate romantic desire" that "does not hold good at all" and yet recurrently appears in terms of emotional intensity and physical sensation in contrast to the deadness avowed by many narrators. In "The Burnt Dancer," the line "Agony nearest to delight" asserts a moment of physical/intellectual fusion, however unworthy the form it seems to allow. That is, the poem has it both ways: the letting go of sensuality and pleasure is made vivid but terrifying: "Of what disaster do you warn us / Agony nearest to delight?" That it is placed in the context of purgatorial fire exaggerates its significance, since the black moth dances "Distracted from more vital values / To golden values of the flame / . . . For mirthless dance and silent revel." The speaker melodramatically contrasts this "twisted dance" that stays in his own brain with the "whiter flames that burn not" from which the "singéd reveller" has strayed. A far more disturbing poem than those of comic marionettes, it nonetheless retains the hyperbole of emotional excess depicted in movement, color, and heat by one who displaces it and finds it still in his own brain.

If Eliot's appropriation of alter selves in forms of puppets, clowns, actors, and mandarins allows a sardonic distance from romantic desires, forms of desire that could then be conventionalized and reduced to the sentimental or absurd, these objectified containers of sensation could not suffice for such terrors as appear in other poems. In many, fears of "madness" and of its dark interiors intensify the modes of disavowal, set aside mockery for a self-absorbing horror, "enlarge sensibility" beyond what is bearable. These desires are beyond foolish or excessive. They are obsessive, violent, sexual, mad – as in, for example, "The Love Song of St. Sebastian," "Oh little voices of the throats of men," "Do I know how I feel? Do I know what I think?," and "Prufrock's Pervigilium." Yet these extreme feelings and desires are also, in different ways, both possessed and dispossessed: the poems enact forms of dissociation in which desire is split off and enclosed in an/other without freeing or easing the speaking persona. Unlike Eliot's marionettes, clowns, and various players, who embody the inchoate desire his speakers sardonically dismiss, his dissociated states, apparitions, hallucinations, and doubles carry unbearable desires that cannot be owned even if recognized in moments of horror. Several poems written in 1914 and several that are undated, for example, explore states of derealization and depersonalization. More disturbed and internal than any of the poems Eliot published, they nonetheless evoke a realm of experience so terrible as to underscore later, more coded expressions, as in the "lost / Violent souls" of "The Hollow Men" or the *The Waste Land*'s images of madness and dissolution or the more controlled representations of horror in "Sweeney Agonistes." When such inner terror appears later, it is usually reframed in abstractions or distanced in allusions or attributed to dramatic characters. In *Inventions,* it is explicit and expressed as direct sensation and emotion. In "Oh little voices of the throats of men," for example, the debate between desire and indifference ends in distraction and sleep, the agitated circling of thought displaced by shadows of lilac that take on human character – dancing, leaping, and crawling: "You had not known whether they laughed or wept." Yet the relation of this figure to whoever speaks is indeterminate. The poem begins in the third person, shifts to "you" in admonishing careful paths, "we" in imagining some balance of pleasure and pain, "he," and then an "I" who may be the voice of "he," to dismiss all possibility of hope, knowledge, or desire. "He" sleeps and "you" would not know whether the voices of the shadows laughed or wept. This dissolution of consciousness into all pronouns so removes and abstracts desire as to nullify it. Only of an unspecified "you" addressed by the unspecified "he" is fear or hope or feeling predicated. And yet the speaker is haunted all night by the shadows of lilac plumes and voices in chimneys that may laugh or may weep. The poem begins with little voices in the throats of men that "rend the beautiful and curse the strong." "We" the readers are left then with emotionally intense potentialities vividly realized and dis-owned, projected onto voices and shadows, yet acknowledged with a kind of anguish. The sensual and engaged obsess – in the early sense of "lay siege to" or "assail" – Eliot's abstracted and indifferent voices.

Such voices are not "hysterical" in the common sense of the word, as in "out of control"; rather they reveal internal states that have been disavowed and in later poems become more enigmatic and distanced, so that the reader is left with a constant sense of something deeply disturbing just out of reach or just beyond vision. Such poems as "The Burnt Dancer," "Oh little voices of the throats of men," "The Little Passion: From 'An Agony in the Garret,'" and "Do I know how I feel? Do I know what I think?" explore states of derealization and depersonalization in which horror of self is pervasive but sense and feeling are removed and watched or are strangely inarticulate. They represent "hysteria" in Janet's terms: a dissociation or disintegration of self so intolerable it is felt as mad. In "Do I know how I feel? Do I know what I think?" elements of both derealization and depersonalization present an "I" so disintegrated as to be uncertain of what is real or even of who he is.

The poem has three sections. In the first a voice questions both knowledge and identity so radically that the "I" is outside even self-awareness: "Do I know how I feel? Do I know what I think? / Let me take ink and paper, let me take pen and ink . . ." With the ellipsis this thread trails off, and the speaker imagines walking softly down the hall to inquire of the porter what he feels and thinks, wondering whether the porter may simply assert a fact of normalcy and say he is the gentleman who has lived on the second floor. But this gives way to fear of what answer may be given:

> Yet I dread what a flash of madness might reveal
> If he said "Sir we have seen so much beauty spilled on the open street
> Or wasted in stately marriages or stained in railway carriages"

This shift from the flattened affect of ordinary existence to a flash of almost visionary insight into the terror of the ordinary is felt as "mad," as a disconnection between the dailiness so frequent in early published poems and some terrible reality behind or beneath or outside it. The speaker is, in terms of "depersonalization," "at an unbridgeable distance from ongoing perceptions." The poem also contains aspects of "derealization" in which "the individual . . . *experiences* the world or its inhabitants as not quite real."[39] The voice of the "I" questions who or what he is and seeks an external definition from some other voice; at the same time, he experiences a hypothetical description of the world and daily life as a revelation of madness.[40] Even the walk down the hall, the inquiry of the porter, the possible response are all conditional, premised on "if."

The second section imagines the self as both unable to grasp reality ("There is something which should be firm but slips, just at my fingertips") and, abruptly, lying dead under a doctor's knife. Seemingly a corpse while an autopsy is performed, the speaker is yet aware that "the cause of death that was also the cause of the life" is probed. This experience of being dead is, as in so many of these poems, sharply imagined in sense images: of smell ("creolin") sight ("a black bag with a pointed beard"), sound ("of something that drips," "whisper in the brain"), touch ("the ancient pain"), and taste ("tobacco on his breath"). Though these sensations are acute, they are placed in a hypothetical future state of death, and the "I" remains dissociated, uncertain of what is known or felt or even of "the secret which I cannot find."

In the third, brief, section, the speaker slides into the numbness of ether, escaping thus the brain's imaginings:

> My brain is twisted in a tangled skein
> There will be a blinding light and a little laughter
> And the sinking of blackness of ether
> I do not know what, after, and I do not care either

What is explicit here as psychological states of derealization and depersonalization is echoed in published poems in ways not overt and explicit.

Prufrock, in the published poem, questions his own identity, imagines others defining him, imagines the evening as an etherized patient. The last two sections of "Preludes IV" envision and then mock a sense of what is real. Gerontion has lost "sight, smell, hearing, taste and touch" and dissolves into a thousand deliberations. The surreal images in Part V of *The Waste Land*, framed in a context of allusion and myth, still represent a sense of personal unreality and dissolution, in the end, into madness, now Hieronymo's. In the *Facsimile*'s original version of the surreal landscape, beginning with the woman drawing out her long black hair, the speaker says the line, "It seems that I have been a long time dead," echoing the voice in "The Little Passion: From 'An Agony in the Garrett'" as well as the experience in "Do I know how I feel?"[41] Here it might well be associated with Dante, with its added line, "Do not report me to the established world," or with Jessie Weston's barren waste lands, but in the poems of *Inventions* the sensations are direct and asserted not only as internal psychological states but as forms of experience definable in Janet's terms of hysteria and dissociation. They reveal the "modernist" sensibility Eliot so extensively sought to resolve by the reconstruction of order through poetic means, through the "role of the artist in the development and maintenance of the mind."

Eliot's earliest poems can be read – even when their langugage seems melodramatic or personally agonized – as a poetic fusing of sensation and thought that have, for the speakers of the poems, fallen apart. In "Do I know how I feel" the loss of sensation is represented as sensation; the experience of numbness or being dead is realized – in its loss – as feeling. Eliot's poetry develops this extraordinary form of representing absence (what has been excluded) as presence (what remains in some sense known) in the published poems, especially through *The Waste Land*.

THE DOUBLE

Depersonalization, derealization, and numbness thus appear in many poems, splitting off sensations, emotions, and desires from immediate consciousness and leaving Eliot's "curiously empty" voices. In other poems, feelings and emotions, so disturbing as to be completely separated from the "I" who speaks, are re-embodied in other selves, "both intimate and unidentifiable." While the marionettes, actors, dancers, and clowns tend to deflect and mock romantic desire and conventional pleasure, and the speakers of poems representing depersonalization and derealization generally express horror of ordinary experience as like death, the doubles tend to reincarnate "madness" in the form of disavowed lust or violation.

While the "double," an other self experienced as external and able to be perceived, even interacted with, may seem quite distinct from experiences of unreality or etherization, it is also defined as dissociation in a more total form. For Eliot this "other" or "alter self" is often the strange old man, who sings and mutters and claims his identity with the horrified and resistant "I" who speaks. In "Prufrock's Pervigilium" he appears, sitting across the street in the dawn, and is named "my Madness." Were it an isolated image, the name might be read as simply similarity or empathy with such a character, but read in the context of a series of interconnected images as well as Eliot's ongoing preoccupation with disintegration, *dédoublement*, internal division, and dissociation, this figure fits a pattern: a dirty, mad, chattering, drunken, and vile old man with whom the speaker identifies and with whom he shares illicit desires. In "First Debate between the Body and Soul," he is blind and stumbling in alleys and gutters. He is senile and he "pokes and prods . . . The withered leaves / Of our sensations." The "withered leaves" of sensation return as a refrain three times, rhyming on "masturbations" and "defecations," and framing a narrator's contemplations of the "pure idea" and the "Absolute." The opposition of the ideal to the physical, seen as degradation, is sustained in other versions of this figure. In "The Little Passion from 'An Agony in the Garret'" the "withered" face in the mirror has a smile of "washed-out, unperceived disgrace." Like Prufrock in "Pervigilium," he has walked the streets, "diving into dark retreats." In "Dans le Restaurant" the old waiter disgusts and horrifies the speaker with his dirty fingernails, his story of a long-ago (at age seven) moment of power and delirium with a little girl in a field, but most of all his recognizable similarity to the speaker himself: "Quel droit as-tu a des expériences comme moi?" This scene reappears in parallel ways in the hyacinth girl episode of *The Waste Land*, where the speaker also feels both longing and incapacity in the face of a young girl with flowers and damp hair, and in "Death by Water," where Phlebas is taken directly from the ending of "Dans le Restaurant" and is, in both poems, in need of purification. In "The Death of Saint Narcissus" the speaker is both a "young girl / Caught in the woods by a drunken old man" and the old man himself: "And he felt drunken and old." As in "Dans le Restaurant," a moment of illicit desire in a country scene is horrifying and remembered with revulsion as one's own act or experience. An elderly waiter with trembling hands tries to intervene in "Hysteria" by urging the couple toward a rusty green table in a garden.

What these figures have in common are age, associations of dirt and disgust sharply contrasted with flowers or gardens or lush countryside, images of "withering" or "disgrace," and a powerful sense of revulsion in the narrator, who experiences both loathing and identification. Although the identification is not direct in "Hysteria," the speaker and elderly waiter share a panicky need to stop the scene of uncontrollable laughter and its effects.[42] Gerontion too is associated with decay and dirt, recalls lost beauty, and experiences a horror of vice and "unnatural crimes." Though the setting differs, he, like the old blind man of "First Debate," the narrator of the hyacinth girl episode, and Prufrock, experiences a sense of dissolution and loss of sensation. Even the "familiar compound ghost" of "Little Gidding," who returns with wisdom, recalls the division when "body and soul begin to fall asunder" – a dissolution comparable to that of Prufrock in "Pervigilium": "And as he sang the world began to fall apart." This figure, much explicated and identified with other poets, is also a transformed version of the double – in this case explicitly identified:

> So I assumed a double part, and cried
> And heard another's voice cry: 'What! are *you* here?'
> Although we were not. I was still the same,
> Knowing myself yet being someone other –.

The streets they walk are "streets I never thought I should revisit." Though this figure is represented as a ghost and a "dead master," he is also represented as the speaker's self, and, like the other doubled figures of old men, one whose memory of tasteless fruit and "expiring sense / Without enchantment" and of the dissolution of body and soul parallels those of other doubles. Yet, as a ghost, he is past the experience itself. The double thus appears from Eliot's earliest to his latest poetry,[43] and it assumes, in various guises, the form of an old man who mirrors the speaker's disintegration or dissolution of mind and world, a disintegration Eliot saw as madness. The senile or mad old man in many incarnations embodies what is worst and most impossible to acknowledge in oneself.

While the old man appears repeatedly in Eliot's work, the most revealing and most striking example is in "Prufrock's Pervigilium," revealing because in this poem he is most directly identified with the speaker himself, both by the pronoun "my" and by the linking of his chatter with the dissolution of the speaker's world (rolled up into a ball). The doubled self of "you and I," long recognized as internal division and presciently defined as a "doppelganger" by Grover Smith as early as 1950, is here addressed as the external double of dissociated selves. While the published poem can be read in other ways, the early version incorporating the "Pervigilium" provides a new lens for Eliot's representation of identity and desire. As he so often did, Eliot gave conflicting accounts of his own text: he wrote to Kristian

Smidt that the "you" was a male companion.[44] Yet in a later interview he claimed that Prufrock was partly himself and partly someone else, a man of about forty who also partly expressed his own feeling.[45] One might, of course, see these claims as consistent if one's male companion is one's alter self. Nonetheless, the companion of the published poem is transformed as "my Madness" into the disturbing figure of displaced and disavowed desire.

The night of the "eve of Venus" evokes this figure. And as Christopher Ricks describes in his extensive notes to this suppressed section of "Prufrock," it alludes both to the resurgence of life, generation, and sexuality and to "the dark sense of *Veneris*, not only Venus but the venereal."[46] The nausea, hallucination, and self-loathing portrayed in "Prufrock's Pervigilium" opens in city streets of prostitutes and evil houses, and leads to madness. According to Lyndall Gordon, this section was apparently written slightly later than the published poem but suppressed before publication.[47]

The Prufrock of the published poem exhibits numbness, aboulia, depersonalization, and derealization, as well as implied doubling. Yet the anxiety and distress, so vividly represented, lack what Eliot calls an "objective correlative"; the anxiety far exceeds any given situation. In the "Pervigilium" such anxiety emerges with particular details in hallucinatory houses leaning, chuckling, and whispering, and in catlike darkness, transformed by tentacles, preparing to leap; the doubling is psychologically explicit as madness. The enigmatic and coded forms of multiplicity, which for Eliot were "mad," are here direct and powerfully expressed as sensation and knowledge. While the material is far more disturbed and dark than that of the published version, the images and experiences – of streets, women, a catlike physical world – are the same in more extreme forms, revealing in sharp outline the re-incarnated experience of internal division and "madness" evasively implicated in much of the published work.

In like manner, anxieties and disturbances, barely beneath the surface of many published poems, are directly represented in the poems of *Inventions*. They offer a kind of vocabulary of modernist dis-ease, as Eliot defined it in his various discussions of the "dissociation of sensibility" and "disintegration": his early characters are both representations of such dissociation and poetic attempts at re-association through sensually explicit awareness of discarnate desire. For Eliot, as for Janet, this experience was "hysterical": the fear it induces troubles his personae, from speakers who displace romantic desire onto singers and puppets yet feel dead in its absence to Prufrock staring out at the world and at his alter self muttering and singing. That Eliot himself may have feared manyness as madness, as something against which the soul struggled, may reveal more about the forms his early poetry took and the directions of his critical claims about sensibility and order than about the meaning of the multiplicity he recognized.

Whether experienced, observed, or known through the psychological theory he studied, dissociation provided Eliot with a model for representing passionate, extreme, even sensational forms of inner experience while separating them from the speaking voices I have called the "ostensible I." By suppressing the "mad" voice, Eliot later developed an increasingly abstract poetry, yet the voices return, even in the compound ghost of "Little Gidding." Reading these voices in terms of Stevenson's "polity" reveals complex, diverse, and often overwhelming forms of identity and desire that Eliot recognized and understood but found it impossible to affirm. In *Inventions* they are vividly realized fragments of consciousness or doubled selves dissociated from the speaking voice yet intensely present in the poem. I speculate that this early poetics of dissociation – its incarnated roles and puppets, its depersonalization of hallucinatory selves and doubles – allowed, even facilitated, the peculiar and distinct coexistence of sensual immediacy and abstraction, desire and detachment in Eliot's early published poems.

NOTES

1. T. S. Eliot, *Inventions of the March Hare: Poems 1909–1917*, ed. Christopher Ricks (New York: Harcourt Brace, 1996), 64–5.
2. See, for example, discussions of "you and I" as two aspects of self in Elizabeth Drew, *T. S. Eliot: The Design of His Poetry* (New York: Scribner, 1949); Grover Smith, *T. S. Eliot's Poetry and Plays: A Study in Sources and Meaning* (Chicago: University of Chicago Press, 1956); and Robert Langbaum, "New Modes of Characterization in *The Waste Land*," in *Eliot in His Time*, ed. Walton Litz (Princeton: Princeton University Press, 1973). Examples of the use of Bergson may be found in Kristian Smidt, *Poetry and Belief in the Work of T. S. Eliot* (London: Routledge and Kegan Paul, 1961); Nancy K. Gish, *Time in the Poetry of T. S. Eliot* (London: Macmillan, 1981); and B. C. Southam, *A Guide to the Selected Poems of T. S. Eliot*, 6th edn. (New York: Harcourt Brace, 1996). James Longenbach discusses Eliot's doubling as ghostly specters in "Uncanny Eliot," in *T. S. Eliot: Man and Poet*, ed. Laura Cowan (Orono, Maine: National Poetry Foundation, 1990). Langbaum also notes that Eliot referred readers to Pierre Janet.
3. T. S. Eliot, "The Music of Poetry," in *On Poetry and Poets* (New York: Noonday Press, 1961), 17.
4. Etzel Cardeña, "The Domain of Dissociation," in *Dissociation: Clinical and Theoretical Perspectives*, ed. Steven Jay Lynn and Judith A. Rhue (New York: Guilford, 1994), 15.
5. Ibid., 19.
6. Ibid., 24.

7. Frank W. Putnam, "Dissociative Disorders in Children and Adolescents," in *Dissociation: Clinical and Theoretical Perspectives*, 176.

8. Cardeña, "The Domain of Dissociation," 24.

9. Ian Hacking describes the development of the term "*dédoublement*" in relation to the famous case of Felida X as a hysteric. See Ian Hacking, *Rewriting the Soul: Multiple Personality and the Sciences of Memory* (Princeton: Princeton University Press, 1995), 160 ff.

10. Erik Z. Woody and Kenneth S. Bowers, "A Frontal Assault on Dissociated Control," in *Dissociation: Clinical and Theoretical Perspectives*, 53.

11. Ibid., 52–3.

12. Ibid., 75.

13. Quoted in Christopher Ricks's notes to "Convictions," in *Inventions of the March Hare*, 103. Ricks comments at length on the parallels in Laforgue and others as well as Symons.

14. Pierre Janet, *The Major Symptoms of Hysteria* (New York: Macmillan, 1907). I first discussed Eliot's use of dissociation in an MLA paper in 1997. Since developing this study in detail, I have read Grover Smith's article, "T. S. Eliot and the Fragmented Selves: From 'Suppressed Complex' to 'Sweeney Agonistes,'" *Philological Quarterly* 77, no. 4 (Fall 1998): 417–37. Smith also notes Eliot's familiarity with Janet and Prince, using their definitions of dissociation in a reading of "Suppressed Complex" and commentary on other poems. While I share his focus on Janet and the accurate representation of clinical dissociation in several poems, my argument extends Eliot's use of this to a complex theory of poetics. Also, I do not share Smith's acceptance of the intrinsic pathology in multiplicity assumed by Janet and Prince. I wish to thank David Mieklejohn for pointing out this article's related discussion.

15. Janet, *Hysteria*, 332.

16. T. S. Eliot, "The Metaphysical Poets," in *Selected Essays* (New York: Harcourt Brace, 1964), 241–50.

17. T. S. Eliot, *The Varieties of Metaphysical Poetry*, ed. Ronald Schuchard (New York: Harcourt Brace, 1993).

18. Hacking, *Rewriting the Soul*, 44. See also Morton Prince, *The Dissociation of a Personality* (New York: Oxford University Press, 1905; 1978). Prince studied the three personalities of a woman he names as Miss Beauchamp and concludes that one is the "real Miss Beauchamp."

19. Janet, *Hysteria*, 3–4.

20. Ibid., 4.

21. Ibid., 5.

22. Throughout the war years, the *Lancet* carried articles on how to cure hysteria in soldiers. For an overview of hysteria in World War I, see Judith Herman, *Trauma and Recovery* (New York: Basic Books, 1977), 20–3.

23. See Lyndall Gordon on Eliot's reading and notes in the Houghton Library. *T. S. Eliot: An Imperfect Life* (New York: Norton, 1999), 37–8.

24. Eliot, *Varieties*, 51.

25. Ibid., 53.

26. Ibid., 53–4.

27. Ibid., 55.

28. Ibid., 213.

29. Ibid., 212.

30. I wish to thank Lavinia-Onitiu for translating and researching etymologies of key French terms.

31. Eliot, *Varieties*, 221.

32. T. S. Eliot, "London Letter," *Dial* 71, no. 2 (1921): 216. The gendering of dissociation appears in a few other places but does not seem to be consistent.

33. T. S. Eliot, "A Commentary," *Criterion* 12, no. 48 (1933): 469. Eliot defines the irony in contrast to that of Anatole France, who represents, he claims, "the age which is past."

34. Eliot, *Varieties*, 284–5.

35. Ibid., 287.

36. See Janet, *Hysteria*, 314–6. For an account of Vittoz's ideas and methods, see Adam Piette, "Eliot's Breakdown and Dr. Vittoz," *ELN* 33, no. 1 (1995): 35–8. Piette notes that Vittoz "may have guided Eliot to confirming a key-word, 'dissociation'" (38), but he does not connect this with the extensive French and American psychiatric literature on hysteria and dissociation.

37. Peter Nicholls, *Modernisms: A Literary Guide* (Berkeley: University of California Press, 1995), 181–2.

38. Quoted in John Jervis, *Transgressing the Modern* (Oxford: Blackwell, 1999), 9. Like Jervis, I draw on this concept for its specific value here, without using its discourse of origin.

39. Cardeña, "The Domain of Dissociation," 24.

40. I am indebted to Dr. Michael Garnett for the recognition that aspects of derealization as well as depersonalization are present in the poem's narrator.

41. Eliot wrote to Conrad Aiken on December 31, 1914 of his own sense of being not quite alive in Oxford. *The Letters of T. S. Eliot*, ed. Valerie Eliot (New York: Harcourt Brace Jovanovich, 1988), vol. 1: 74.

42. The "hysteria" has been read as either the man's or the woman's. I suggest that in terms of then-current views of hysteria, both characters are hysterics. The uncontrollable laughter is, in Janet's terms, one form of "automatic agitation" (see *Hysteria*, 257–62), while the male speaker experiences a kind of hallucination of himself being swallowed. Moreover, the old waiter's trembling hands and urgently repeated suggestions to take tea "mirror" the speaker's anxiety.

43. A ghost prefigures as well as follows and transforms Eliot's "mad" doubles. In Eliot's first poem, "A Fable for Feasters," written in 1905, a "wicked and heretical old sinner" returns as a ghost to terrify monks given up to gluttony and sensation. T. S. Eliot, *Poems Written in Early Youth* (New York: Farrar Straus Giroux, 1967), 3–8.

44. Smidt, *Poetry and Belief in the Work of T. S. Eliot*, 85.

45. See Southam, *A Guide to the Selected Poems of T. S. Eliot*, 48–9. Eliot did not, however, use the specific term "split personality" as Southam claims.

46. For a discussion of Pater's treatment of this theme and Flavian's death from venereal disease in *Marius the Epicurean*, see Ricks's notes in *Inventions*, 176–8. Flavian, in Pater's version, writes the "Pervigilium Veneris" while dying of the disease.
47. Lyndall Gordon, *Eliot's Early Years* (New York: Oxford University Press, 1977), 45; cited in *Inventions*, ed. Ricks, 176–7.

CHAPTER 6

Mimetic desire and the return to origins *in* The Waste Land ·

Jewel Spears Brooker

Charles Darwin's *On the Origin of Species*, published in 1859, was recognized within a year of its appearance as a monument in natural philosophy. But it was much more than an event in the history of science. It effected a revolution in the social sciences, with enormous consequences for the arts, especially naturalism and modernism. Although sometimes associated with notions of discontinuity, Darwin's work was in fact a vindication of the great Newtonian principle of continuity. He succeeded where his predecessors failed in part because his hypothesis included the "missing link" that connected present to past and contemporary humans to their remotest ancestors. Throughout the rest of the nineteenth century and the early part of the twentieth, scholars in the human sciences attempted to follow through on Darwin's claim that lost origins could be reconstructed through the use of surviving fragments. As Darwin claimed to have discovered the origin of species, they tried to find the origins of religion, society, and mind. In *Religion of the Semites* (1889), William Robertson Smith attempted to trace the evolution of the Jewish religion; in *The Golden Bough* (1890–1915), James G. Frazer tried to reconstruct the original all-encompassing myth; in *Themis*, Jane Harrison tried to track Greek religion to its roots; and in *From Ritual to Romance* (1920), Jessie Weston traced the Grail romances to primitive rituals. In sociology, Emile Durkheim in *The Elementary Forms of Religious Life* (1915) and Lucien Lévy-Bruhl in *Les Fonctions mentales dans les sociétés inférieures* (1910) tracked primitive society and the primitive mind.[1] In fact, what T. S. Eliot said of *The Golden Bough* can be said of all these works: they should be read "as a revelation of that vanished mind of which our own is a continuation."[2]

The late nineteenth- and early twentieth-century flowering of the social sciences is part of the context of the rise of modernism in the arts. Most of the modernists assimilated the obsession with origins from the general culture or from Frazer. T. S. Eliot, however, absorbed it from his superb education in philosophy and the social sciences. Between 1911 and 1914, as

130

a student in Harvard University's doctoral program, he took a number of seminars in myth, philosophy, and religion, and it is clear from his papers in the Eliot Collection at Harvard that he not only absorbed, but also criticized the work of such masters as Frazer, Tylor, Durkheim, and Lévy-Bruhl.[3] A few years later, as a struggling young writer in London, he wrote a series of sometimes brilliant book reviews of major works in the human sciences. Eliot also integrated his knowledge of the social sciences into his reviews of artistic works, including Wyndham Lewis's *Tarr*, Stravinsky's *Rite of Spring*, and Joyce's *Ulysses*. He argued that an understanding of primitive man is a prerequisite for understanding civilized man, adding, in one review, "The maxim, Return to the sources, is a good one."[4] Eliot recommended this return not only for poets, but also for critics: "If literary critics, instead of perpetually perusing the writings of other critics, would study the content and criticize the methods of such books as *The Origin of Species* itself . . . and *Primitive Culture*, they might learn the difference between a history and a chronicle, and the difference between an interpretation and a fact."[5] *Primitive Culture* is E. B. Tylor's landmark study of the origins of mythology, religion, language, and art.[6]

Even before his formal studies in the social sciences, Eliot was aware of the thin line separating cultured contemporaries from their primitive ancestors. In 1910, for example, in "Portrait of a Lady," the lady's voice and her desires are associated with violins, but the gentleman caller's silence and his desires with a "tom-tom" (surely a pun): "Among the windings of the violins / . . . inside my brain a dull tom-tom begins / Absurdly hammering a prelude of its own." The speaker's malaise in these early poems is vague ("Are these ideas right or wrong?"), approximating the angst found in Baudelaire, Kierkegaard, and Edvard Munch. Once Eliot begins his graduate studies, however, the vagueness disappears. First, he draws a line between the artist and everybody else, the distinction being that the artist is in touch with primitive life; he is a sort of missing link in the consciousness of the race. In a review of Wyndham Lewis's *Tarr*, for example, Eliot argues that "The artist . . . is more primitive, as well as more civilized, than his contemporaries; . . . Primitive instincts and the acquired habits of ages are confounded in the ordinary man. In the work of Mr. Lewis, we recognize the thought of the modern and the energy of the cave-man."[7] In retrospect, we can see that the portrait of the narrator in "Portrait of a Lady" is a portrait of the artist as a young man. Second, Eliot begins to feel that artists have a responsibility to reconnect the primitive mind to the modern mind, part of his emerging argument on "unified sensibility," most fully articulated in his essay on the Metaphysical poets and in

his 1926 Clark Lectures at Cambridge.[8] Third, Eliot begins to highlight
the connection between religion, sexuality, and violence. He censored the
poems in which the connection is most graphic (for example, "The Love
Song of St. Sebastian" [1914]),[9] but published many pieces (for example,
"Sweeney Erect," *The Waste Land*) in which the connection is only lightly
veiled. Fourth, he begins to focus his interest in origins on "survivals,"
i.e., fragments of behavior and ritual which survive in contemporary culture long after their function is lost or forgotten. The survivals are crucial
because, once recognized, they become part of the link between primitive
and modern. Fifth, although Eliot does not drop his assumption of continuity ("that vanished mind of which ours is a continuation"), he increasingly
emphasizes stratification and simultaneity.[10] His best-known discussions of
simultaneity are in "Tradition and the Individual Talent" and his review
of *Ulysses*.[11] But his reviews are replete with references to "stratifications"
of primitive and modern life. In "War Paint and Feathers," for example,
he argues that the artist "should be aware of all the metamorphoses of
poetry that illustrate the stratifications of history that cover savagery."[12] In
"Sweeney Among the Nightingales," Eliot creates a textbook example of
stratification in which Tereus, Agamemnon, Christ, and Sweeney are seen
not only as a temporal sequence, but as a spatial construct, simultaneously,
in the present moment.

Eliot's writings, not least *The Waste Land*, bear ample testimony to his
concern with origins, with the nexus of religion/sexuality/violence, with
the conscious use of survivals, with stratification as an element of form,
and with the artist as an essential link between primitive and modern. The
poem, as Joseph Bentley and I argued in *Reading* The Waste Land, can be
seen as a probe sent in search of lost unity, a probe which both accelerates
and disintegrates in the closing lines of the poem.[13] The surface is littered
with fragments of contemporary life (including fragments of primitive ritual
unrecognized by the poem's characters), and the allusions provide a running
commentary linking religion, sexuality, and violence. Especially important
in *The Waste Land* is the role of the artist as a mediator between primitive
and modern, part of Eliot's larger argument that the mind of the artist
resolves binaries such as present and past, feeling and thought, personal
and impersonal.[14] *The Waste Land* is at once impersonal, a reflection of
a crisis in culture in postwar Europe, and personal, a reflection of Eliot's
own life. While Eliot famously argued that art is impersonal,[15] he also
admitted that it is personal. *The Waste Land*, he conceded, is the "relief of a
personal . . . grouse against life."[16] The ostensible contradiction disappears
when one looks beyond proof texts to the whole of his criticism. In a

number of essays, including his review of *Ulysses*, he distinguished between the "material" of art, which is real life, and its "method," which involves the use of myth to effect a metamorphosis into something rich and strange.[17] Eliot's poetry, like all great art, is personal in that it begins in what Yeats calls the "foul rag and bone shop of the heart."[18] Moreover, it is personal in that his choice of mythic fragments was guided by desire, much of which must have been subconscious. In 1921, as he was writing *The Waste Land*, Eliot explained that the selection of a myth is not random, but, rather, directed by one's point of view, one's self-image, and one's desires. "The myth that a man makes has transformations according as he sees himself as hero or villain . . . Man desires to see himself . . . as more admirable, more forceful, more villainous, more comical, more despicable . . . than he actually is. [A myth] is not composed of abstract qualities; it is a point of view, transmitted to importance."[19] The conscious use of fragments of myth, then, is not only a means of achieving impersonality, but also a means of expressing a point of view, "transmitted to importance." In 1917, Eliot approvingly quoted Stanley Cook's view that "The doctrine of survivals is entirely inadequate when it forgets that we are human beings and do not accept beliefs merely because they happen to lie within our reach." Eliot added "Survivals are . . . subconsciously selected."[20]

The following analysis pursues Eliot into the labyrinth of mimetic desire.[21] First, I will look briefly at two of the elements which guided his choice of "material" – his life in the city and his marriage. The contemporary characters and the survivals in *The Waste Land* were not chosen simply because they happened to be at hand; they were "subconsciously selected" from his experience, from his desires. Second, I will look at the boudoir scene in "A Game of Chess," with emphasis on the allusion to Philomel from Ovid's *Metamorphoses*. "A Game of Chess" and the Philomel allusion are particularly interesting for my purposes, because they invite consideration of the distinction between life and art, and also because they illustrate the importance of desire in the subconscious selection of material for the poem. My argument is grounded in what Eliot consciously brought from his studies, but more importantly in what he "subconsciously selected," in the interest of which I will use the theoretical work of René Girard, a critic whose main insights came from psychologically/sociologically informed readings of ancient and modern literature, including biblical texts, Greek drama, and nineteenth-century French and Russian novels.

Girard's work is an extension of the late nineteenth- and early twentieth-century advances in the social sciences studied by Eliot. Like Tylor, Frazer, Durkheim, Weston, and Eliot himself, Girard returns to origins by studying survivals in contemporary culture, especially in modern literature. Like them, he focuses on the ancient connection of religion, violence, and sexuality in culture, particularly discussed in *Violence and the Sacred* (1972) and *The Scapegoat* (1982). Girard goes beyond his predecessors, however, in his understanding of the nature of desire and in the connection he makes between desire and the return to origins.

Girard's understanding of desire, first outlined in *Deceit, Desire, and the Novel* (1961), is particularly helpful in understanding Eliot. In Girard's view, desire is more psychological than biological. It comprehends sexuality, but is not restricted to it, involving rather "the dynamics of the entire personality."[22] Desire is usually understood as a spontaneous response to a desirable object, but according to Girard desire arises less as a response to an object than as part of a nonconscious imitation of another desiring subject. People tend to think of their desires as unique, but in fact they desire what others desire, and the awareness that another desires the same object feeds not only desire but rivalry with the other desiring subject. Desire, then, is mimetic. Girard also claims that desire is triangular, involving not only a subject and an object, but a mediator, with the primary psychological bond being between the subject and the mediator. Desire is thus mediated rather than direct and secondhand rather than original or spontaneous. It is part of an infinite chain without origin and, because its object is constantly being displaced by a mediator, without end. Girard sees this serial displacement as an indication that the ultimate object of desire is metaphysical; that is, the real object is not *having* but *being*, not acquiring an object, but constructing and protecting a self. On the subconscious level, desire is part of infinite longing, longing that involves a desire to return to origins. The mimetic nature of desire and its association with infinite longing are evident in the nineteenth-century novels Girard uses in his analysis. The heroine of Flaubert's *Madame Bovary*, for example, appropriates her desires from models. The premium Emma places on objects is not related to their intrinsic value, but to the value attached to them by others. And the ultimate object of her desire is existence itself.[23]

Girard distinguishes between two types of mediation. In "external mediation," the mediator between the subject and the object is temporally or spiritually or intellectually remote from the subject and superior in status, or at least perceived to be so. The subject tends to admire the mediator from afar. In "internal mediation," conversely, the model is at hand, and he is an equal or inferior. In this situation, the subject perceives the mediator as a rival and tends to despise him. Moreover, in external mediation, the subject feels proud of himself for imitating his model; in internal mediation, the subject experiences shame and self-disgust in his desire. Classic examples of external and internal mediation can be seen in *Don Quixote* and *Notes from Underground*, respectively. Both the Don and the Underground Man take their desires from others, but the first from esteemed superiors and the second from despised equals or inferiors. In external mediation, with its focus on remote mediators, the impulse to return to origins is strong. In internal mediation, with its focus on equality, the impulse to return is obscured or absent. In internal mediation, desire feeds resentment and leads through rivalry to violence.[24] Internal mediation is characteristic of democratic societies, especially modern industrial democracies.

Girard's distinction between "external" and "internal" mediation is helpful in understanding desire in *The Waste Land*. Desire entering the poem through the mediation of cultural memory could be thought of as "external" – that is, involving mediators who are remote in time and high in stature – lovers such as Aeneas or spiritual leaders such as Augustine. In external mediation, the subject admires the model and does not consciously enter into rivalry with him. Desire related to personal memory and contemporary history, on the other hand, could be thought of as internal – that is, involving mediators who are within the speaker's own circle and roughly equal in class and prestige. Certainly, in the contemporary world of the poem, hierarchies and distinctions are minimal. For the crowd flowing over London Bridge in the morning and the office workers having intercourse after work, internal mediation is the only possibility, for everyone is a clone of everyone else. For instance, the narrator in the "Unreal City" section of "The Burial of the Dead" is part of the crowd flowing over London Bridge and down King William Street. One source of his anguish is the realization of identity ("mon semblable, – mon frère"), the awareness that his desires are not original, but preexistent in the reader and in those others whose eyes are fixed before their feet on London's dirty pavements. As Girard points out, this sort of mediation leads to resentment and self-contempt, and, not surprisingly, such feelings are pervasive in this poem. But it must be noted that the distinction between external and internal is fluid in *The Waste Land*. As Eliot's note on Tiresias says, the characters melt into each other – the men are "not wholly distinct," the women "are one woman," and the "two sexes meet in Tiresias." This melting not only transgresses boundaries of chronology, class, and gender, but also crosses the bright line between myth and history. For example, a contemporary woman suffering from "nerves" melts into Cleopatra; both melt into Philomel, a purely mythical character; and Philomel is our contemporary, our double. Collapsing external mediators into internal ones creates an overall effect of crisis which remains unresolved after the poem's final "shantih."

Girard also connects mimetic desire with violence. The prelude to violence, of course, is conflict, usually seen as the result of aggression. He argues, conversely, that conflict proceeds from "appropriative mimicry," by which he means secondhand desire that involves an impulse of acquisition or appropriation. If the impulse to mimesis is present in both desiring subjects, the situation leads to reciprocal violence. Reciprocal violence involves the back and forth of revenge, and thus by its very nature tends to accelerate toward crisis. From earliest times, people have partially understood the tendency of violence to spread and accelerate in terms of contagion. To avoid being pulled into violence, one must avoid contact with people who are or have been involved in violence and must avoid contact with blood, known to be impure because of its unquestionable connection to violence. "When violence is unloosed, blood appears everywhere . . . and stains everything it touches."[25] This means, for example, that warriors returning from battle must be decontaminated and that women must be segregated during menstruation and after childbirth. "The fact that the sexual organs of women periodically emit a flow of blood . . . seems to confirm an affinity between sexuality and those diverse forms of violence that invariably lead to bloodshed."[26] The association between sexuality and violence is firmly rooted in religion, where the two meet in agricultural/fertility rituals; it is also rooted in social reality, where they meet in rape, defloration, sadism, and other situations. There are many other connections between sexuality and violence. Both, for example, tend to fasten upon surrogates, and both are associated with explosive emotions.[27]

Almost from the moment *The Waste Land* appeared in October 1922, knowledgeable readers associated "A Game of Chess" and its allusions with Eliot's marriage. Within weeks of its publication in London, Ezra Pound, who had served as midwife for the poem, had dinner with John Peale Bishop. Immediately afterward, Bishop wrote to Edmund Wilson that according to Pound the first part of "A Game of Chess" was an account of Eliot's marriage – "Eliot's version . . . is contained in 'The Chair she sat in like a burnished throne.'" Bishop added his own interpretation, presumably deduced from Pound's comments – "The Nightingale passage is, I believe, important: Eliot being Tereus and Mrs E., Philomel."[28] Bishop's equation is too simple, of course, but it is not entirely wrong. In 1923, Eliot said in his *Ulysses* review that the material of art includes "the emotions and feelings of the writer himself . . . The question, then, about Mr. Joyce, is: how much living material does he deal with, and how does he deal with it?"[29] The two main subjects in the Philomel sections of *The Waste Land*, sexual violence and the struggle to speak/sing, are clearly weighted with "the emotions and feelings of the writer." Without going into great detail and without claiming any one-to-one correspondence, I wish to comment on two clusters of emotion and feeling which involve violence and sexuality – Eliot's response to the city and his marriage. Both are part of the reservoir of "living material" which guided his selection of mythic fragments in the poem, and both are richly illustrative of mimetic desire.

Eliot was at once attracted to and repelled by life in the city. His ambivalence stems in part from a simultaneous attraction toward and fear of violence in the city at night, in part from a quickening of sexual desire combined with a need to check that desire. "Rhapsody on a Windy Night," written in Paris in 1911, was born of this ambivalence. A young man walking through the red-light district of a big city in the middle of the night senses danger and observes ("remarks") prostitutes and other creatures of the night. He is pushed to the edge of madness by simultaneous attraction and disgust as stained women hesitate toward him in open doorways.[30] On New Year's Eve, 1914, Eliot wrote from London to his college friend Conrad Aiken to complain of having "nervous sexual attacks which I suffer from when alone in a city . . . [T]his is the worst since Paris. I never have them in the country . . . One walks the streets with one's desires, and one's refinement rises up like a wall whenever opportunity approaches. I should be better off . . . if I had disposed of my virginity . . . years ago."[31] A few months later, in April, he met Vivienne Haigh-Wood, and in late June, with nudging from Ezra Pound, he married her. In so doing, he disposed of his virginity and of whatever innocence he might have had. The honeymoon was a disaster. Vivienne confided in Bertrand Russell (never a good idea), who confided in his mistress that the Eliots' "pseudo-honeymoon at Eastbourne [was] a ghastly failure. She is quite tired of him . . . [and] in the lowest depths of despair."[32] Eliot's version is preserved in "Ode": "When the bridegroom smoothed his hair / There was blood upon the bed."[33] These lines clearly point to "living material," for it is now known that Vivienne suffered from a disorder which caused profuse vaginal bleeding. Soon after their marriage, he learned that she was ill, that she suffered from problems associated fairly or unfairly with female sexuality, problems such as "nerves" and hysteria.[34]

Even this thumbnail sketch reveals the strong presence of mimetic desire. Eliot's desire was stimulated by being in the city because of what was happening there – what others were doing – and by his ambivalence about imitating them. His desire to be married was mediated not only by the presence of prostitutes in London, but also by Pound, who urged him to marry an English girl and remain in London. Eliot was evidently virginal when he married, and thus the bloody honeymoon must have underscored for him the primal connection between blood and female sexuality. And no matter how devoted Eliot may have been to his wife, he could not but have been impressed (consciously or subconsciously) by the fact that sex always resulted in blood upon the bed. If Girard is right, Eliot (again, consciously or not) must have associated female sexuality with violence, with pollution, and with contagion. It is easy in retrospect to see that the marriage was doomed from the start, and indeed, within a month or so, Vivienne was involved in an adulterous relationship with Bertrand Russell. In Girardian terms, the squalid affair with Russell can be seen in terms of mimetic desire, contagion, and an acceleration of psychological violence. Eliot, with some reservations, admired Russell, and his admiration was appropriated by Vivienne. Her unwitting husband, then, served as a mediator in the emerging sexual triangle. In addition, her friends acted as mediators between her and Russell, for he was a famous man and an intellectual icon. In admiring him, she was admiring a man others admired and envied. Russell's admiration for Vivienne, however, was mixed with disgust for her and, because he was intellectually and socially her superior (like Dostoevsky's underground man with the prostitute), with contempt for himself. He described one of his trysts with her in terms that open a window on Eliot's marital situation. The night with Vivienne, Russell complained, was "*utter hell*. There was a quality of loathsomeness about it which I can't describe." He grumbled that sex with Vivienne left him with "nausea" and "horrible nightmares."[35] Eliot himself did not comment on his sexual life, but if Vivienne had this effect upon a seasoned philanderer, one can only imagine the effect she had upon a shy and sexually inhibited puritan.[36]

There is one other observation I would make regarding the "living material" behind "A Game of Chess," the marriage section of *The Waste Land*. Although the Eliots, in their fashion, remained devoted to each other, it is clear that very early in their marriage the relationship changed. To use Girard's terminology, the desire changed from the desire *to have* to the desire *to be*. In my view, they became rivals in a psychological battle for being, and each seems to have considered his or her own existence threatened by the existence of the other. That Eliot considered her a rival for being is evident in his poems. In the honeymoon poem already quoted, the bridegroom describes the bride as "*succuba eviscerate*," and in an even earlier poem, "Hysteria," the male speaker reveals a fear of literally being engorged.

Eliot's anxiety over sexuality could not have created these problems *de nilo*, but must have compounded them.[37] That Vivienne considered Eliot a rival in some fierce psychodrama is clear from the comments of their friends. Russell, for example, told Ottoline Morrell that Vivienne "has impulses of cruelty to him . . . It is a Dostoevsky type of cruelty, not a straight-forward every-day kind."[38] Eliot's defense in this psychological battle of attrition seems to have been melancholy silence and measured coldness. Like all reciprocal violence, the hostility between the Eliots fed upon itself and generated fear. By the time he was writing *The Waste Land*, the crisis was full-blown, with loss of distinctions in his psychological life and his marital life echoing those in the postwar culture around him. The tragic cluster including his wife's illness and their increasing rivalry, Eliot feared, might have blocked his poetic efforts. He felt that he, like Philomel, had been silenced. A year after his marriage, he confided in his brother Henry that he was afraid that "Prufrock" would turn out to have been his "swan-song."[39]

The stress of city life and the miserable marriage did not silence him, however, but gave him more "living material" for poetry, a gift on full display in "A Game of Chess." This part of *The Waste Land* consists of a two-part exploration of contemporary sexual relationships, the first in a lady's dressing room, the second in a pub. The dressing room scene, at issue in this paper, features characters resembling Eliot and his wife. He invited both his wife and Ezra Pound to comment on the typescript, and both noted the parallel. Vivienne clearly approved. Beside the lines "'My nerves are bad tonight. Yes, bad. Stay with me. / Speak to me'" she wrote "WONDERFUL." Pound, however, disapproved of such obvious realism, writing "photography" in the margin beside the same lines and "photo" beside the line "'Are you alive, or not? Is there nothing in your head?'"[40]

The dressing room section is itself divided into two parts, the first a description of the room and the second a "dialogue" between a man and (presumably) his wife. In the first part, the wife is alone. In the second, her husband is present and the point of view shifts from the unnamed narrator to him. The room is filled with "withered stumps of time," survivals such as the sevenbranched candelabra and fruited vines, the significance of which are probably lost on the woman. The centerpiece in the room is a *trompe l'oeil* painting of Philomel:

> Above the antique mantel was displayed
> As though a window gave upon the sylvan scene
> The change of Philomel.

Through the window thus opened, the woman could glimpse, if she looked, a flowering woodland ironically described in language taken from Milton's description of Eden in *Paradise Lost* and, in the center, Philomel at the moment of her change into the nightingale. For the narrator, the painting suggests not only metamorphosis, but its antecedent violence. He is aware, as the description makes clear, that Philomel has been "So rudely forced" by a "barbarous king," that the "change" is the last in a series that includes betrayal, rape, and mutilation. He is also aware that in compensation she has been given a voice that cannot be violated.

The most complete account of Philomel is contained in Ovid's *Metamorphoses*, and it is to *Metamorphoses* that Eliot directs us.[41] As Ovid tells the story, Tereus, King of Thrace, comes to the aid of the King of Athens, whose city is under siege. The siege is lifted, and as a reward the King of Athens gives his elder daughter Procne to Tereus in marriage. The marriage begins under a cloud, attended not by the marriage deities but by the Furies, spirits of vengeance for blood spilt within families. Tereus takes his bride to his kingdom, and they have a son, Itys. Procne misses her sister Philomel, and Tereus volunteers to go to Athens and bring her to Thrace for a visit. But on the return trip, overwhelmed by lust, he rapes her in the woods. When she threatens to tell what he has done, he cuts out her tongue and leaves her to die, later telling Procne that she has been killed by animals. With the help of a maidservant, Philomel survives and weaves her story into a tapestry which is delivered to her sister the Queen. Procne finds Philomel, brings her to the palace, and tends her wounds.

The rape and mutilation of Philomel, however, is only half of the story; the other half recounts the revenge taken by the sisters and the metamorphosis of the three principals into birds. Procne's first impulse is an eye for an eye and a tooth for a tooth: for mutilation, she would mutilate; for rape, she would castrate. "I would cut out his tongue . . . / cut off the parts which brought you shame." But such revenge against a warrior king would be impossible, and so she turns to a substitute, killing their beloved son Itys and serving him to his father for dinner. Once Tereus has enjoyed his cannibalistic feast, Procne calls Philomel, who hurls the child's bloody head at the father. Reciprocal violence escalates to an incredibly high pitch here and would have continued, except that it is interrupted by gods who turn the fleeing women and their sword-drawn pursuer into birds – the red-breasted swallow, the sonorous nightingale, and the hoopoe bird with its sword-like beak.[42]

The painting of Philomel in "A Game of Chess" shows Eliot's preoccupation with "all the metamorphoses of poetry that illustrate the stratifications of history that cover savagery."[43] The painting displays a paradisial scene sketched over a dark wood of horror. Its prominence and detailed description point to the Ovidian/Eliotic themes of sexuality, violence, and metamorphosis. For example, the link between sexual desire and violence can be seen in the various shadings of "Jug jug" – at once a parody of sounds of sexual intercourse, a slang expression for prostitution, the sound of a mutilated singer, and the dark undersong of the nightingale, itself a figure for the poet. Each of these shadings points to stratification from the shadowy woods of prehistory through the nineteenth century, and the sudden change of verb tense in the line "And still she cried, and still the world pursues" brings the story into the twentieth-century urban bedroom, bridging past and present, myth and history.

The presentation of desire is continued in the second part of this section of "A Game of Chess." With the entry of the woman's husband into the room, a pseudo-dialogue ensues in which the desires of both parties become more evident. The woman is loquacious and nervous, a cauldron of human wishes. Her desire is unfocused, lacking an object – "'What shall I do now? What shall I do?'" She wants something but nothing in particular; she wants to do something, but doesn't have any idea what to do. The man is silent and repressed; his less visible desire is not articulated to the woman, but for the reader of the poem it is mediated through language – in part through Shakespeare, in part through personal memory. When she asks him "'Do you remember / 'Nothing?'", he reflects "I remember / Those are pearls that were his eyes," suggesting that he too is thinking of metamorphosis.

One might expect that an encounter between a man and his wife in her dressing room would deal at least peripherally (even if ironically) with sexual desire. The desire in this scene, however, is not biological but psychological. Desire is clearly revealed in the woman's hysteria and the man's cynicism, but the desire lacks a specific object. This absence of the object is evident in the repetition of the word "nothing" – "'Do / 'You know nothing? Do you see nothing? Do you remember / 'Nothing?' . . . 'Is there nothing in your head?'" I would argue, based on my reading of René Girard, that the presence of unattached desire represents the endless deferral of the objects of desire. In this reading, desire in "A Game of Chess" turns out to be primarily metaphysical in that it is not a desire *to have* but a desire *to be*. The woman's insistent questions – "'What shall I do now?'" – can be read as expressions of desire for desire, of desire that another human subject, her husband, acknowledge her existence. In withholding the recognition she craves, he is trying to protect himself from absorption by her, trying to shore up the boundaries that support his own existence. Their memories may include the self-transcendence involved in sexual love, but their present attention is on self-preservation. They have become rivals in a struggle for being, and the tone suggests that it cannot end happily for both.

A striking feature of Eliot's use of the myth is his unambiguous sympathy with Philomel. Ovid's story is objective, carefully balancing an action and a counteraction – male aggression followed by female revenge, rape/mutilation followed by murder/cannibalism. Dante's version, which Eliot knew well, is unsympathetic to the sisters. In the *Purgatorio*, he points to them as examples of wrath, but ignores Tereus' crimes against them. Eliot's version moves in the opposite direction, lingering on Philomel as victim – "So rudely forc'd. / Tereu" – while entirely omitting the second half of the tale in which she takes disproportionate revenge. Dante's motive for skewing the narrative is straightforward and didactic; Eliot's is less clear. It is evident from the pseudo-dialogue that follows that the woman is obsessed with her own suffering and her status as the victim of a male; at the same time, she is oblivious of her own vengeful acts. She is acutely aware of her need to escape and in desperation considers running out in the street in her dressing gown with her hair down. She suffers from paranoia and seems to feel that the world is pursuing her; she also seems to intuit that she is trapped and will not be rescued by the gods. The poem's sympathy with Philomel, however, is not limited to lines revealing that the woman thinks of herself as a victim; it remains constant across the shifting voices, male and female. This sympathy with the female and lack of sympathy with the male seem to be related to the overarching focus on the suffering land, a strongly feminine symbol, and one which colors point of view throughout the poem.

The structure of the boudoir scene is elegant in its careful balance of linguistic and narrative elements. It is a dance of opposites that conveys mutual suspicion but also facilitates reciprocal imitation, evident in the way the man's thoughts echo and reshape the woman's words and in the way her words correspond to his thoughts. The choreographed mimicry and controlled conflict are evident in the analogy between their actions and movements in a chess game. In the allusion to Middleton's play *A Game of Chess*, chess provides cover for sexual politics and sexual violence. In Eliot's poem, the male contemplates a game of chess as a way of giving structure to their meaningless lives; at the same time, he conveys by gesture and thought that the chess game would be a way of managing the continuation of psychological violence.

The boudoir scene in "A Game of Chess" illustrates Girard's notion of mimetic desire and infinite longing. More important, it connects desire and the endless deferral of desire to memory and a return to origins. This scene also shows the literary effects of Eliot's immersion in the social sciences. First, there is the return to origins, moving backward from a postwar scene roughly contemporary with the composition of the poem through centuries of recorded history to the earliest prehistoric myths. Less important than the journey, however, is the destination, for all of the allusions, all of the women from Philomel to Cleopatra, lead back to monomyth which Frazer claims encompasses all history, all religion, and all art. Second, there is the clear attempt to access the original by the use of its surviving fragments. As noted above, "A Game of Chess" is littered with "withered stumps of time" appropriated by contemporaries for personal use. Third, the dressing room survivals link religion, sexuality, and violence. Most of the survivals are part of ancient religious rites (for example, the fruited vines), most include sexuality (tragic lovers such as Dido and Aeneas), and most are streaked with violence (above all, the story of Philomel). And fourth, stratification is a basic element of form in the scene, for the characters are organized not only in time but also in space, simultaneously.

The allusion to Philomel is the most important in "A Game of Chess." Compared to Philomel, the other women (Cleopatra, Dido, and Eve) are only supporting players. They are unnamed and barely present. Eve, for example, comes in through the phrase "the sylvan scene" from Milton's description of Eden, a phrase most readers would miss without a guidebook. Philomel, on the other hand, is named and is given seven consecutive lines. Moreover, she is given four lines in "The Fire Sermon" and one in "What the Thunder Said." As the archetypal violated and silenced female, she takes her place beside the land itself as one of the great symbols in the poem as a whole. As a figure of mimetic desire, she is our contemporary, but as one of our oldest ancestors she provides a link between mimetic desire and a return to origins. Her story was old by the time of Homer, in fact, and sufficiently familiar for use as an allusion in *The Odyssey*.[44] To use a phrase Eliot used of Frazer's *Golden Bough*, her story extends human consciousness as far into the dark and "backward . . . abysm of time" as it can go.[45]

The second Philomel passage in *The Waste Land* appears in the middle of "The Fire Sermon," which also happens to be the center of the entire poem. Although Eliot superimposes many times and places in this poem and deals with all at once, he makes postwar London the primary location in this middle section. He carefully places most of its incidents on London's streets or on London's river, and mentions pubs, fish markets, and the Thames-side church of Magnus Martyr. He names the streets running beside the river and remembers the empty bottles, sandwich papers, and cigarette butts left on the riverbanks by summer's departed lovers. Most of the characters are Londoners – office workers, city directors, prostitutes, and royals. The opening and closing scenes are set beside or on the Thames. The emphasis on London is even stronger in the manuscript. A long section, omitted before Eliot shared the poem with Pound, begins "London, the swarming life you kill and breed" and describes London as "responsive to the momentary need," as "vibrat[ing] unconscious to its destiny," and Londoners as "bound upon the wheel."[46]

The city, as suggested earlier, is for Eliot the scene of mimetic desire, pollution, and violence. These Ovidian themes dominate "The Fire Sermon," with the main action consisting of tawdry and mechanical sexual encounters. Thus it is not surprising to hear the voice of Philomel in the "Unreal City":

> Twit twit twit
> Jug jug jug jug jug jug
> So rudely forc'd.
> Tereu

In "A Game of Chess," the focus was on the "change" of Philomel, but here it is on her violation. Gone are the painting's positive elements – the Edenic woodland, the metamorphosis, and the reference to the "inviolate voice," but the rapist, the rape, the mutilated victim, and the mocking sounds of dirty sex remain. The intrusion of the Philomel motif at this point associates sexual relations in "The Fire Sermon" with rape and the humiliation of women. In this part of the poem, arguably, all of the women, like the land itself, have been "rudely forc'd." The Philomel reprise is followed immediately by a return of the "Unreal City" theme. In *The Waste Land* drafts, the link between Philomel and the city is more pronounced. The "Unreal City" scene appears twice, the two almost identical passages constituting a frame enclosing Philomel's violation and emphasizing the interplay between sex, violence, and the city.[47]

Pollution and contagion, ubiquitous in cities ancient and modern, are major motifs in this part of the poem. The air is brown at noon; the river sweats oil and tar; the riverbanks are littered with the detritus of desire – sandwich papers, empty bottles, cigarette butts, and "other testimony of summer nights." The vignettes of contemporary characters – loitering prostitutes, Sweeney and Mrs. Porter, Mr. Eugenides, the typist and clerk, and the various Thames maidens – indicate that the pollution is moral as well as environmental. The central event in this poem of crisis is rape, and as both violence and desire are contagious, the effects of Philomel's violation have spread from the center to the periphery in all directions. Contagion is evident in the presence of disease-carrying rats, in the movement of the polluted river, and in the air circulating in and out of unwholesome lungs.

In Ovid's version of Philomel, the emphasis is primarily on the link between violence and desire, but in postclassical versions, particularly in Romantic and modern traditions, the emphasis is on music and desire. The connection between music and desire is foregrounded in "The Fire Sermon," for everything in this section, including rape, is performed to music. The section opens with a river minstrel singing "Sweet Thames, run softly, till I end my song." In quick succession, he is followed by the crooner of a bawdy ballad from Australia, by children *"chantant dans la coupole,"* by Philomel's plaintive song, by the mechanical music of the gramophone and the "pleasant whining" of the mandoline, and finally by the songs of the Rhine maidens reincarnated as Thames maidens. The typist and clerk scene ends with the lovely lady putting a "record on the gramophone," and the next paragraph begins, "This music crept by me upon the waters." In all these passages, the disturbing effect of music upon a listener is highlighted. The association of mimetic desire and music goes back to Eliot's Harvard poems. In "Portrait of a Lady," for example, the narrator remains self-possessed "Except when a street piano, mechanical and tired / Reiterates some worn-out common song . . . Recalling things that other people have desired."

The final references to the Philomel story appear in "What the Thunder Said," the last section of *The Waste Land*. The final paragraph begins with a question, "Shall I at least set my lands in order?" which is answered with a cascade of fragments from various times and cultures and in several languages. Two fragments, contained in a single line, refer to Philomel – *"Quando fiam ceu chelidon* – O swallow swallow." The first (translation: "When shall I be as the swallow?") comes from the anonymous Latin poem *Pervigilium Veneris*, celebrating the return of spring. The second – "O swallow swallow" – is from a song in Tennyson's *The Princess*. That Eliot wanted the reader to recognize the allusions in this paragraph is clear from the fact that he cross-referenced this line to the Philomel references in "A Game of Chess" and "The Fire Sermon." There is also a reminder of Philomel in the snippets from Kyd's *The Spanish Tragedy* – "Why then Ile fit you. Hieronymo's mad againe." In this drama of revenge and blood (that is, reciprocal violence), Hieronymo, like Tereus, has been driven mad by the slaughter of his son, and he arranges that the murderers be killed in the performance of a play. He then avoids speech under torture by biting off his tongue and spitting it at his tormentors. He is both torturer and tortured, and thus, in this desperate self-mutilation, he echoes Tereus and Philomel at once.

The line from the *Pervigilium Veneris* – "*Quando fiam ceu chelidon*" – is a reminder of the connection between mimetic desire and music. This second-century Latin poem describes the "Vigil of Venus" – that is, the eve of the festival of the goddess of love. This ancient springtime fertility festival is launched with a night of feverish foreplay during which sexual desire in humans and animals reaches a crescendo in anticipation of release on the morrow. Such desire is richly mimetic, in that it is related more to the desires of other subjects than to the desirability of any object. Human beings join in the lovemaking in spring, one might say, because the birds and bees are doing so. The spirit is perfectly caught in the refrain – "tomorrow let loveless, let lover tomorrow make love."[48] Such festivals, in which the participants wear disguises, are characterized by loss of individual identity and violation of norms related to sexual behavior. Of the twenty-two stanzas in the *Pervigilium*, the first twenty describe sexual foreplay. Then suddenly, from the dark wood, the music of the nightingale is heard over the amorous sounds of the creatures below. The discordant song undercuts the rest of the *Pervigilium* with a reminder of a connection between mimetic desire and violence, but, as Allen Tate suggests, something new is introduced into poetry here. That is "the poet's sudden consciousness of his own feeble powers. When shall I, he says, like Philomel . . . , suffer violence and be moved to sing?" This unexpected shift from narrative to lyric, from desire in nature to desire in the poet, gives this otherwise conventional poem enormous power.[49]

The richness and complexity of Eliot's poetry owes much to his early work in the social sciences. His increasingly comprehensive understanding of the implications of Darwin's work as it was absorbed by Frazer, Durkheim, and others provided the context in which he worked out his poetics. Of the principles he derived from Darwin and Frazer, none is more important than the maxim that wisdom requires a return to origins. Eliot's poetry, however, is much more than the versification of social theories; it is a continuing meditation on desire, a meditation informed by his own experience in the city, in his marriage, and in other contexts. His understanding of desire, as Maud Ellmann suggests, must have been influenced by Freud. She associates *The Waste Land* with Freud's theory of repetition, which maintains that human beings have a compulsion to repeat, and with his notion of the uncanny, which is "whatever reminds us of this inner compulsion to repeat."[50] Freud's theory of repetition, a component of his own attempt to reconstitute origins, is part of the theoretical background of

Girard's understanding of mimetic desire, explored at length in this paper. *The Waste Land* is a study in mimetic desire, highlighted in the famous opening lines of the poem. April is cruel because she mixes "memory and desire." Memory not only *looks* backward, searching for what might have happened last week, but also *repeats* backward toward origins. Desire looks forward but is continuously fed by memory and imagination. Eliot's continuing meditation on the intersection of memory and desire culminates in the beautiful closing paragraph of "Little Gidding" which reveals that "the end of all our exploring / Will be to arrive where we started / And know the place for the first time."

NOTES

1. For a discussion of the emphasis on returning to origins, see Jeffrey M. Perl, *The Tradition of Return: The Implicit History of Modern Literature* (Princeton: Princeton University Press, 1984), 3–57, and Jewel Spears Brooker, *Mastery and Escape: T. S. Eliot and the Dialectic of Modernism* (Amherst: University of Massachusetts Press, 1994), 1–22.
2. T. S. Eliot, "London Letter," *Dial* 71, no. 4 (October 1921): 453.
3. There is a substantial body of criticism on Eliot's studies in the social sciences. See especially Piers Gray's *T. S. Eliot's Intellectual and Poetic Development, 1909–1922* (Brighton, Sussex: Harvester Press, 1982). Gray's book includes long excerpts from Eliot's important 1914 essay "The Interpretation of Primitive Ritual." Other excellent books include Robert Crawford's *The Savage and the City in the Work of T. S. Eliot* (New York: Oxford University Press, 1987), indispensable for relating Eliot's childhood and college readings to his early poems; and William Skaff's *The Philosophy of T. S. Eliot 1909–1927* (Philadelphia: University of Pennsylvania Press, 1987).
4. Eliot, "War-Paint and Feathers," *Athenaeum* (October 17, 1919): 1036.
5. Eliot, "The Beating of a Drum," *Nation & Athenaeum* 34, no. 1 (October 6, 1923): 11.
6. E. B. Tylor, *Primitive Culture: Researches into the Development of Mythology, Philosophy, Religion, Language, Art, and Custom*, 2 vols., 3rd edn. (London: John Murray, 1891).
7. Eliot, "*Tarr*," *Egoist* 5, no. 8 (September 1918): 106.
8. Eliot, "The Metaphysical Poets," in *Selected Essays* (New York: Harcourt Brace, 1950), 241–50; and Eliot, *The Varieties of Metaphysical Poetry*, ed. Ronald Schuchard (London: Faber and Faber, 1993).
9. The censored poems are now available in *Inventions of the March Hare: Poems 1909–1917*, ed. Christopher Ricks (New York: Harcourt Brace, 1996).
10. In Joseph Frank's terminology, Eliot's interest expands to include spatial form. See Frank, "Spatial Form in Modern Literature," in *The Widening Gyre: Crisis and Mastery in Modern Literature* (Bloomington: Indiana University Press, 1963), 3–62.

11. Eliot, "Tradition and the Individual Talent," in *Selected Essays*, 3–11; "*Ulysses*, Order and Myth," *Dial* 75, no. 5 (November 1923): 480–3.

12. Eliot, "War-Paint and Feathers," 1036.

13. Jewel Spears Brooker and Joseph Bentley, *Reading* The Waste Land: *Modernism and the Limits of Interpretation* (Amherst: University of Massachusetts Press, 1990).

14. Eliot, "The Metaphysical Poets," in *Selected Essays*, 241–50.

15. See, for example, "Tradition and the Individual Talent," 3–12.

16. *The Waste Land: A Facsimile and Transcript of the Original Drafts*, ed. Valerie Eliot (New York: Harcourt Brace, 1971), xxxiii.

17. For a discussion of the important distinction between material and method in Eliot's work, see Jewel Spears Brooker, "The Case of the Missing Abstraction," in *Mastery and Escape*, 110–22.

18. W. B. Yeats, "The Circus Animals' Desertion," in *The Poems of W. B. Yeats*, ed. Richard Finneran (New York: Macmillan, 1983), 348.

19. "The Romantic Englishman, the Comic Spirit, and the Function of Criticism," *Tyro* 1 (Spring 1921): 4.

20. Review of *The Study of Religions* by Stanley Cook, *Monist* 26, no. 3 (1917): 480.

21. For a linguistically based reading of Eliot and desire, see Harriet Davidson, "The Logic of Desire: The Lacanian Subject of *The Waste Land*," in *The Waste Land: Theory in Practice*, ed. Tony Davies and Nigel Wood (Philadelphia: Open University Press, 1994), 55–82. For a Freudian perspective, see Maud Ellmann, *The Poetics of Impersonality: T. S. Eliot and Ezra Pound* (Cambridge, Mass.: Harvard University Press, 1987). For a feminist perspective, see Colleen Lamos, *Deviant Modernism: Sexual and Textual Errancy in T. S. Eliot, James Joyce, and Marcel Proust* (New York: Cambridge University Press, 1998).

22. *The Girard Reader*, ed. James G. Williams (New York: Crossroad, 1996), 268. Girard's notion of desire can be profitably compared/contrasted to that of Jacques Lacan. Both see desire as fundamentally psychological and as related to insufficiency, and both see desire as intersubjective. In Lacan, the focus is on desire and language; in Girard, on desire and cultural mechanisms for controlling violence. See Jacques Lacan, *Ecrits: A Selection* (New York: Norton, 1977).

23. See René Girard, *Deceit, Desire, and the Novel*, trans. Yvonne Freccero (Baltimore: Johns Hopkins University Press, 1965), chapter 1.

24. See Girard, *Deceit, Desire, and the Novel*, chapter 1.

25. René Girard, *Violence and the Sacred*, trans. Patrick Gregory (Baltimore: Johns Hopkins University Press, 1977), 34.

26. Ibid., 35.

27. Ibid., 34–6.

28. Quoted in *T. S. Eliot: The Modernist in History*, ed. Ronald Bush (New York: Cambridge University Press, 1991), 193.

29. Eliot, "*Ulysses*, Order and Myth," in *Selected Prose*, ed. Frank Kermode (New York: Harcourt Brace, 1975), 177.

30. Such ambivalence, of course, is not unique; it can be found in Joyce's *Portrait of the Artist*, in *Ulysses*, and in many poems of the night from James Thomson to Robert Lowell.
31. *The Letters of T. S. Eliot*, ed. Valerie Eliot (London: Faber and Faber, 1988), vol. I: 75.
32. Quoted in Ray Monk, *Bertrand Russell* (London: Jonathan Cape, 1996), 440.
33. Eliot, *Inventions of the March Hare*, ed. Christopher Ricks (London: Faber and Faber, 1996), 383.
34. Peter Ackroyd, *T. S. Eliot* (New York: Simon and Schuster, 1984), 67–8.
35. Quoted in Lyndall Gordon, *T. S. Eliot: An Imperfect Life* (New York: Vintage, 1998), 126.
36. For an interesting account of the triangular relationship between Eliot, his wife, and his former teacher, see Ronald Schuchard, *Eliot's Dark Angel: Intersections of Art and Life* (New York: Oxford University Press, 1999), 57–8.
37. For a more antagonist feminist reading of "Hysteria" and "Ode," see Colleen Lamos, *Deviant Modernism*, 82–8; 96–108.
38. Bertrand Russell, *Autobiography* (Boston: Little Brown, 1951), vol. II: 64.
39. Eliot, *Letters*, vol. I: 151.
40. *The Waste Land: Facsimile and Transcript*, 11, 13.
41. Quotations from Ovid are from *Metamorphoses*, trans. Rolfe Humphries (Bloomington: Indiana University Press, 1955), Book VI.413–678.
42. In the earliest versions of the myth, Philomela becomes the swallow and Procne becomes the nightingale. See for example *Odyssey* XIX.518–24 and Aeschylus, *Agamemnon*, lines 1142–50 (*Oresteia*, trans. Robert Fagles [New York: Penguin, 1977]). Ovid, in *Metamorphoses* VI, is unclear about which woman becomes which bird. Later writers, confused by Ovid's obscurity and depending on a dubious etymology for Philomela ("song-lover" instead of the far more probable "song-less"), made her the nightingale. It is thus Philomela who enters English literary history as the nightingale.
43. Eliot, "War-Paint and Feathers," 1036.
44. *Odyssey* XIX.518. Aristotle in *Poetics* XVI.41 refers to a lost play by Sophocles on Tereus and Philomela. See also Ovid, *Metamorphoses* VI.412 ff.; Dante, *Purgatorio* IX.13–15, XVII.19–21; Shakespeare, *The Rape of Lucrece*, ll. 1128 ff.; *Cymbeline* II. ii. 18–21, 44–6; Milton, "Il Penseroso"; Keats, "Ode to a Nightingale"; Coleridge, "The Nightingale"; Arnold, "Philomel"; and Swinburne, "Itylus."
45. Eliot, "A Prediction in Regard to Three English Authors," *Vanity Fair* 21, no. 6 (February 1924): 29.
46. Eliot, *The Waste Land: Facsimile and Transcript*, 37.
47. Ibid., 43.
48. "Pervigilium Veneris," trans. Allen Tate, in Tate, *Collected Poems 1919–1976* (New York: Farrar Straus Giroux, 1977), 151–61.
49. Ibid., 148.
50. Ellmann, *The Poetics of Impersonality*, 59.

CHAPTER 7

Theorizing emotions in Eliot's poetry and poetics

Charles Altieri

The history of Eliot criticism offers a depressing form of justice: the very vocabulary for appreciating poetry that he did so much to shape has turned out to be in large part responsible for the decline of his power and influence in the academy. Ambivalence now becomes effeteness, complexity idealism, and the desire for intricate unities a defensive projection of mastery by which to ward off threats of castration. Consequently, what had been staged as a revolutionary modernism now gets taught primarily as a reactionary evasion of historical realities from which we can be freed by a less pretentious modernism or, even better, by an enlightened postmodernism.

This volume's concern with the topic of Eliot and desire provides an opportunity to escape this entire revenge cycle. For we are invited to look carefully at how his formal and thematic elements are woven into specific emotional configurations, so that we have to develop for those elements an imaginative density not easily subsumed under the now standard litany of complaints about his impersonality and abstraction. This does not mean we cannot be critical of Eliot. Indeed focusing on how desires are staged within his work may reveal an even more monstrous fascist or patriarch than our more tepid thematizing has allowed us. But at least this Eliot can have an imaginative life that we might envision winning the degree of influence, admiration, and antagonism that Eliot did from many quite considerable poets and critics, including influential figures on the left like Christopher Caudwell and Raymond Williams.

My Eliot will not be such a monster; at least he is not intended to come off as one. I will use this occasion to speculate on what seems to me still distinctive and powerful in his rendering of emotions, in part because this focus will make it possible for me to demonstrate how, even in our hyper-critical age, we can develop historical stances toward his work that find more to admire and to use than they do to condemn and moralize upon.[1] This demonstration will require two overlapping projects. First I want to elaborate the historical force of Eliot's formal innovations by fleshing out

how fully he responded to what he saw as the dissociated sensibility dominating his culture. This entails specifying what he thought problematic in
dominant ways of representing and valuing emotions, and then it requires
clarifying the specific elements comprising his own projected alternative
model for affective life. Second, I want to supplement this looking backward by turning to its possible projections into the future. Therefore I will
explore the possible differences Eliot's work might make in our present
attitudes toward the nature of emotional life, especially in relation to the
now dominant philosophical and therapeutic paradigms on this topic. If
I am right, the analysis might also help indicate that Eliot's influence or
impact on his peers and his heirs was not because of the ideologies of race,
class, and gender that he helped enforce. Rather it was because, conservative
as he was, he developed at least this one substantial modeling of affective
life that has claims to alter how his heirs could deploy their imaginative
energies.

To make good on my ambitions I will have to show how Eliot's own
poetry both establishes and tests ways of making affective investments.
Deeply suspicious of received renderings of emotional life and increasingly
dissatisfied with a poetry grounded primarily in such suspicion, Eliot exper-
imented with modes of presenting and projecting desire more immediate
and also more inherently social than the culturally dominant modes of linking affects to causal narratives. And in doing that he developed an abstract
modern imaginative space radically new for English poetry. In order to
characterize these achievements, I will have to build a context by engaging recent philosophical discussions of the emotions – not to apply these
directly to Eliot's work but rather to show how Eliot provides quite different
and important responses to the fundamental topoi developed within these
philosophical discussions.[2]

In particular I will use these topoi to argue that much of Eliot's poetry
from "The Love Song of St. Sebastian" through *Ash Wednesday* makes available the following transformations in dealing with lyric emotion: it presents
a quite different speaking agent, more abstract and elemental than those
presented by his predecessors; it puts the abstract staging of spiritual conditions in the place that plot and scene had occupied so that the new poetry
directly implicates its readers in the most fundamental questions about
the values they commit to; it modifies our ways of thinking about how
passive and active aspects of our affective lives interpenetrate; and it resists
narrative causality, thus finessing standard therapeutic and philosophical
models for assessing emotions, and aligning imagination with emotional
structures closely paralleling those developed by non-representational work

in the other arts. Able in his own eyes to create a prose that could cut to the
core of his culture's dilemmas, Eliot eventually demanded of himself a corresponding intensity, scope, and public resonance for the affects elaborated
in his poetry.

Ultimately an account of these affects will have to focus on the poetry.
But here I want only to suggest what might be at stake in our taking
Eliot's ambitions seriously. So I will try first to place what I take to be
general outlines of his treatment of the affects in a philosophical context.
In his prose Eliot often distinguishes between "feeling" and "emotion."[3]
And his writing on Bradley develops concepts like "immediate experience"
that provide a significant context for this distinction. But since Eliot never
sets himself explicitly to developing a theoretical account of the affects, I
think it is prudent to concentrate on his poetry. There we find his richest
rendering of the qualities of affective life most compelling for him, and
there we find self-reflexive activity that can help us engage and modify
contemporary theorizing. As our means of identifying the relevant issues,
I propose that we place Eliot's work in a framework provided by isolating
what I take to be the four basic topoi that any philosophical account of the
emotions has to address. This will dramatize the pressures on and pressure
points within philosophical treatments of the emotions. And having that
context will help foreground Eliot's differences from the dominant lines of
thinking while providing a background for making comparisons with how
other poets evoke and interpret affective intensities.

1 *Establishing intentionality.* Any account of the emotions has to articulate
what role thinking and imagination play in characterizing human emotions
and in connecting these emotions to beliefs and to actions. We cannot deal
adequately with emotions if we treat them simply as drives or behavioral
modifications because we cannot be sufficiently concrete about how agents
experience them or about what might produce changes in specific cases.
Interpreting emotions seems to require delineating a person's relevant particular beliefs, enabling fantasies, and projections connecting the mental
state to possible behaviors or future states. Without these concerns we cannot account for variations in affective intensity or for the different ways
agents deploy and modify investments in what extensionally seem the same
states. For example, contempt and pity can look very much alike unless we
inquire into specific beliefs or into how the emotion gets oriented toward
specific actions.

When we ask what form these interpretations best take we find ourselves
at the core of modernist poetics. For modernist art gathers much of its
energy from its critique of the still standard narrative formats that have

been considered the obvious mode for contextualizing emotions within intentional contexts. Narrative formats encourage our thinking of the emotions in temporal, causal terms. So it seems reasonable to act as if we could develop persuasive stories about what triggered the affect and hence recognize what might satisfy it. Agents try out narratives, and therapists imagine that the best way to change emotional behavior is to modify the narratives by which agents frame their own senses of themselves. What we cannot treat causally we have to ignore or relegate to moods.

Notice how this reliance on narrative shapes the kind of agency to which we attribute the intentionality. We assume that the one who expresses the emotion is a distinct individual capable of playing all the roles that protagonists play in our plot structures, especially the role of coming to take responsibility for the very dynamics that set the plot in motion. This version of agency makes our acknowledging and owning our emotions the fundamental value in reflecting upon them, perhaps even of experiencing them in the first place. And we best adapt this principle of ownership by subsuming the basic constituents of affective life under the overall rubric of ego-psychology. Identity is a matter of the ways one represents and takes responsibility for one's emotional commitments. This in turn means that the only good emotion is a dead one or, less figuratively, that our task as agents is to become persons by demonstrating our abilities to keep the emotions within the bounds of the plots our culture provides us. If we fail at living within this explanatory regime, we are treated as if we are not coherent selves and need therapy.

Clearly there is a good deal of sense in this perspective. But the perspective also brings substantial limitations. The model of identity that I have just been describing places emotions center stage in what Lacan has shown is a theater of *méconnaissance* perhaps inescapable within ego-psychology. Having a stable ego becomes inseparable from treating emotions as states to be understood and mastered. For psychological identity depends on our being able, not only to represent ourselves within plots, but also to make ourselves the challenged actors whose efforts at mastery make the plots worth attending to. We simultaneously need intensity, so that the plot matters, and control, so that we matter as masters of the plot. Under such contradictory demands, the possibilities of self-delusion within fictions of self-mastery multiply. It proves all too easy to exaggerate particular emotional moments as conditions to be valued, so social life begins to approximate the conditions of opera.

These problems would haunt the activity of judgment even if we could plausibly project ourselves as capable of cogent self-analyses. But, Lacan adds, we never find ourselves in this minimally mediated position. Our plots for our emotions, or for ourselves as emoters, also invite a second theatrical dimension produced by our inescapable relation to projected audiences. There are at least two relevant aspects of this relation – the grammatical relation through which cultural frameworks impose the terms by which we formulate these identities, and the imaginary relation that we rely on for ultimately sanctioning our performances by providing the signifier we desire for the fantasies that we need signified. Even as we pursue specific ends such as helping someone we pity, we find ourselves imagining an audience who desires us for that action, and our need for that approval will affect our judgment about what does and does not count as the adequate carrying of our pity into action.

2 *Relating active and passive aspects of our involvement in emotions.* The basic reason that identity is so problematic when we reflect on emotions is that these phenomena involve complex relations between what seems passive or contingent about an individual in a situation and what seems active or self-defining in the person's behavior. We earn identities by being active in relation to forces that otherwise would determine us. But if we attribute too much activity to ourselves, we trivialize the emotion by denying its emergence any power over us. Without substantial passivity nothing can move us to the point that we attempt to modify our priorities. So theorizing about the emotions has to find ways of acknowledging both sets of impulses – toward control and toward allowing our feelings to lead us into potentially new relations with the world and with other people. Without elaborating both poles we cannot tell whether a radical act of self-definition like Bartleby's is an assertion of freedom or a submission to compulsion.

But how do we develop the conceptual terms or imaginative strategies by which to keep both poles in dynamic interaction? If we approach questions of passivity and activity from traditional rationalist and humanist philosophical perspectives, we find it almost impossible not to treat passivity as problematic and consequently to emphasize the active, self-interpreting component in affective life – so powerful is the idealist tradition in our conceptual lives. Autonomy becomes inseparable from rationality. For, as Eliot pointed out in speaking about Kant, we can only establish a clear idea of freedom if we can imagine how it might be possible to produce "the identity of cause and effect."[4] But basing one's account of the emotions on the affective qualities presented will not allow that identity. The terms of feeling are too passive, too bound to the empirical self, to allow the spirit to bind itself to its own laws. Only reason has the power at once to conceive laws that are fundamental to its own nature and to give such law substance in its own activity, transmitting reason's causality into effects that simply embody those laws.

From this Kantian perspective, which in its turn abstracts from deep features of Christian values, surrender to the emotions can make us literally monstrous – humanity transformed into pure appetite. When we succumb to the emotions, we give up the kind of self-definition that reason provides, and we bind ourselves to satisfactions that stem from our contingent dispositions rather than from what is most internal and most distinctively human. Yet in this Kantian scheme, what is most human is also most abstract and impersonal. We are most human when we are least particular. Clearly this cannot do, however much it allows a sublime sense of human powers. So recent philosophy tries on many fronts to restore power to this particularity by insisting that much of what matters about our humanity consists in ways that we are passive so that our environment can attune us to its contours. The romanticism that Eliot hated returns as philosophy, telling us that we are most active precisely when we allow ourselves to be passive and hence when we subordinate consciousness's eagerness to impose structure to the roles of heeding and focusing on particular flows of energy. We are even promised by arch-romantics like Gilles Deleuze that we may be able to suspend the entire dynamics of identity production if we allow our emotions to provide in themselves the intensity and connectedness that we want our reasoning to produce. From this perspective we are most monstrous when we let our desire for control repress those relational structures which can provide concrete connections worth seeking control for. But in pursuing those relations, how do we not also repeat the worst excesses of romanticism? How do we avoid simply granting authenticity to any claim asserting the intensity of feeling and the pleasures of attunement to local circumstances? How can there be any sense of direction or focus or even community when we find our emotions epitomized in Robert Creeley's plaintive cry, "O Love! where are you leading me now?"

3 *Relating emotion and reason.* So far I have concentrated on what we might call the psychological aspects of the tension between passive and active relations to emotional force. A third topos adapts essentially the same structures to the public question of what place emotions can have in the practical decisions we make. Our reflections on the emotions seem inescapably divided between the need to trust the supplements they provide to reason and the need to suspect their ways of misleading us, if only into operatic self-indulgence. So we have to find ways of determining to what degree emotions are compatible with reason and hence with prudent

decisions, and to what degree they are dangerous because they warp our sense of priorities and block our using universal principles.

Speaking of Matthew Arnold, Eliot provides a good (and characteristic) version of the suspicious rationalist: "'The power of Christianity has been in the immense emotion which it has excited,' he says; not realizing at all that this is a counsel to get all the emotional kick out of Christianity one can, without the bother of believing it."[5] Yet Eliot also came increasingly to realize that there could be no Christianity, no relief from instrumental reason, unless the affects had the power to influence or to determine ends, which reason might then help us secure. Reason's lack of affect enables us to see clearly, without distraction. But that lack of affect means reason cannot in itself move us from seeing to acting. Emotions make actions possible because they establish scales of salience among particulars. Salience gives judgment a direction that guides its decisions. And then judgment can operate in terms of that outworn but perhaps necessary Arnoldian notion of the best self. For the stronger the image of character we bring to our actions, the richer our possibilities of keeping our actions continuous with what we project as our identities. How else are we to distinguish which of the mind's constructs seems most appropriate for individual dispositions and for specific socially embedded relationships? Yet every temptation to idealize where the emotions lead us takes place in an imaginary world pervaded by seductions to various operatic postures and, more important, by tendencies to let postures substitute for commitment and intensities for identity.

4 *Valuing emotions and the roles emotions play in establishing values.* Assessing the relation of reason to emotions is closely related to the question of how we attribute significant values to our emotional states. This is not quite as standard a topos as the other three because most philosophers still do not grant the emotions such power, at least when we are to speak of making judgments about values. Rather, the philosophers are content to deal with the values that emotions produce in instrumental terms: what happens within the emotional state matters much less than the consequences the particular affects produce for our practical lives. Yet there are those like Deleuze who in my view make it necessary to understand how emotions also constitute substantial sources of value in themselves. This need makes for substantial complications. For we then have to address the fact that dealing conceptually with value in relation to our affective lives requires our reconciling two distinct models of judgment. The first is the familiar one oriented toward actions: judgment is based on using rational criteria to

make decisions about probable outcomes that follow from letting certain emotions shape our projects. The second model of judgment is much more difficult to thematize. For here the relevant aspects of our decision making cannot be articulated in terms that readily fit our habits of making and testing arguments. In such cases values are embedded in the dispositional traits that the emotion brings into focus.

The one area where traditional philosophy gestures toward this second model is in its accounts of aesthetic experience, since in that domain the entire field depends on articulating modes of judgment based on particular states rather than on chains of argument. Aesthetics allows us to concentrate on how we might talk about phenomena where the play of interrelated elements is far more important than any thematizable conclusions we arrive at about or through our explorations. But in contemporary aesthetics the relevant language of values is typically about objects. The theory of emotions needs analogous models of value about subjects. (Aesthetics does also deal with subjects, but usually simply by celebrating freedom and participation, not by characterizing particular states that comprise value-laden modes of being.)[6] That is why modernist art becomes an important analogue for those attempting this more difficult course. Much of it adapts Nietzsche's powerful distinction between the defensive and impersonal structures sustained by the "will to truth" and the working of a "will to power" creating value out of its own intensities and imperatives. The values it seeks then depend on how its emotional investments organize our energies and dispose us to seek to continue the states they afford (or the transitions they provide) rather than shift into more practical (or more theoretical) orientations. Such values satisfy in much the same way that music satisfies – that is by the play of internal structures brought to intensity and given resonance as they pass through time. Perhaps it will help to imagine this internal structure as the effects of a gravitational field set in motion by certain experiences. When we find satisfaction within an emotion, when we want to dwell in the world it helps organize, we see specific details of our lives coming into sharp focus and into new possibilities of significance – both in their organization and in the degree of intensity they bear. Think of being angry or being in love or just becoming fascinated by something we feel we are observing unfold for the first time. We enter a field where states of mind consist primarily in a vividness of sensual details and their concrete interrelations. It matters to us how perceptions and projections fuse or pull apart at various rates and angles of intersection, how patterns begin to be formed that will shape our desires and our memories, and how new boundaries get constituted in relation to what seems to fit or to matter and what seems exiled to some "other" realm no longer capable of eliciting our full attention. Even if god may not reside in the details, anger and shame do. Such emotions fix details in time and hence invite obsession, while other affective orientations like being in love or just caring about some practice cultivate a fluid responsiveness to change.

It is of course difficult to know what to trust or to treasure in these expanding and intensifying fields of relationship. No theorizing can change this. But theorizing can at least attempt to provide reasons why we need not foreclose on such embodied workings of the imagination simply because of difficulties in bringing the discourse of knowledge to bear. Hence the inescapable core of this fourth topos is the need to so characterize these gravitational fields that we come to understand our uncertainties as in large part a positive response to intensities and mobilities that simply cannot be processed adequately by the understanding. Two consequences follow. We have to find as public as possible an alternative to relying on standard epistemic hierarchies in theorizing about our emotional lives. Perhaps we can replace criteria that we attribute to reason with a sense of the shape given to our sense of affects simply by our education into cultural grammars. On that basis it becomes clear why the passive and the active are so intricately interwoven, since we have to yield to what then allows our intensities. And we make it possible to appreciate how our satisfactions depend on letting complex affective fields take various forms while we bracket as much as possible our demands for discursive intelligibility and practical decision making. At times this temporal folding will simply be a matter of letting talk go on, at others talk will seem a violation of the relevant modes of attention.

Given this framework of four topoi, I can now return to Eliot. If we concentrate on how Eliot resists letting the life of affects be contained within his culture's narrative frames, we can show how his poetry provides perspectives on all four of our topoi that are more responsive to the problems we have been considering than are the accounts of the emotions that still dominate philosophical discourse in America. In making this case I will also be arguing indirectly the historical claim that much of Eliot's importance for other modern poets stemmed from an analogous accomplishment. Eliot developed imaginative sites that showed poets how they could engage what seemed quite new and radical modes of feeling elaborated in the other modernist arts.

One of Eliot's earliest poems, "Opera," sets the stage for his interest in modes of consciousness that provide alternatives to narrative forms for understanding affective states. Ease of narrative interpretation seems to him inseparable from self-aggrandizement, and hence from tendencies to appropriate emotions rather than to let oneself fully encounter forces that may well not be readily subsumed under prevailing cultural practices or what Wittgenstein would call "cultural grammars." Therefore the social world is best staged as a domain of appearances and screens that one must read against in order to have a decent sense of what is acting upon the psyche. In order to make visible the sources of such resistance, the poems have to call attention to some alternative mode of processing. So they flirt with emotional economies appropriate for allegory and dream vision that the novel had to resist in order to make dominant its own visions of self-understanding. Hence Eliot's interest in Baudelaire – dazzling new possibilities of spirit seem released by producing Dantean allegory in frag- mented modern forms. Eliot argued that where much romantic poetry exploits "the fact that no human relations are adequate to human desires" and does not believe in any "further object for human desires," Baudelaire refuses to rest in this alienated secular psychology. Instead he tries to pen- etrate the inner workings that might make possible "the adjustment of the natural to the spiritual, of the bestial to the human, and of the human to the supernatural." Baudelaire has "created a mode of release and expression for other men," establishing a renewal of sincerity that is not caught up in the "superficies of sincerity" that one finds in his peers.[7]

"The Love Song of St. Sebastian" dramatizes this Baudelairean cult of an intensity not containable within the images used to express it. Most of the poem keeps its affects contained within fairly standard links of penitence to masochistic fantasies. But the last stanza proves far more strange, insisting on an affective leap that challenges all received emotional grammars, as well as established principles of good taste. In its opening sentence the poem almost coyly suspends action in order to let the speaker linger over the details of the head Sebastian holds on his lap, as if the poem were gathering energies that the position we see from a distance will not be able to contain. Then the poem in effect makes clear the radical impulses deferred and intensified by that delay. It establishes a delicious economy between the other loving the speaker "because I should have strangled you / And because of my infamy," while the speaker recognizes, "And I should love you the more because I had mangled you / And because you were no longer beautiful / To anyone but me."[8]

The subjunctives here derive from the psychic worlds of "Prufrock" and "Mandarins." But the emotions asserted have none of the overprecision of measuring "out my life with coffee spoons." Rather they display a direct- ness and absoluteness of feeling that cannot be explained, yet is clearly too intense and focused to be dismissable. The lines insist on causality, yet there is no available framework by which to interpret that causality. Psychoanalysis might try, but if it insisted on explanation it could do little more than provide explanatory substitutes for concrete obsessions. Were we to handle this poem as a practical expression, we would be likely to tell the speaker, "you do not really mean that; you want only to get the other's attention and express your feelings of dependency and demand." But Eliot's speaker does seem to mean exactly what he says. So there remains only the option of taking the assertions quite literally by locating some world or level of the world in which the expressions seem to make cogent sense in themselves. These lines invite allegory but repudiate allegorical interpretation. And they use that refusal as their means of insisting that we stay as much as possible within their quite specific fantasy-driven desires. Sainthood requires such strangeness. Reaching out toward the limits of logic becomes our means of reaching in to the intricacies and excesses of Sebastian's expressive activity.

I doubt we need much additional comment to link this "Love Song" to Eliot's experiments in *Poems 1920* and in *The Waste Land*, as well as to the more positive use of allegory enabled by his conversion. *Poems 1920* vacillates between poems that try to subsume desires into forms so tight that pure statement prevails and poems that create a scene so stretching dramatic coherence that we have to postulate some psychological space for the speaking which no practical narrative can contain. "Sweeney Among the Nightingales" epitomizes this second option even in its rendering of narrative. For we move from the particulars of Sweeney's appearance out to the physical and mythological environment, then back to intense concentration on aspects of the concrete scene. Yet these images cannot even come close to containing the emotions that get elicited. We can participate in the relevant emotions only if we make ourselves identify with the shifts in perspective – from Sweeney's need for a position outside the window that remains ridiculous to an observer situated with a more capacious view, to the extreme distance that registers the timeless physical consequences of the nightingales' presence in the woods. The concluding perspective invokes the abstractness of allegorical space, but it insists that this space can only be adequately filled by the literal image the poem stages. As he withdraws, the speaker sees the host conversing with "someone indistinct." That scene magically expands from sight to hearing as attention shifts to the "nightingales . . . singing near / The Convent of the Sacred Heart." And having stretched vision, the singing then also opens into a domain where the present fuses with the past. The last stanza begins with the nightingales singing "within the bloody wood" where "Agamemnon cried aloud." Then this opening allows the past to offer its judgment on Sweeney's experience as the poem shifts to the fact that these nightingales and all they represent "let their liquid siftings fall / To stain the stiff dishonoured shroud."9

The Waste Land goes on to seek voices for these various perspectives. But there we cannot even provide a social identity for the speaker because that position has to become more abstract, has to be constructed as a mode of consciousness capable of hearing the need and desire pervading the poem's various voices. If Tiresias can be suggested as the speaker, that is only because he embodies the allegorical role of an eternally suffering consciousness paralyzed by the very access it has to the underlying conditions of our most basic desires. But if one can appreciate what that consciousness sees, if one can embrace a poetic dream of cultural therapy putting an entire civilization's voices on the couch, one finds oneself terrifyingly open to the logic of Christianity, which is after all primarily a theory about the consequences of hearing a Word within the word.

These brief observations should provide context sufficient to allow me to return to my four topoi, now, to measure how the distinctive responses Eliot gives to each can help modify how we imagine ourselves as affective beings and why we might care about such imaginings.

1 *Establishing intentionality.* My strongest claims for Eliot's developing new modes of intentionality all circulate around his handling of affective agency – in part because his criticisms of the standard narrative and operatic modes are so sharp and in part because he provides a powerful "transpersonal" alternative for grounding his lyrical intensities. Let me first rehearse the substantial criticisms that Eliot's work enables us to mount against the prevailing ways that the dominant narrative-centered views construct intentionality in affective life. We have already noted that his suspicions of these habits have substantial parallels to those developed by Lacan, another ascetic Christian in his overall sense of values. Now I will dwell for a moment on two correlated features of those criticisms that concern projections of agency.

The first parallel is philosophical. Central to Eliot and to Lacan is a profound suspicion of all romantic expressivist notions of identity, notions that emphasize getting in touch with some core self and locating basic values in how we make those deep aspects of the self articulate. In their view selfhood is not some property that we possess, or that possesses us, but a construct we offer so as to make particular organizations of experience for specific purposes.10 Therefore persons can project many selves, each coherent so long as we recognize the specific work we are trying to do, for example in proposing a self interested in writing about emotions or one whom we use to explain why such writing seems otiose. We cannot locate one self for these selves. Attempting that leads us into the labyrinth of substitutions and projections and pseudo-identifications that Lacan shows continually deflect desire into demand. Such projection subsumes the fluidity of our interfaces with the world into fantasies of substance so that we then have to become defensive and often violent in order to provide for them a tenuous stability.

The second parallel follows logically. In effect Lacanian psychoanalysis and Eliotic irony both take their departure from a strong sense of how these efforts to stabilize a self end up only in displacing our proprial feelings into endless chains of unsatisfying substitutes demanding further substitutes. Interpretation of the self seems never to lead back to those necessary sources of our intensities that probably cannot be represented or possessed in personal form. Consequently, rendering intentionality in relation to emotions is not for Eliot simply a matter of clarifying what someone believes and projects. We are invited to understand how such beliefs and projections are so deeply pervaded by complex tonal registers that we cannot adequately describe intentionality unless we also characterize the audiences projected as giving the agent the identifications he or she seeks.[11]

Ultimately I want to show how this sense of being pervaded by voices has as its positive counterpart the capacity to imagine transpersonal dynamics for our individual emotional states. But first I have to elaborate the building blocks of this transpersonality. From Eliot's perspective we know a character only when we recognize how the speaking voice is part of a state of mind projecting its own being heard and reacting to that anticipation. The audience will range from the ladies who come and go to the God who asks us to sit still. Consider for example how Prufrock's relation to those ladies gets transformed into the similar yet much more intricate structures shaping the speaker in "Portrait of a Lady," who cannot even speak to himself without hearing how his voices might be overheard. And Sweeney's sense of self seems both so fragile and so needy that everything he encounters becomes a threat to what he projects onto it as possibility. So understanding his desire seems to require recognizing a dimension of fantasy that is not available to simple narrative but that operates as a pervasive modifier of all our descriptions. In all these cases, images offered as markers of intimacy seem staged for unseen auditors who are imagined as conferring on the speaker the desired sense of identity. Yet his unspecifiable presence in the speaker's intentional stances actually dooms the speaker to constant frustrated repetition of the same structure of appeal. What moves him and what it seems will satisfy him just will not come into accord.

Eliot's essay on Dante (1929) makes articulate the positive possibilities latent in this fluid interplay of layers of identification. Discussing Dante's *Vita Nuova*, Eliot insists that in order to understand what is deeply personal in the poem, we have to accustom "ourselves to find meaning in final causes rather than in origins."[12] Searching for origins leaves us trapped in a modern attitude shaped by Rousseau in which confession becomes our primary access to individuality. Searching for causes, on the other hand, requires returning to Dantean concerns for how dream states carry allegorical force. But the Eliot closer to Baudelaire's "fractured Dante" could not rely on a Dantean version of these final causes. He could, nonetheless, keep present a sense of how the confessional mode of lyric expression had a tendency to blind itself to its own imperatives. So the task of *The Waste Land* was to reframe the understanding of need and demand that in his culture usually issued in confessional stances. Even though final causes could not be specified, the authorial presence had to keep visible what was strikingly inadequate in relying on individual confessional acts. Pure satire could indicate these inadequacies. But it could afford no sympathy, and it would give the illusion that the author had somehow escaped the dilemma. Instead Eliot wanted to emphasize his complicity with his speakers. Only in such complicity could one evoke the full range of emotions involved in learning to hear one's own efforts to be confessional. He wants to dramatize a situation where efforts at self-expression become so busy demanding an audience that the agent cannot look adequately at either the causes of its pain or the consequences of its using assertion as a vehicle for continuing that pain by other means. No wonder then that Eliot counterposes to those voices a strong but indecipherable authorial presence reminding us of how much necessarily escapes our efforts at self-representation.

This foregrounded, yet depersonalized, work of desire plays two fundamental roles in Eliot's poetry. First it dramatizes within the poem a presence that suffers from the delusions sustained by the voices in the particular scenarios. And then it stages for this suffering an appeal to allegorical levels that establish a bond with its audience unique in English poetry. The audience is brought to its intensities of self-awareness by hearing the pain of self-betrayal in voices that seek to establish personal identities. So it has to locate for itself a site where it can take seriously the kinds of forces to which those characters blind themselves. Therefore Eliot's poetry transforms the confessional basis for emotion into a ritual basis for enacting and reflecting upon more transpersonal aspects of desire, where attention can be paid to the shared needs and shared despair that these voices embody without fully recognizing their common plight. The poem embodies a condition of sheer desire so concrete as to be abstract and to implicate quite general aspects of our intentional lives. Characters and readers emerge into a space where, as in Dante, we feel that "speech varies but our eyes are all the same."[13] And insofar as we allow ourselves any affect at all in our exploration of these allegorical implications, we find ourselves occupying a strange and compelling aspect of imaginative or dream experience. What we share with the condition of the poem seems more definitive of what counts as final causes for us than does any projection we can make of individual identity or individual destiny. The intentionality fundamental to our affective lives may be much more mysterious and much more deeply social than our philosophers have the tools to discover.

I will be more concise on how the remaining three theoretical topoi help us characterize Eliot's distinctiveness.

2 *Relating active and passive aspects of our involvement in emotions.* Eliot the philosopher sympathetic with idealist projects knew well what can be claimed for the active, self-possessing spirit, especially as the abiding presence in works of art. Yet the Eliot concerned with Eastern religions remained sufficiently attuned to the importance of passivity to come to imagine the highest grace as learning to sit still, understanding how our peace is in God's will. His various interests put him in a good position to understand how his own culture's obsession with active spirit easily becomes the self-perpetuation of illusion. But Eliot was not an ascetic, not quite. For him passivity was not an end in itself; it was a means for attuning to whatever spiritual forces one could locate within a world of suffering. Two particular locales for such response were especially important for him – the resources possible within a common language, especially voices that come to seem inseparable from the culture that this language sustains, and the imaginary space where fantasy opens into dream and dream seems to merge with philosophy. There the literalness of poetry opens into allegorical thinking.

Both these locales depend on there being a force of desire not satisfied by narratives of the self. That sense of force then affords Eliot a clear model of active spirit that nonetheless cannot meaningfully function or understand itself unless it grasps how it is distinct from those versions of active emotion that confession does satisfy. One must sit still in order to let the imagination's waiting and listening inhabit the gaps its dissatisfactions produce. It is only by such waiting that one can participate in the energies informing mystic and visionary experience. And, equally important for Eliot, it is only when desires cannot be satisfied in the present that we are likely to turn our attention to the historicity implicit in them. Memory affords a concrete register for aspects of activity too abstract and perhaps too elemental to be interpreted simply in terms of empiricist models of intelligibility and human control. This historical dimension is clearest for Eliot in the forms of continuity and ritual celebrated in *Four Quartets*. But even the Eliot of "Tradition and the Individual Talent" saw the need to present desire as inseparable from typology and therefore most fully intelligible through the historical transformations it generates. However much a pure sense of contingency and hence of horizontality came to seem distinctive of modern experience, for Eliot there was always a latent vertical dimension partially compensating desire for its frustrations and partially promising that its intensities can also become modes of listening and of waiting. Desire offers for self-reflection a means of passing from history as appearance to history as the manifestation of forces with which active identifications might be attempted.

3 *Relating emotion and reason.* Virtually every important poet in English saw his or her work as somehow combating the ancient dichotomy between the irrationality of emotions and the kind of rationality offered by instrumental or empiricist models of the understanding. Does emotion set the criteria by which we decide what kinds of reasons are salient, or do we decide on what kinds of emotions matter by relying on some kind of instrumental reason? Eliot helps us develop two distinctive ways of addressing this issue. First, he insists on a version of lyrical affectivity that is impersonal and objective. Negatively, this means that, while there are usually strong affective components to experience, emphasis on the empirical subject is not the appropriate locus for appreciating their overall form and force. Instead the articulated affective field takes on something approximating an objective existence to be examined in its own right. And, positively, this sense of objectivity helps show that the affects are in many ways parts of public life. It makes sense to postulate modes of judgment that then treat these emotions as direct features of those public lives. We can learn from studying how desire is embodied to recognize some of the basic pressures on a culture, and we can as a public sustain a conversation about which of these emotional dispensations are most beneficial and most harmful to communal life.

Second, Eliot can use this model of judgment to suggest how this conversation may be carried out without quite having to rely on the pragmatic criteria usually used for thinking about public values. The relation between affect and judgment staged by his work is dramatistic, not instrumental. So we need not limit our interpretations to concerns with how discrete emotions affect our actions. Instead emotions appear as aspects of overall situations which have to be interpreted holistically. Reasons do not stem directly from specific emotions, and actions do not emerge directly from reasons. Motive is wound up in complex affective fields and in how those fields are culturally transmitted in image and in linguistic structures. Judgment then is a matter of accurately interpreting the most relevant fields and of elaborating how the paths of engagement and of projection that they foreground might produce particular consequences. Thus *The Waste Land* is less a congeries of specific emotions than the articulation of a single complexly interrelated affective state with claims on the lives of an extensive public. It offers judgment to the degree both that it allows sympathy with the conditions articulated and that it lets us hear through all the pain some possible terms on which alternative commitments might get formulated. And *Four Quartets* offers a profound meditation on interpretation and judgment because it places so much attention on what we might call preparatory contexts out of which certain kinds of action might come to seem desirable. This poem has to make us appreciate a range of feelings for which the society needs a language. And then it can offer its own formulations as the exploration of modes of speaking that bring Christian values into a plausible, unembarrassed relation with the modes of judgment needed for public life. *Four Quartets* presents faith as the willingness to rely on these sentences as adequate means of forming and representing the value commitments forming a person's vision of ultimate affective satisfactions. Eliot's earlier poetry does not have the same sense that what had been diffuse affects now can be the basis of a speech clarifying how they are elements within a comprehensive public life. But from "Prufrock" on, he understood poetry to be the articulation of how emotional complexes have consequences for the ways that agents dispose themselves in relation to possible actions.

4 *Valuing emotions and the roles emotions play in establishing values.* Eliot may be most useful on the topos of how we attribute significant values to our emotional states, in part because he was so disillusioned by the models of valuation dominating Enlightenment culture. Most lyric poetry has a role to play in relation to this struggle, especially in areas where the search for plot causalities and modes of coherence seems especially clumsy. For poetry's focus on complex, mutually qualifying, internal modes of linkage has rich parallels with the ways that psyches produce intensity and even

a sense of internal balance. Eliot deepens this contribution along several registers. For example, his is a distinctive lyrical eloquence. He exaggerates the possible precision of diction in order to insist on the role of word choice in creating the quality feelings have for their own sake, even if this means making narrative more opaque. As Eliot put it, the poet "has the privilege of contributing to the development and maintaining the quality, the capacity, of the language to express a wide range, and subtle gradation, of feeling and emotion."[14] Moreover, the attention to language that this diction demands finds reinforcement in Eliot's insistence on the prominence of cadence. For this emphasis presents the affects as continually exerting their own promise of satisfactions and mysteries pulling against the imperative to connect affect to action.

Eliot's juxtapositional strategies provide an additional twist to this sense of affective activity as an end in itself. These quick shifts are not merely exercises in a Bergsonian cult of the multiplicity and mobility of feelings, although they decidedly are that. Juxtapositional strategies also help address Eliot's concern that Western culture faces a dissociation of sensibility within which feeling and thinking seem locked in separate, unreconcilable agendas, a division that leads agents to align with either romantic religiosity or self-congratulatory cults of rational lucidity. For the poet can keep our attention focused on the work of what we might call "strange attractors" in our affective lives. Poetry not only provides terms for emotions, but also keeps us aware of the various forms of passage and linkage to which all our intensities are subject.

If we understand how emotional elements combine, we have at least a chance to produce new combinations that may actually modify our cultural grammars, especially if we recognize the close intimacy between how we feel and how we construct feeling in language. But it is even more important to notice the kinds of power that are involved in the sites composed as various affects enter these new combinations. For the poems develop something like a volumetric tensional space, something not unlike the rich tensions in cubist painting. In such plasticity the art becomes a direct measure of the intensities possible when one can bring full consciousness to the affective states one is experiencing.[15] And value comes to reside not in what such states produce but rather in how the person comes to make investments in this awareness of his or her own capacities for focused investment.

For most of Eliot's career this awareness was primarily of pain and dissociation, with consciousness itself torn between hating what it saw and having only the intensity of its seeing as recompense for the sight. Even in this work his resistance to narrative insisted that whatever counted as value had to do so in terms of the immanent relation between intensity and will that the poetic states maintained. The *Four Quartets* turned that mode of self-consciousness into a heuristic instrument: poetry could take on the task of exploring the modes of speaking and of investing that faith made possible. It found its richest satisfactions when there emerged a deep correlation between being moved, wanting to be where one is moved, and wanting to be the person so moved.

I worry that it will be easy to dismiss my arguments as too abstract. Might my abstraction be primarily a means of blinding myself to the probability that Eliot's ideas are in fact inextricable from his social vision and from the social projects of those like him who are zealous to restore unified sensibilities by political means. So before I can leave this topic, I want to show that the framework I have been developing affords ways of separating the thinking on affect within Eliot's work from three specific charges regularly leveled against him. These charges are that all of Eliot's ideas are contaminated by the politics they so seamlessly supported, that Eliot's very concern for unified sensibility makes him an anachronism in a postmodern culture now able to thrive on contradiction and multiplicity, and that Eliot was simply aggrandizing his own imaginary identity in his laments about dissociated sensibility as a historical crisis.

Let me take the last of these first. I do not dispute Frank Kermode's argument that there is little historical support for locating a debilitating dissociation of sensibility at a particular moment in Western history. Instead I suggest that Eliot's concerns may be worth attending to precisely because they have no historical specificity: the dissociation of sensibility may be a permanent cultural possibility that the arts are always addressing. Of course that makes it all the more pressing to engage the postmodern line of critique. But by taking on that challenge we may develop a richer sense of those ways in which Eliot need not fit historicist parameters but instead provides a phenomenology still worth attending to.

First we have to distinguish between postmodern interest in "multiplicity" and Eliot's worries about "dissociation." Dissociation is not just another form of multiplicity or way of engaging contradiction. Dissociation is paralyzing, not liberating. It is multiplicity gone amuck or contradiction become debilitating. And no confident general assertion about accepting fragmentation can assure us that some fragments will not interact much more problematically than others. There is dissociation whenever dissonance prevents our fully inhabiting our own perceptions, acts, and desires. Moreover, the opposite of dissociation need not be a "unified sensibility," at least not a contemporary projection of unified sensibility as rigidly defended identity. It is true that Eliot idealized that unified sensibility – but at the same time he tried to avoid basing that unity on how an ego asserts identity for itself. The relevant unity need not be derived from any kind of explanation or invocation of some abstract criterion for unity. A unified sensibility, like a unified poem, is one that is not frustrated by those contradictions that occupy its attention and engage its affects. A unified sensibility can be considered simply one that can will its own range of affects without having to thematize them and seek criteria from the outside.

If my arguments about dissociation take hold, I can provide a response to the question whether Eliot's politics have to be seen as contaminating his various ideas and psychological commitments. In my view Eliot's specific politics simply do not matter much if we can show that the cultural analysis generating the politics is far more telling than are the proposed social solutions. And the more we take the dissociation of sensibility as a phenomenological concern rather than a specifically historical one, the more license we have to treat Eliot's responses to it as themselves to be judged simply in terms of the ways they help us negotiate that phenomenology. Judging these responses is inseparable from assessing the possible values for contemporaries of preserving Eliot's thinking on the emotions. So far I have tried to represent these values in terms of how Eliot can modify how we think. Now I will conclude by shifting to two aspects of how the concrete affective life within the poems can actually modify how we come to invest in certain ways of feeling. Such modifications then can have substantial cultural consequences even if one refuses the political interpretations Eliot put upon them.

First there is the concrete range of distinctive affective forces that Eliot makes available to us by grounding his work in such fundamental desires. At their best the poems do not allude to emotions or simply express emotive states. Rather they attempt to transform "observations into states of mind" and to integrate complex levels of experience into unforgettable structures like the configuration at the close of "Sweeney Among the Nightingales" or the remarkable blend of levels and ranges of reference in *The Waste Land*. These configurations establish an intricate system of exchanges: as ideas are transmuted into sensations, sensations dramatize the conditions of voicing that these frameworks have in our culture.[16]

Eliot on the metaphysical conceit adds a second aspect to these specific modes of embodiment. For the scope of the conceit is inseparable from the pressure brought to bear by "the operation of the poet's mind."[17] This means that conceits not only explore new affective connections but also foreground the tension between the discursive and emotional fields within which the sensations are typically coded. This tension in turn plays an intricate double role: it serves as the glue binding the elements into one aspect of a state of mind, and it serves as a wedge securing the distance between these concrete states and the kind of emotions that fit easily into standard narrative frameworks. Therefore the metaphysical conceit can flaunt the limitations of our usual emotional grammars, in the process inviting us to link the affective sensations to an underlying source beyond narrative. We experience not only new emotional configurations but also the new possibilities of lyric agency which I have been stressing, here as resistance to the dominant ways of mapping affects and hence as potentially building new sensibilities and new emphases within cultural life.

Stein transformed painterly abstraction into the foregrounding of syntax and sound. Williams reconfigured point, line, and plane into a focus on the disposition of energies organized by line breaks and composed by the visual force the grammar of a sentence can take within taut short lines. But only Eliot among his peers fully took advantage of those modernist breakthroughs to mine the elemental forms of our affective life woven into language. Critically, this enabled him to clarify the prices we pay when emotional theatricality displaces the fine contours of that language. And, creatively, it enabled him to formulate a version of constructivism that took as its cultural role the direct modification of our most intimate dispositions and ways of viewing our own powers and needs as agents. As Eliot put it, emotions "have their own laws of growth which are not always reasonable, but must just be accepted by the reason."[18] For him that view made it possible to envision poetic experiment as charged with the task of modifying what become the parameters within which reason operates. Now there remains for us the critical task of defining just how that vision can be formulated and used.

NOTES

1. Were I to situate my project within Eliot criticism, I would say that it has two basic antagonists. The first is Hugh Kenner, who dismissed all the Symboliste aspects of desire in Eliot as mere romanticism compared to Pound's concrete efforts to make the object adequate to the emotions it elicits. This stance simply ignores the tension between desire and its immediate objects fundamental both to Eliot's own sense of experience and to the French tradition fundamental to shaping his ambitions for poetry. The second antagonist consists of work by critics such as Maud Ellmann, *The Poetics of Impersonality: T. S. Eliot and Ezra Pound* (New York: Cambridge University Press, 1987) and Michael North, *The*

Political Aesthetic of Yeats, Eliot, and Pound (New York: Cambridge University Press, 1991) that dwells on what Eliot exhibits or reveals about desire rather than how he understands and deploys it self-consciously. Where this now dominant approach is bound to the fundamentally passive conditions of being caught up in imaginary structures, my perspective emphasizes how both authors and readers can envision themselves taking active responsibility for their imaginary lives. It is more difficult to list allies because I have learned a great deal from so many Eliot critics, in particular from the work of such scholars as Richard Shusterman, *T. S. Eliot and the Philosophy of Criticism* (New York: Columbia University Press, 1988); A. D. Moody, *Tracing T. S. Eliot's Spirit: Essays on His Poetry and Thought* (Cambridge: Cambridge University Press, 1996); Sanford Schwartz, *The Matrix of Modernism* (Princeton: Princeton University Press, 1985); and Jeffrey M. Perl, *Skepticism and Modern Enmity: Before and after Eliot* (Baltimore: Johns Hopkins University Press, 1989) who attend to the intellectual contexts fundamental in his formative years.

2. I offer full summaries of contemporary philosophical positions on the emotions and on feelings in my book *The Particulars of Rapture: An Aesthetics of the Affects* (Ithaca, N. Y.: Cornell University Press, 2003). For this essay it should suffice to say that the most useful versions of mainstream "cognitivist" theories are those proposed by Ronald de Sousa, *The Rationality of Emotions* (Cambridge, Mass.: MIT Press, 1987) and by Keith Oatley, *Best Laid Schemes: The Psychology of Emotions* (New York: Cambridge University Press, 1992). (Martha Nussbaum's *Upheavals of Thought: The Intelligence of Emotions* [New York: Cambridge University Press, 2001] proposes a new version of cognitivism, but I argue at length in my book that her model cannot work.) The best criticisms of the standard cognitivist position are Richard Wollheim's *On the Emotions* (New Haven: Yale University Press, 1999) and Sue Campbell's *Interpreting the Personal* (Ithaca, N. Y.: Cornell University Press, 1997). Wollheim argues that cognitivism cannot handle the imaginary, fantasized ways that emotions connect to the world. And Campbell is quite good on the ways in which the orientation toward belief and judgment in cognitivist theory cannot handle the pressure of inchoate aspects of affective life that drive us to seek greater specific articulation. Finally, for a good overview of contemporary discourse on the emotions, see Paul R. Griffiths, *What Emotions Really Are* (Chicago: University of Chicago Press, 1997). Griffiths's book is also an example of how even when philosophers are critical of cognitivism they are likely to retain a version of its emphasis on the importance of judgment and belief for how we construct affective intensities.

3. Probably Eliot's most basic formulation of the difference between emotions and feelings takes place in his essay "Tradition and the Individual Talent," in *Selected Essays* (New York: Harcourt Brace, 1932), 8–11. For analogous distinctions contemporary with Eliot's, see Norman H. Gardiner et al., *Feeling and Emotion: A History of Theories* (London: Greenwood Press, 1937).

4. T. S. Eliot, *Inventions of the March Hare: Poems 1909–1917*, ed. Christopher Ricks (New York: Harcourt Brace, 1996), 105.

5. Eliot, *Selected Essays*, 385.

6. I. A. Richards's work offers a historically important exception to this claim, as indeed does Nietzsche's. See below, note 15.

7. Eliot, *Selected Essays*, 372, 379, 378–9. Albert Cook's *Prisms: Studies in Modern Literature* (Bloomington: Indiana University Press, 1967) made an important argument for the roles that allegorical frameworks play in modernist writing, but the force of his argument was lost to what I consider the much less interesting model of allegory proposed by Paul de Man.

8. Eliot, *Inventions*, ed. Ricks, 78–9.

9. T. S. Eliot, *Collected Poems 1909–1962* (New York: Harcourt Brace, 1970), 50.

10. For illustrations of this concept, see T. S. Eliot, *Knowledge and Experience in the Philosophy of F. H. Bradley* (London: Faber and Faber, 1964), 19, 49.

11. It is worth noting that this affinity for Lacanian thinking also helps us handle the fantasy dimension of emotions in ways that have considerable relevance for contemporary theory. Eliot both continues and extends Richard Wollheim's argument against cognitivist theory that we simply cannot explain the specific intensities emotions take on in individual lives if we accord them the same intentional structure that we do beliefs. Were beliefs the source, we would expect emotional investments to have the same submission to social control and social negotiation that accrue to beliefs. Since this is not the case, there must be distinctive projections based in a person's specific psychodynamics. To explain those psychodynamics, Wollheim is content with a Freudian model of fantasies shaped by a person's childhood. Both Lacan and Eliot, on the other hand, treat affective investments as more complexly related to modes of identification based on projections about audiences that we hope can provide for us the significations we desire.

12. T. S. Eliot, "Dante," in *Selected Essays* (New York: Harcourt Brace, 1950), 199–237, 234.

13. Ibid., 205.

14. T. S. Eliot, *On Poetry and Poets* (London: Faber and Faber, 1957), 37.

15. I. A. Richards tried to explain the nature of these emotional states in his *Practical Criticism* (see *Selected Works* [New York: Routledge, 2001], vol. IV). But if one relies on a behavioral or mechanical model, one cannot establish sufficiently complex intentional states for the qualities of intensity and intensification fundamental to feeling oneself as empowered by the affects. In contemporary thinking the fullest accounts of such states are in the work of Gilles Deleuze, but in my view we have to bring his vocabulary into richer connections with standard Anglo-American discourse, and we have to find ways of keeping his stress on intensity without attaching that to his romantic politics.

16. Eliot, *Selected Essays*, 249.

17. Ibid., 243.

18. Eliot, *On Poetry*, 24.

PART III

Modern women

CHAPTER 8

Through schoolhouse windows: women, the academy, and T. S. Eliot

Gail McDonald

From the vantage point of the twenty-first century, the trajectory of Eliot's career in the twentieth appears to have two major stages: a long, high ride for forty years, with a few significant but impermanent dips, followed by a precipitous decline in the last forty. The present volume suggests the possibility of a correction to the decline – or at least a rekindled interest. Not coincidentally, this revival occurs as critics have become less sure of the usefulness of meta-narratives about modernism and more inclined to inter-rogate the components of the big story: might it not be more accurate to consider multiple modernisms?[1] T. S. Eliot has been central to every phase of the project of modernist scholarship. An adjustable model of the modern artist, he seems capable of accommodating decades of incommensurable assessments. Since, as Eliot himself expected, these reconfigurations are inevitable, their origins and effects should themselves be objects of study. What makes a critical assessment plausible, even compelling, for one gen-eration and unconvincing for another? Putting aside the obvious (and rare) cases like a new piece of evidence or a previously undiscovered manuscript, what forces power the hydraulics of literary reputation? Contrary to the maxim, there *is* a way of accounting for taste – indeed multiple ways.

This essay undertakes one piece of what must be a complex accounting – Eliot's reception among female readers in the context of women and their place (or lack thereof) in the academy. Why female readers? The importance to Eliot studies of female readers, particularly those situated on campuses, has much to do with educational history: viewed together, the time-lines charting the fortunes of women in the academy and the rise and fall of Eliot's reputation intersect at vital points. The first, prodigious spread of Eliot's influence was concurrent with the incursion of female students on previously male ground. At the beginning, the poet's particular brand of newness was associated with feelings of change and breakthrough, as was the women's, and change was unwelcome in many precincts. Then the novelty wore off, on both counts.

Two images of campus trespass make the point another way. In *A Room of One's Own*, Virginia Woolf, excited by a "little fish" of an idea, finds she cannot sit still:

It was thus that I found myself walking with extreme rapidity across a grass plot. Instantly a man's figure rose to intercept me . . . His face expressed horror and indignation. Instinct rather than reason came to my help: he was a Beadle; I was a woman. This was the turf; there was the path. Only the Fellows and Scholars are allowed here; the gravel is the place for me.

Woolf's narrator returns to the path, the Beadle relaxes his guard, and order is restored. "No very great harm was done," she writes, but the Fellows and Scholars "in protection of their turf . . . had sent my little fish into hiding."[2] Her scene of turf-tussle, too decorous to call a "war," is justly famous. Here is a more obscure scene of intrusion: "I was always on the other side of the wall," the speaker recalls. "On one occasion . . . when I ventured into the schoolyard a little too early when there were still [girls] on the premises and I saw them staring at me through a window, I took flight at once."[3] The speaker is T. S. Eliot; the occasion, the centennial celebration of the Mary Institute in St. Louis, a girls' school next door to the Eliot family home. When school was out, the yard was Eliot's playground. The little boy, like Woolf's walker, finds himself in the wrong place at the wrong time and, like her "little fish," darts away.

Eliot's recollection, recorded by a note-taker at the occasion, has little of the stylistic or intellectual richness of Woolf's, but I cite it as a complement to hers for two reasons. First, as a diptych of academic enclosures, the two scenes suggest that the gendering of academic space is not one narrative, but many. Its characters are both women and men, the points of view mobile, and the resultant tones mixed – wry, jocular, angry, frightened. Second, this picture of Eliot as startled interloper on female territory reverses Woolf's far more familiar scene of the woman chastised for walking on the academic grass. The staring girls – perhaps hostile, perhaps merely curious – undermine the equally familiar scene of Eliot as a welcome presence in places academic. Woolf's image of the outraged Beadle depicts the academy's reception of women in the early decades of the century; the second image of the unwelcome boy captures Eliot's campus reception in recent decades. We see in the juxtaposition that the space itself, whether a real or an imaginary campus, has a multivalent significance comprising social goals, individual desires, class privilege, forces of liberation or of oppression; it is a repository for often conflicting aims, an enclosure welcoming to some, suspicious of others. The preferred list of visitors is subject to change.

As I have argued at length elsewhere, Eliot's fortunes have, to an unusual degree, been wedded to the academy's self-definition.[4] Historically, the academy has had two, sometimes contradictory, mandates: one is to create new knowledge; the other is to preserve and pass on tradition. The humanities have struggled with this dual role, and the canon has been a particular source of ongoing dissension within the ranks. At the heart of this division are questions about jurisdiction: by what right does any one group of people privilege any one group of texts? And by what standards are such judgments to be made?

In the university, whatever the answer has been, however it may have been challenged, one thing remained certain until the twentieth century: the judge was male. Women's presence on campus has changed the complexion of authority. Thus my focus is on the symbolic weight of gender as it relates to academic practices and values, in particular to matters of professional authority and scholarly objectivity. Professionalism and disinterestedness are significant markers of academic "impersonality," one of the most disputed terms in Eliot's oeuvre. Inquiring into the meanings of such weighted terms requires attention to the circumstances in which they are deployed. In *The Gender of Modernity*, Rita Felski suggests a method of interrogation: "Rather than simply subsuming the history of gender relations within an overarching meta-theory of modernity articulated from the vantage point of the present, feminist critics need to take seriously past women's and men's own understandings of their *positioning* within historical processes."[5] It will not do to assume that the most recent views are the most enlightened or that past readers were benighted. An analysis of Eliot's significance to female critics must instead attend to the rhetorical situations in which their views were expressed. The position of the academic woman has been, I suggest, a significant and changing site of such expression.

A Room of One's Own had its genesis on campus, growing out of two talks Woolf gave at Cambridge in October 1928, one to the Arts Society at Newnham and another to the Odtaa Society at Girton, where Muriel Bradbrook heard her speak. "We enjoyed Mrs. Woolf," she recalled, "but felt her Cambridge was not ours." Woolf's portrait of being relegated to the gravel emphasized, no doubt rightly, that women were not welcome in the academy. And yet Bradbrook seems to take pleasure precisely in her role as interloper. "Her" Cambridge, as she explains, belonged to T. S. Eliot. "The poetry of *The Waste Land* gave us a new world . . . 'Bliss was it in that dawn to be alive!'"[6] By the time of Woolf's talks, Eliot had not only published *The Waste Land* (1922) but had also delivered the prestigious Clark Lectures (1926).[7] As these dates suggest, Eliot's academic acceptance was astonishingly swift in some quarters. The poet Kathleen Raine had not heard of Eliot until she arrived at Cambridge, but as a first-year undergraduate studying botany she found the effects of her first encounter with the poems "instantaneous and tremendous."[8] Eliot was for the students a poet of youth and change, Bradbrook recalls:

> The effect of *The Waste Land* was not gloomy but exhilarating and intensely stimulating. Our confusion was understood, our time had found a voice. No other encounter can have the effect of great contemporary poetry met in youth, which not only interprets experience but is itself experience. It grew within my privileged generation, became part of ourselves, and has remained so.[9]

Declaring her affiliation with Eliot, Bradbrook aligns him with positive change, even, in the earlier allusion to Wordsworth's blissful dawn, with revolution. He is a comrade-in-arms. Bradbrook's Eliot is not Sandra Gilbert and Susan Gubar's:

> [T]he wastings of *The Waste Land* are epitomized by the hysterical speech of women who can "connect nothing with nothing" . . . [T]he language of these women embodies "the horror, the horror" that the poet spells from an impotent sibyl's leaves and leavings. For ultimately . . . Eliot transcribes female language in order to transcend it, thus justifying Joyce's claim that *The Waste Land* ended "the idea of poetry for ladies."[10]

Bradbrook's generational struggle in the aftermath of world war is here replaced by a war between the sexes, the shaping metaphor of *No Man's Land*. Whereas Bradbrook's tone is nostalgic and celebratory, Gilbert and Gubar's is accusatory. No longer an ally, Eliot has become an iconic enemy of the new. In their reading, the really new in the early twentieth century is the work of women, a creativity thwarted and suppressed by male writers: "Indeed," they argue, "it is possible to hypothesize that a reaction-formation against the rise of literary women became not just a theme in modernist writing but a motive for modernism."[11] Attention-getting as the three volumes of *No Man's Land* were, they were not an isolated phenomenon: an adversarial construction of gender relations in the making of modernism underwrites many of the most often cited texts of first-wave feminist scholarship.

How is it that Eliot, Bradbrook and Raine's champion of a new, progressive generation, is also Gilbert and Gubar's enemy of the new? The answers vary in plausibility. Eliot changed. Knowledge about Eliot changed. Criticism changed. On the surface, Eliot did appear to change in 1927 when he declared English, Anglican, and conservative allegiances. Some of his contemporaries – Ezra Pound, Conrad Aiken – decried the move as a betrayal of the iconoclastic agenda of modernism. More recently, critics have been inclined to see the 1927 announcement as simply formalizing inclinations there from the beginning of Eliot's public career. *The Waste Land*, his most overtly experimental poem, of course predates the announcement, but again, by reading the conservative elements of Eliot's thought back into the poem, some analyses treat the technical innovations as a kind of window-dressing, not central to the poem's ideas. Along with *Sweeney Agonistes*, the portraits of Fresca and Grishkin, "Hysteria," and other creations, the poem is frequently cited as damning evidence of Eliot's misogyny. Since apparently misogynist attitudes are in evidence early and late in the career, there is relatively little reason to seek an explanation for changed critical assessment in some dramatic shift in Eliot's way of thinking. Knowledge about Eliot has also changed, of course. The publication of the facsimile of *The Waste Land*, the first volume of his letters, the edition of *Inventions of the March Hare*, and, especially, the attention paid to Eliot's literary and personal relations with women in major critical texts have deepened our understanding of his working methods, poetic development, and private life.[12] But again there have been few major revelations that would, in themselves, turn the critical tide. The words of the poems are the same as ever, but the number of critics interested in studying and judging the darker implications of those words has substantially increased.

Changes in literary criticism offer the most plausible explanation for the differences between the Eliot of Bradbrook and Raine's Cambridge and the Eliot of Gilbert and Gubar's no man's land. That explanation lies readily to hand in histories of academic literary study.[13] The oft-told tale normally cites the hegemony of New Criticism in the United States (traced back to tenets of Eliot's critical essays, especially those of *The Sacred Wood*) followed by the rise (usually dated from the 1960s) of methods less formalist, more contextual, and more interested in the social and political implications of texts. While the history in England is quite different in other regards, it is the same in its turn away from a curriculum centered in New Critical practice and thus – directly or indirectly – away from its putative sponsor, Eliot. A comparable turn occurs in poetry, where the generations of the 1950s and 1960s (beat, angry, confessional) consciously smash the poem as polished artifact, a poem often labeled "academic."

What this condensed version of the story leaves out is the shift in tone and the role of gender in its making. For Bradbrook and Raine, praise of Eliot is of a piece with their sense of possibility, a thrilled pleasure in the radically different. For Gilbert and Gubar, the thrill is gone, replaced by indignation. Strong language has not, of course, been limited to female commentators. To take a single but typical example: Kenneth Rexroth praised Denise Levertov by damning Eliot and his followers: "At first she fell under the influence of the Southern Colonels . . . We were all horrified. 'So and so is a lot like our Empson,' said she to me. Said I to her, '[Y]ou are a leader of the very generation of revolt against the impostures of Empson, Richards, Eliot and their sycophants.'"[14] Enthusiastic embrace followed by angry expulsion is in keeping with the model Gerald Graff outlines in *Professing Literature*. "How," Woolf wonders about academic enmity in *A Room of One's Own*, "explain the anger of the professors?" (32). Her wonderfully direct question may be adapted to the treatment of Eliot in the first phase of feminist rereadings. But the question needs a counterpoint to encompass the phenomenon of Eliot's early academic adoption: "How explain the thrill of the professors?" And not just professors, of course, but also professional critics, little magazine editors, and so on, as the whole critical enterprise became increasingly joined to – at times inseparable from – the academic.

The predictable clash between old and new, hegemonic and marginal, accounts in part for the rise and fall of Eliot. It may be argued that his fall from academic grace would have come whether or not any woman ever entered the academy. The list of male detractors is, after all, also long and distinguished. But such an explanation fails to account for the striking degree to which the rhetoric of praise and blame around the figure of T. S. Eliot has itself been colored by gender stereotyping. In a review comparing *The Waste Land* to a book by Lew Sarett called *The Box of God*, for example, Harriet Monroe characterizes Eliot (to his detriment) as an "indoor thinker": "the miasma which afflicts Mr. Eliot is as remote a speculative conceit, as futile a fritter of mental confectionery, as Lyly's euphemism must have been to Elizabethan sailors." By contrast, Mr. Sarett's work "is an outdoor man's poem of faith . . . the creed of the pioneer . . . the hero who has the future in his keeping."[15] Similar formulations worked to undermine the dignity of professors of literature, largely an "indoor" population in the public imagination; the increase of women entering the profession reinforced that view, as angels left the hearth to go to the library. Suzanne Clark's *Sentimental Modernism* amply demonstrates the gender-coding of intellectual life: rigor, precision, and tough-mindedness are preferred to nurture, openness, sympathy.[16] In the first half of the twentieth century, this value-system was especially critical to a humanities professoriate under pressure to demonstrate its worth and seriousness. Two of the most important developments in twentieth-century academic and literary history centrally involve women and their relationship to such academic protocols: first, a growing population of women students entered a formerly male dominion; then, influential critic-scholars put gender at the center of the literary curriculum. For the first group of women, Eliot served as an emblem of the rigorous mind; for the second, as an emblem of exclusion.

Eliot, a Harvard man given to learned allusion, was distinctly not "non-U" and therefore was an apparently easy fit for the classroom. At once an insider and an outsider, he crafted a position as keeper of the cultural flame at the same time that his most famous poem appeared to many readers to question whether there was any flame left to keep. Universities, by turns preservers of heritage and champions of free thought, were at that historical moment growing familiar with the contradiction. The presence of Woolf's woman on the quadrangle grass was an instance of just that dilemma. The most significant trend in that century's history of higher education was the progress toward democratization; arguably incomplete, this movement has meant that the quadrangle no longer belongs exclusively to white, economically privileged males. In the early twentieth century, the flashpoint of the debate over entry into the symbolically gated enclave was gender. Andreas Huyssen argues that

in the age of nascent socialism and the first major women's movement in Europe, the masses knocking at the gate were also women, knocking at the gate of a male-dominated culture. It is indeed striking to observe how the political, psychological and aesthetic discourse around the turn of the century consistently and obsessively genders mass culture and the masses as feminine, while high culture . . . clearly remains the privileged realm of male activities.[17]

By the time Woolf spoke to the women of Girton and Newnham and Eliot delivered the Clark Lectures, the mass education movement in England was about fifty years old. The newly founded "redbrick" universities provided an alternative to "Oxbridge"; operating costs at these more accessible schools caused them to be relatively hospitable to women, while Oxford and Cambridge remained overwhelmingly male. The deaths of young men during World War I, however, created a serious loss of fee income for the two traditional universities and, in a highly unusual move, both institutions sought help from the Treasury in 1919. These financial pressures add an important footnote to the "men of 1914" narrative familiar to modernist scholars. In part because of the loss of men, women were conceded degrees at Oxford in 1920. Cambridge resisted for the time being, admitting women only to "titular" degrees in 1921, but the gates at which women had knocked were ajar.[18] There would be repeated attempts to close them. The number of females to be admitted to Oxford was limited by statute in 1927, and the women's colleges would not receive full recognition there until 1959. The Supplement to the Cambridge Historical Register for 1921–30 lists 183 new lectureships, of which 11 were awarded to women. Although these figures suggest an impressive increase in the role and influence of women, Rita Tullberg reports that, during the same period, the heads of Newnham and Girton "attended University functions and ceremonials by courtesy only and were counted as 'wives' at social gatherings."[19] Full membership rights for Cambridge women, including a vote in University governance, would not be extended until 1948.

In the United States, the first two decades of the twentieth century saw a 1000 percent increase in the number of women enrolled in state-supported colleges.[20] Most major universities admitted women to doctoral programs by the 1890s, with some notable exceptions: Radcliffe, but not Harvard, made the Ph.D. available to women in 1902; Princeton, Yale, and Virginia did not admit women to the university fully until 1969–70. The percentage of women with earned doctorates rose steadily in the early decades of the twentieth century (from 6 percent in 1880 to 15 percent in 1920), but acceptance of women as advanced students and faculty members was, with few exceptions, grudging. Fellowships for women were fewer and less generous than for men; some professors resented that attention should be diverted from male students; and there were predictable crises as female enrollments grew and women began to excel.[21]

Coincident with the increased presence of women at both English and American universities was an equally historic shift in the curriculum from classical languages to the mother tongue. In many cases, the vernacular curriculum entered through the "back door" since the women's colleges were employed as laboratories for curricular experiment. Prior to this development, the study of English literature was stopped well short of contemporary work: the Oxford English curriculum ended at 1830. The causes for the decline of classical languages in favor of modern are, of course, numerous and not solely gender-based. Nevertheless, contemporary commentators routinely declared a causal connection between women students and relaxed academic standards. Where once female biology had been invoked to explain why women were not suited to higher learning of any kind, now the same facts of nature were rehearsed to explain why women could excel in the "softer" subjects like literature – with the consequence that literature itself lost status as a field of study. The effort to professionalize literature and literary criticism was strongly motivated by a desire to rid literature of this aura of femininity. The experiments of I. A. Richards, William Empson's *Seven Types of Ambiguity* (1930), and Laura Riding and Robert Graves's *Survey of Modernist Poetry* (1927) may all be viewed through this lens.[22]

These are the contexts in which Eliot's first female critics read. Even for those readers outside the academic quadrangle, practicing poets and magazine reviewers, this sense of the "feminization" of literary production and study was pervasive, as various aspects of the "woman-question" were argued in newspapers and magazines. What is the *positioning* of these readers vis-à-vis their reading and their articulations of opinion about that reading? Reading practices declare one's allegiances and affiliations. In the academy, they also declare one's brand of professionalism, as anyone knows who has ever admitted shamefacedly to not having read some canonical novel or breakthrough critical book. Given the histories of government, patrimony, and paid work in England and America, it will be noted immediately that "allegiance," "affiliation," and "professionalism" are themselves words with gendered etymologies, all denoting vows of loyalty to a superior person or ideal – normally male. In addition, professional standards depend upon measurements (statistics, tests for certification) and upon hierarchical structures fostering competition (ranking, promotion), models associated with the traditionally male fields of science and business. Eliot's reception gauges a shift in the conception of affiliation, one brought about in part by a shift in the gender of the affiliates. Over time, that change would serve to diminish his stature.

But not at first. "Tradition and the Individual Talent," now often a touchstone for readings that construe Eliot's "mind of Europe" as an exclusionary model inimical to the development of female talent, was published in 1919. In 1922, I. A. Richards became a lecturer in the new Cambridge School of English and shortly thereafter declared Eliot "the one hope" for the school. Eliot's following was at first limited to the younger dons and the students: by 1924, the undergraduate magazine *Granta* referred to him as "the most discussed of contemporary highbrows." But it is important to emphasize that the poet's influence was then viewed by the academic power structure as subversive – he *was* the "really new" and thus for traditionalists unproven, unwelcome. In Bradbrook's time, enthusiasm for Eliot in the face of donnish snobbery marked one as thoroughly modern. Students jammed the hall for the Clark Lectures; the *Cambridge Review* noted that "the whole of both Newnham and Girton colleges" turned out.[23] A centerpiece in the reclamation of contemporary poetry as a serious pursuit for the ambitious, Eliot's work was undergraduate contraband for both men and women, the book no one has to force you to read because it is *yours* – an affiliation so deep that it becomes an identity. Such identifications are also a means of declaring what one is not.

The phenomenon was felt off campus, too. May Sinclair responded to a negative review of *Prufrock and Other Observations* in terms evoking both gender and class: "I know that Mr. Waugh is simply keeping up the good old manly traditions of the *Quarterly* . . . with its war cry: ''Ere's a stranger, let's 'eave 'arf a brick at 'im.'" She admires Eliot precisely because his genius is "disturbing"; he is "dangerous," not a poet whom "comfortable and respectable people can see, in the first moment after dinner."[24] Remarks of this sort capture the energy and pleasure with which a younger generation debunks the values of an older. Insofar as modernist poetry in the person of Eliot was perceived to be heady in its experimentalism, its widening of subject matter, even its darkness, the women of Eliot's own generation could see their pioneering energies mirrored in his work. And insofar as modernist poetry was considered a serious and culturally significant endeavor requiring erudition, the women found their own intellectual aspirations validated.

During this same period, Bradbrook was bracketed with William Empson in the examination results; she "had done all that would have entitled me, if [I had been] a man, to graduate as a B.A." Sir Arthur Quiller-Couch still commenced his lectures with the salutation "Gentlemen," refusing to acknowledge the women who sat in front of him.[25] Newspaper cartoons in both England and the US routinely pictured the female intellectual as a sterile old maid. While the "true-woman" ethos could comfortably coexist with the idea of teaching other people's children, women who chose to teach adults in universities had cause to see themselves as anomalies. For American female professors, a telling indication of their position outside the mainstream is the set of statistics gathered by the AAUW covering the period up to 1924. Of 1,600 women surveyed, three-quarters were unmarried, divorced, or separated – a startling statistic in view of woman's expected destiny as wife and mother. M. Carey Thomas, the founder of Bryn Mawr, said, "Our failures only marry."[26]

To be as modern as T. S. Eliot, in this context, was to regard oneself as a serious intellectual and a social progressive. Neither affiliation could be comfortably linked in that era to the female body in its heterosexual, reproductive capabilities. The life of the mind was understood to preclude the life of the sexed body, a residue of the monastic foundations of many institutions of learning. To the extent that progress for women was impeded by assumptions about reproductive destiny, a life apart from that destiny could be experienced as liberating. In *Growing Up in Revolution*, Margaret Cole recalled the Girton of 1911 in just such terms: "My first impression of College was one of freedom . . . to be *where* you liked, *when* you liked and with *whom* you liked . . . to get up and go to bed when you pleased and, if desirable, to go on reading, writing or talking till dawn."[27] The ironic line Vivien Eliot contributed to *The Waste Land* comes to mind: "'What you get married for if you don't want children?'" Eliot wrote to Aiken in 1915 that he was leaving Oxford, "with its pregnant wives [and] sprawling children . . . Come let us fly to a land where there are no Medici prints, nothing but concubinage and conversation."[28] Not only does he express distaste for traditional (and clearly impoverished) family life, he also indicates a preference here for the exotic – a seraglio, not the drawing room of a faculty wife. Two months later, however, he puts family life in a somewhat different light, one more relevant to women who sought a livelihood outside of traditional marriage and family:

The great need is to know one's own mind, and I don't know that: whether I want to get married, and have a family . . . and compromise and conceal my opinions and forfeit my independence for the sake of my children's future; or save my money and retire at fifty to a table on the boulevard, regarding the world placidly through the fumes of an aperitif at 5 p.m. – How thin either life seems![29]

Eliot here views the burdens of care for a family as toxic to his creative capacities and integrity. The choice for women who wished not to "compromise and conceal" was similarly limited – indeed more so. The life of the *flâneur* was not an option for them, its nearest equivalent made possible only by extraordinary self-possession and sufficient money to maintain oneself. Shari Benstock copiously documents the lives of some who sought artistic and sexual independence in *Women of the Left Bank*.[30] The motives of these adventurous women and of the confused T. S. Eliot of 1915 are not dissimilar: they are united by aversion to conventionality, provinciality, and the deadening effects of a life imposed rather than chosen.

Among the many impositions faced by the female professoriate of the years 1910–19 were conventional demands for ladylike behavior and the assumption that motherhood is woman's natural state. These expectations provide an angle for rereading the apparently misogynist comments of male modernists: the poetic "Portraits" of ladies; Joyce's remark about ending "the idea of poetry for ladies"; Eliot's image of "Lady Precocia Pondoeuf" composing poems in her nursery; Pound's assertion that "the female / . . . Is a chaos"; Eliot's likening of his *Poems* to female "discharge."[31] These instances and scores of others have by now become familiar through frequent citation and analysis. Prima facie, they seem either deeply disturbing or pitiably juvenile. Independent-minded women of the 1920s, however, also refer to "ladies" derisively, deflating the pretensions of the guardians of gentility. Bradbrook recalls in "My Cambridge": "In her talk to the freshers in 1927, the Mistress concluded, 'And remember, my dears, the eyes of the Cambridge ladies will be ever upon you!', advising us to don hat and gloves at Storey's Way" (120). Or consider Djuna Barnes's provocatively titled *Ladies Almanack* and *The Book of Repulsive Women*, which play upon notions of acceptable and unacceptable behaviors for ladies. A desire for unladylike intellectual and artistic ventures was not limited to the male modernists.

As for misogynist revulsion from the female body, women's attitudes could hardly be expected to correspond. Nevertheless, being at ease with one's body was neither socially nor institutionally mandated. As the AAUW statistics cited earlier indicate, there was a disincentive among female intellectuals within the academy to "embody" themselves through marriage and childbirth. Marriage could mean job loss, and maternity leave was nonexistent. In 1930, Helen Gardner covered classes at Birmingham for Elsie Phare when her Newnham friend was refused a few days' absence to deliver a child.[32] Doubtless, when Eliot wrote to his father, "I distrust the Feminine in literature," he shared the then-common view that a writing desk in a nursery was unseemly.[33] In an era when the "Feminine" was coded as weak-minded, sentimental, conventional, and maternal, women of Bradbrook and Raine's generation also had cause to distrust it. It was this construction of the "Feminine" that had kept the women students invisible to Quiller-Couch. Eliot's much-discussed theory of impersonality, I suggest, spoke persuasively to women for whom the various attributes of the personal – emotions, vulnerabilities, confidences – were, for professional reasons, best kept at bay. Disinterested reading, broad learning, and disciplined poetic expression were for these readers, as for many of their male colleagues, allegiances that helped to insulate them from accusations that their life's work was a trivial or unnatural pursuit. In short, a wholly agonistic depiction of relations among the young moderns – male versus female – tells part of the story, but wrongly minimizes their shared aims: defense of the arts they practiced and the unconventional lives many of them wished to live.

Searching the work of some of Eliot's most distinguished female critics, one finds, if not precisely gender-blind readings of the poems, then at least readings in which gender is not a central issue. Helen Gardner's *The Art of T. S. Eliot*, still an unexcelled reading of *Four Quartets*, begins with an acknowledgment that the critic from whom she has learned the most is "Mr. Eliot himself."[34] Her considerable powers are trained on largely formal concerns. Elizabeth Drew's *T. S. Eliot: The Design of His Poetry* employs a

Jungian framework of analysis to examine the poetic career, and, while a psychological slant is more clearly personal than one devoted to prosody, the book does not seek to judge the private life.[35] Both writers, insofar as they speak of the poet rather than the poem, are sympathetic to the spiritual dimension of the poetry. Neither work has the quality of a mind struggling with ideas personally offensive to the reader.

From the late 1920s through the 1950s, invective directed at Eliot came much more from men: Max Eastman, Yvor Winters, Malcolm Cowley, Waldo Frank, Stanley Edgar Hyman, Murray Krieger, to name the best known. Certain complaints recur. Eliot is pedantic and purposely mystificatory; he is a fastidious mandarin without sympathy for the lives of ordinary people; his critical precepts are self-contradictory and unsystematic; he is a dictator who has had a deleterious effect on literary taste. Babette Deutsch briefly referred in a review of 1918 to Eliot's "indifference to the strife of nations and classes," and this charge would be reiterated by mostly male critics throughout the 1930s.[36] In a similar vein, Genevieve Taggard and Meridel Le Sueur saw Eliot as misanthropic and pessimistic, an influence detrimental to social meliorism.[37] In general, the commentaries had much more to do with class than with gender. Women's voices were infrequent, and the simplest explanation is one of numbers – there were simply fewer women teaching and writing criticism in the scholarly journals or the literary reviews. Among these few, Eliot had more adherents than detractors.

Rebecca West, however, offers a critique of Eliot's influence that warrants particular attention because of the way she considers gender and authority together. In "What is Mr. T. S. Eliot's Authority as a Critic?," a 1932 review of *Selected Essays*, West admires Eliot's poetry but suspects his criticism of exercising a "pernicious" influence on English letters. Emphasizing Eliot's training at Harvard and his appointment to the Chair of Poetry there, West finds that "he has made his sense of the need for authority and tradition an excuse for refraining from any work likely to establish where authority truly lies, or to hand on tradition by continuing it in vital creation." "He appears," she continues, "unable to distinguish between vices and vigour, the attempts to find new and valid classifications in place of old ones which have proved invalid, and the pressing of the analysis of emotion to a further stage." As a result, he has become lazy, sneering, and repetitious. In the same essay she grants that Irving Babbitt and Paul Elmer More have taught Eliot "certain facts" useful for the practice of criticism, but lampoons them for their fastidiousness, labeling them types who "like to call trousers unmentionables."[38] To summarize bluntly, West depicts Eliot and his teachers as having the temperaments of persnickety old ladies. This view is especially interesting given her response to D. H. Lawrence's article "Goodboy Husbands," where she disputes Lawrence's thesis that female schoolteachers have robbed men of their virility. Lawrence, she feels, has got things backward. It is not the working man taught by female teachers who "seems languid and effete. It is, as a rule, the man who got his education at a preparatory school and a public school from male teachers."[39] For West, the trouble with Eliot and his followers is that, in seeking to maintain the appearance of control and authority, they have forfeited the vitality that first brought Eliot to scholarly and critical attention. In 1932, having just returned from the United States, she reported on the politics of authority at work there: "Any dull young man who could put up a show of scholarship . . . [and] express a hunger for authority and tradition, could claim to be under the leadership of Professors Babbitt and More or Mr. Eliot, and be exalted to a position (academic or other) far above that attainable by any writer who omitted this rite and set to honest work."[40] Ritual veneration of Eliot had become the mark of the ambitious male professional, and the old hierarchies continued unbroken.

After the historic admission of women to colleges and universities, the second most significant event for women in literary studies is, in the estimation of many, the rise of feminist approaches in criticism. Begun amid the general cultural and political upheaval of the 1960s, the methods of feminist criticism were designed to bring attention to people and ideas excluded from the academic mainstream. This essay is not the place to rehearse the history of feminist literary theory, not even if the topic were limited to its academic manifestations. However, it is fair to say that within modernist studies, feminist work has added appreciably to the store of information by unearthing the roles women played in modernism as artists, publishers, editors; reexamining the relationships among men and women who played significant roles in modernism; redefining the contours of literary modernism by focusing attention on previously undervalued texts; revising the conception of modernist style by questioning the tenet that a work must be experimental to be modern. For purposes of comparison, I will concentrate on just two issues especially relevant to readings of T. S. Eliot. These issues concern how we understand tradition and how we understand the impersonal, particularly in the establishing of academic authority. The two are bound together and also imply their opposites – innovation and the personal. Whether tradition is viewed as a key or a padlock depends on who the observer is and where she stands. For professors like Bradbrook or Gardner, the tradition Eliot espoused was the heavy key to the gate of the college; yet it is clear that carrying this weight did not prohibit their seeing themselves as innovators whose presence would ultimately alter the tradition they earned through study. They were in this sense enacting the dynamic Eliot lays out in "Tradition and the Individual Talent," whereby the new revises the old: "the past should be altered by the present as much as the present is directed by the past."[41] For that generation, the expectation was that they were the vanguard of change and that tradition, truly understood, was not at odds with innovation.

But there is another way to look at tradition and that is to question its source and value. It is difficult to take this stance effectively, however, until one is within the gates. Woolf again furnishes an apt metaphor for the dilemma: "I thought how unpleasant it is to be locked out; and I thought how it is worse perhaps to be locked in" (24). Increasingly, as the students became teachers and their students became teachers, women in the academy grew to sufficient numbers so that, while still not in the majority in departments of literature, they were no longer an oddity behind a lectern. Statistics from the US Department of Education, for example, show that in 1910 women received 10 percent of the total number of doctoral degrees awarded; in 1990 they received 40 percent of those degrees and these continued to be clustered in the humanities and education.[42] The demographics of higher education show a campus far more diversely populated in the mid- to late twentieth century than could have been imagined in the mid-nineteenth. Moreover, women rose not just in numbers but in influence, publishing significant scholarship, assuming leadership roles in professional organizations, and in general making a discernible impact on the conduct of literary study. This impact had a great deal to do with the perception of being locked in: the outsiders were now in, but what did they find inside? By the late 1960s, the Eliotic notion of tradition had become associated with a static canon, an overwrought veneration of male writers, and a systematic suppression of difference in artistic expression and critical methods. Tradition, in this guise, was increasingly understood as a barely veiled form of oppression. May Sinclair's 1917 assertion that "Mr. Eliot belongs to no tradition at all" seemed an absurdity given Eliot's sway over academic criticism and teaching.[43] In such an atmosphere, being inside the gate signaled complicity with the most deadening aspect of tradition – endless reproduction of the same systems of hierarchy, including gender hierarchy.

One manifestation of the turn appears in first-wave feminist attention to the treatment of women's bodies in Eliot's poetry. The lines from *Sweeney Agonistes* about doing a girl "in" have been a *leitmotif* of these analyses.

Both psychoanalytic and feminist approaches to literature have found the violent treatment of women a significant, even defining, element of his work. The impulse to assess Eliot's treatment of the body is also linked to a changing ethos about the place of the personal in the academy, one that has continued to affect feminist work on Eliot. Impersonal or disinterested reading is no longer an unquestioned tenet of scholarship; it has become customary for critics to bring personal identity directly into the discourse of criticism. Lyndall Gordon, for instance, cites a 1997 review of an Edinburgh production of *The Cocktail Party*: "'the ending is . . . repugnant, condemning an inconvenient girlfriend to a grisly death.'" Gordon notes that "this reviewer was a woman, and as women's voices grow strong Eliot's 'bullying' is rightly questioned. Bodies are women's creations; we don't want to see them killed or tortured or throttled."[44] Gordon identifies the critic as a woman, emphasizes with "we" that she is a woman, and then links the treatment of the fictional Celia to the treatment of the real Emily Hale. All separations – between the reader and the text, the play and the artist's life – are blurred in a general disapprobation of both text and author.

Was Muriel Bradbrook any less personal in claiming Eliot for her "privileged generation"? Paradoxically, the answer must be "yes." In identifying herself with Eliot, she affirmed a set of values that, in her view and at her historical moment, acted to separate intellectual activity from the particulars of personal identity in an institutional atmosphere where those particulars often posed obstacles to her freedom. It was unfair that she should have had to repress or evade issues of gender, but acknowledging the inequity does not take us far beyond self-righteous outrage. Eliot's insistence on the autonomy of poetry put the focus of criticism on the poem, not the reader, in ways that made "impersonality" a positive attribute. A "continual extinction of the self" in the interest of either art or scholarship seems to many readers of the current generation a far more troubling proposition than it did when Eliot wrote the words in 1919.[45] Maud Ellmann summarizes the implications of disinterestedness in the conclusion of *The Poetics of Impersonality*: "To some extent, critics have used the doctrine of impersonality to rescue modernism from its racism and homophobia: to purify the poems of their authors' politics and hence to insulate aesthetics from history . . . However, the closer one examines the theory of impersonality, the more its ideological objectives reappear; and it becomes impossible to separate its politics from its poetics."[46] The inseparability of politics, poetics, and the personal creates a criticism in which the politics of both text and reader are scrutinized. Whereas enthusiasm for Eliot had once signaled a commitment to the innovative energies of *les jeunes*, contemporary feminist readers of the male modernists must address misogyny directly, if only to move beyond it to more complicated readings of gender-inflected aspects of their work. Colleen Lamos, for example, asserts that "Facing up to the errant female sexual energies within [Eliot's] poems . . . is necessary if we are to continue to read Eliot with something other than hostility or incomprehension."[47]

For those inclined to be hostile, Eliot's corpus of work is as plentiful a source of evidence as it is a treasury for those inclined to be reverential. Increasingly, however, criticism appears to eschew either/or depictions of Eliot. Lamos, for example, finds that "the feminine 'other' that his poems continually abject are interior to their imaginative structure." Her reexamination of Eliot's errant poetic energies depends upon a conception of modernism as having "divergent elements" and "differential, multivalent effects."[48] Bonnie Kime Scott in *Refiguring Modernism* also appears to seek a more comprehensive reading of Eliot: "The subjects of the emotions, the feminine, and the disorder of sexuality recur in Eliot's writing and make him a more confused figure than we found in the gender-blind critical accounts offered through the 1960s, or in more recent accounts that cite only his most violent texts on women."[49]

The temptation to see the trajectory of Eliot's reception as having arrived now at a reasonable and accurate middle ground between adulation and condemnation must be resisted. To begin with, the pattern is suspiciously neat, and density should be favored over neatness in writing literary histories. Narrative form favors the resolution of conflict, but inherent in that resolution is an assumption that present-day interpretation offers a clearer view of matters than was possible in the past. Of course the academic enterprise is founded on the notion that the more we study, the more we learn, yet this model is not always applicable to literary interpretation and, in any case, can lead to an arrogance that wrongly discounts the voices of the past, voices that will eventually include our own.

NOTES

1. An influential example of this shift is Peter Nicholls, *Modernisms: A Literary Guide* (Berkeley: University of California Press, 1995).
2. Virginia Woolf, *A Room of One's Own* (1929; reprint, San Diego: Harcourt Brace, 1989), 6. All further references to Woolf are to this essay in this edition.
3. T. S. Eliot, "Address," in *From Mary to You* (St. Louis: Centennial Issue, December 1959), 134.
4. See my *Learning to Be Modern: Pound, Eliot, and the American University* (Oxford: Clarendon Press, 1993).

5. Rita Felski, *The Gender of Modernity* (Cambridge, Mass.: Harvard University Press, 1995), 8.

6. M. C. Bradbrook, "My Cambridge," in *Women and Literature, 1779–1982*, (Brighton, Sussex: Harvester Press, 1982), 115.

7. For the story of Eliot and the Clark Lectures, see T. S. Eliot, *The Varieties of Metaphysical Poetry*, ed. Ronald Schuchard (San Diego: Harcourt Brace, 1993), 1–31.

8. Quoted by Muriel Bradbrook, "Growing Up with T. S. Eliot," *DLB Yearbook 1988* (Detroit: Gale Research, 1988), 110.

9. Ibid., 112.

10. Sandra M. Gilbert and Susan Gubar, *No Man's Land: The Place of the Woman Writer in the Twentieth Century*, vol. 1: *The War of the Words* (New Haven: Yale University Press, 1988), 235–6.

11. Ibid., 156.

12. See the following editions: *The Waste Land: A Facsimile and Transcript of the Original Draft Including the Annotations of Ezra Pound*, ed. Valerie Eliot (New York: Harcourt Brace Jovanovich, 1971); *The Letters of T. S. Eliot*, vol. 1: *1898–1922*, ed. Valerie Eliot (New York: Harcourt Brace Jovanovich, 1988); *Inventions of the March Hare: Poems 1909–1917*, ed. Christopher Ricks (London: Faber and Faber, 1996). Among significant critical works paying particular attention to gender are Nancy K. Gish, "T. S. Eliot," in *The Gender of Modernism: A Critical Anthology*, ed. Bonnie Kime Scott (Bloomington: Indiana University Press, 1990), 139–54, and Bonnie Kime Scott, "T. S. Eliot: Playing Possum," in *Refiguring Modernism*, vol. 1: *The Women of 1928* (Bloomington: Indiana University Press, 1995), 113–44. Also see Lyndall Gordon, *Eliot's Early Years* (Oxford: Oxford University Press, 1977), *Eliot's New Life* (Oxford: Oxford University Press, 1988), and *T. S. Eliot: An Imperfect Life* (New York: Norton, 1999). The last of these combines and revises the earlier two books.

13. See John Guillory, *Cultural Capital: The Problem of Literary Canon Formation* (Chicago: University of Chicago Press, 1993) and Gerald Graff, *Professing Literature: An Institutional History* (Chicago: University of Chicago Press, 1987).

14. Kenneth Rexroth, "The Poetry of Denise Levertov," in *Denise Levertov: Selected Criticism*, ed. Albert Gelpi (Ann Arbor: University of Michigan Press, 1993), 12–13.

15. Harriet Monroe, "A Contrast," in *The Merrill Studies in* The Waste Land, ed. Bradley Gunter (Columbus, Ohio: Merrill, 1971), 20. The review originally appeared in *Poetry* in 1923. John Lyly is, of course, associated with *euphuism* (artificial and affected style) and not *euphemism*. Elizabethan sailors would likely employ neither, so Monroe's point remains clear.

16. Suzanne Clark, *Sentimental Modernism: Women Writers and the Revolution of the Word* (Bloomington: Indiana University Press, 1991).

17. Andreas Huyssen, *After the Great Divide: Modernism, Mass Culture, Postmodernism (Theories of Representation and Difference)* (Bloomington: Indiana University Press, 1986), 214.

18. Carol Dyhouse, *No Distinction of Sex: Women in British Universities, 1870–1939* (London: UCL Press, 1995), 239–40.

19. Rita McWilliams Tullberg, *Women at Cambridge* (Cambridge: Cambridge University Press, 1998), 178.

20. William Chafe, *The American Woman: Her Changing Social, Economic, and Political Roles, 1920–1970* (New York: Oxford University Press, 1972), 89.

21. Barbara Miller Solomon, *In the Company of Educated Women: A History of Women and Higher Education in America* (New Haven: Yale University Press, 1986), 133, 58.

22. For a discussion of William Empson's work in the context of quantum physics, see Jonathan Bate, *The Genius of Shakespeare* (New York: Oxford University Press, 1998), 313–16.

23. Eliot, *Varieties of Metaphysical Poetry*, ed. Schuchard, 5–6, 13.

24. May Sinclair's 1917 review of *Prufrock and Other Observations* is reprinted in *Gender of Modernism*, ed. Scott, 448–53.

25. Bradbrook, "My Cambridge," 113, 116.

26. Solomon, *In the Company of Educated Women*, 138 (AAUW statistics), 84 (quotation from Thomas).

27. Quoted in Bradbrook, "My Cambridge," 116.

28. Eliot, *Letters of T. S. Eliot*, 74.

29. Ibid., 88.

30. Shari Benstock, *Women of the Left Bank: Paris, 1900–1914* (Austin: University of Texas Press, 1986).

31. The poems include Eliot's "Portrait of a Lady" and Pound's "Portrait d'une Femme." "Lady Pondoeuf" is described in Eliot's "A Brief Treatise on the Criticism of Poetry," *Chapbook* 2 (March 1920): 2. The reference to female "chaos" is from Pound's Canto 29 in *The Cantos* (New York: New Directions, 1986), 144. For the reference to "discharge" see Conrad Aiken, *Ushant* (Boston: Little Brown, 1952), 233.

32. Dyhouse, *No Distinction of Sex*, 162–3.

33. Eliot, *Letters of T. S. Eliot*, 204.

34. Helen Gardner, *The Art of T. S. Eliot* (New York: Dutton, 1950), preface.

35. Elizabeth Drew, *T. S. Eliot: The Design of His Poetry* (New York: Charles Scribner's Sons, 1949).

36. Babette Deutsch, "Another Impressionist," *New Republic* (February 16, 1918): 89.

37. Gilbert and Gubar, *No Man's Land*, vol. 1: *The War of the Words*, 216.

38. Reprinted in *Gender of Modernism*, ed. Scott, 587–92.

39. See *Gender of Modernism*, ed. Scott, 584–7. The letter was sent to *Sunday Dispatch* in 1929, but was never printed.

40. Quoted by George W. Watson, "The Triumph of T. S. Eliot," in *T. S. Eliot: Critical Assessments*, ed. Graham Clarke (London: Christopher Helm, 1990), vol. 1: 358.

41. T. S. Eliot, *Selected Essays* (1932; reprint, New York: Harcourt Brace, 1952), 5.

42. US Department of Education, *Digest of Education Statistics 1998* (Washington: US Government Printing Office, 1998), 195. There was a decline in both doctoral degrees and women faculty members between 1940 and 1960, followed by a recovery in the mid-1960s. For a discussion of both setbacks and progress in women's education during this period, see Catharine R. Stimpson, *Women's Studies in the United States: A Report to the Ford Foundation* (New York: Ford Foundation, 1986), 6–7.

43. *Gender of Modernism*, ed. Scott, 449.

44. Gordon, *An Imperfect Life*, 418.

45. Eliot, *Selected Essays*, 17.

46. Maud Ellman, *The Poetics of Impersonality: T. S. Eliot and Ezra Pound* (Brighton, Sussex: Harvester Press, 1987), 199.

47. Colleen Lamos, *Deviant Modernism: Sexual and Textual Errancy in T. S. Eliot, James Joyce, and Marcel Proust* (Cambridge: Cambridge University Press, 1998), 103.

48. Ibid., 81, 3.

49. Scott, *Refiguring Modernism*, vol. 1: 121.

CHAPTER 9

T. S. Eliot speaks the body: the privileging of female discourse in Murder in the Cathedral and The Cocktail Party

Richard Badenhausen

Many of T. S. Eliot's readers have concluded that his treatment of women in the poetry is generally unsympathetic if not entirely unfair. Joseph Bentley once explained that every time he taught Eliot's work, students would ask why the poet seemed not to like women. Sandra Gilbert and Susan Gubar have suggested that Eliot "responded to the threats posed by women . . . with fantasies of femicide," while M. Teresa Gibert-Maceda points out that when discussing "Eliot's treatment of women . . . most readers just label [him] 'misogynist.'"[1] In light of Prufrock's inability to communicate with the women coming and going around him, the unflattering monologue of the self-absorbed woman in "Portrait of a Lady," Gerontion's fear of History and her "many cunning passages,"[2] and the shrieking epileptic of "Sweeney Erect," those responses make sense.

It is useful to ponder, however, the implications of Marianne DeKoven's comment that such "vicious representations of women have been *allowed* to define Eliot's relationship to the feminine."[3] Actually, Eliot's relationship to the feminine is far more complex than critics usually concede. The poet's attitude toward women alternated at times among fear, disgust, worship, fascination, hostility, attraction, sympathy, and even understanding. In portions of his later work, Eliot's positive representations of the feminine produce some of the strongest characters in all his writing, the Chorus of the Women of Canterbury in *Murder in the Cathedral* (1935) and Celia Coplestone in *The Cocktail Party* (1949). Each ends up serving as a symbolic representation of the benefits of self-transcendence while at the same time playing a fundamental role within the framework of each drama. The Chorus articulates the emotional "underpattern" that rests beneath the drama of Becket's martyrdom,[4] and Celia's personal journey makes the failure of the conventional cocktail-party set that much more pathetic.

But I would like to focus in particular on the language of these plays, for Eliot has crafted a theatrical design that isolates male and female discourses and sets them against each other. This allowed the poet to explore the tensions inherent in "the structure of the binary," which Domna Stanton reminds us is "the dichotomy between such culturally determined oppositions as rationality and emotionality, activity and passivity, presence and absence, in a word, 'male' and 'female.'"[5] In applying this model to a reading of Eliot's plays, I see the Chorus and Celia adopting an experiential language of the body diametrically opposed to the world of logos,[6] a logos articulated by the male characters in *Murder in the Cathedral* and all the characters surrounding Celia in *The Cocktail Party*. These women embrace the kind of semiotic communication, as outlined by Julia Kristeva, that results in an "unsettling process" rather than a reinforcement of logical discourse.[7] But instead of negating this bodily discourse, as might be expected, Eliot's plays actively privilege key components of its power – a celebration of the emotional and physical – over the rational and spiritual, even though the poet has typically been represented as an upholder of the latter tradition. Situating Celia within such a framework allows us to understand her martyrdom not as an example of offensive, gratuitous violence, but as a bodily protest with which Eliot sympathized, given his lifelong attraction to the notion of martyrdom as a signifier of one's moral seriousness and spiritual devotion. My rereading of the drama proposes a major repositioning of Eliot by offering an artist far more interested in writing and privileging an experimental female discourse and doing so in the plays, work that is usually thought to contain his least meaningful poetry. Similarly, it serves as an important corrective to the all-too-frequent casual placement of Eliot within generalized versions of modernism, like Andreas Huyssen's, that seek to locate misogynist impulses at the core of the movement; for the poetry of the plays reveals a writer who has traveled a great distance from the material he generated from 1910 through the 1920s.[8]

I am using the term "female discourse" both literally, to signify the language spoken by women in the plays, and rather broadly, to mark a type of language that transgresses the patriarchal social structure as a way of resisting and finally transcending it. It borrows from, and in fact assimilates, as much as that is possible, Hélène Cixous's notion of an *écriture féminine*, Kristeva's postulation of the "semiotic," and Luce Irigaray's construction of a fluid, "bodily" discourse separate from dominant forms of speech, even though these three writers vary in the degree to which they restrict the writing of such a language to women. My essay suggests Eliot's explorations into writing for female characters can be profitably critiqued and better understood when aligned with French feminist assumptions about language, since the poetry spoken by the Chorus and Celia fits into (to a surprising degree, at times) the models assembled by these writers. Overlaying these theoretical

works onto Eliot's poetry helps dislocate it from traditional modes of interpretation that tend to be the norm in Eliot studies; for, if I may borrow
Carolyn Burke's observation about employing female modernists to better
understand their male counterparts, "we may find that their syntactical and
rhetorical solutions to gender issues suggest to us more flexible, and imaginative ways of reading."[9] While sensitive critical readings of Eliot have
dwelt on the poet's attraction and revulsion toward female "waste" or efflu-
via – most notably, Maud Ellmann's exploration of Kristevean "abjection"
in *The Waste Land* and Wayne Koestenbaum's positing of a homosocial
collaboration between Eliot and Pound over the "hysterical" textual body
of the same poem – I am adopting the rather innovative stance of demonstrating how Eliot's employment of female, bodily language actually calls
into question the strict polarities of male and female.[10] My essay also breaks
new ground by examining the turn toward female discourse in Eliot's later
work.

The valorization of a female language signifies an extreme shift for the
mature Eliot in the middle of his career; early poems such as "Hysteria"
evince a fear of female discourse and its attendant otherness. In that short
1917 prose poem, in which the speaker is literally inhaled by a laughing
female, his anxiety manifests itself specifically as a fear of engulfment.
Eliot's syntax is revealing: the employment of passive voice demonstrates
the lack of control felt by the speaker, while the progression of verbs –
from signifying mere involvement to confusion about one's surroundings
to pain – expresses the increasing alarm of being taken in (literally) by the
feminine. Cixous volunteers a telling explanation of this type of anxiety
when she notes how man "might feel resentment and fear of being 'taken'
by the woman, of being lost in her, absorbed or alone."[11] As a result, the
threatening figure of woman is distanced by Eliot. Stripped of her identity
and shut off from human contact, Eliot's early women are more often
presented obliquely – as "female smells in shuttered rooms" (*CPP*, 25) –
and thus safely, as in this example from "Rhapsody on a Windy Night"
(1917).

It is not until *Murder in the Cathedral* and *The Cocktail Party* that Eliot
creates two versions of a female character who follow Cixous's urge that
woman work toward "*seizing* the occasion to speak" and "forge for herself
the anti-logos weapon."[12] The action of *Murder in the Cathedral* is composed
almost wholly of masculine enterprises, as any 1935 audience might expect
of a drama set in medieval England that turns on political and religious
questions. The plot consists entirely of power plays among various groups
of men. Becket challenges the king's authority by returning to Canterbury

to prepare for his martyrdom; male tempters seek to derail his pilgrimage by dangling images of power before his eyes; the loyal Priests try to shield Becket from danger by offering the sanctuary of the Church; and the murderers carry out their orders with brutal efficiency when they kill the future saint and then justify their action by boldly addressing the live theater audience. The drama sets up an environment dominated almost entirely by logos and positions at its chronological and symbolic center a sermon, the quintessential logocentric text. It is almost redundant to cite Derrida's acknowledgment that "phallocentrism and logocentrism are indissociable," but the key in such environments is that there exists, according to Jonathan Culler, "a transcendental authority and point of reference: truth, reason, the phallus, 'man.'"[13] In such a setting, the male point of view is validated even before it is articulated. The male characters of *Murder in the Cathedral* drive the plot, and the Women of Canterbury (the sole female presence in the drama) avoid its various conflagrations. In their initial ode, the women confess to preferring the safe, tranquil atmosphere of their households and ask explicitly to be left alone. Their first words – those that open the play – stress the passivity of their character: "Here let us stand, close by the cathedral. Here let us wait" (*CPP*, 239). Thus after the first few minutes of the opening scene, the drama has established the conflict between two different groups, two different value-systems, two different discourses.

Since *Murder in the Cathedral* begins by presenting the Chorus within the confines of the rigid hierarchy of twelfth-century England, a system that emphasizes women's status as a subordinate class, audiences are invited initially to minimize the role of the Chorus. Indeed, close to the start of the action the Second Priest encourages that response when he replies to one of the choral odes with a series of sharp dismissals: "You are foolish, immodest and babbling women" and "You go on croaking like frogs in the treetops" (*CPP*, 245). Eliot forces audiences to confront their own prejudices by asking members early on to make a choice between the two groups. In what might be read as an enactment of Cixous's call to "break out of the snare of silence"[14] – after all, their lengthy ode opens the play – the Women of Canterbury have committed the ultimate public transgression of the logocentric world: they have spoken. A reinforcement of the dominant institutional hierarchies would require that they be subsequently chastised.

Yet a funny thing happens on the way to the whipping. Not only are the women not punished, they are allowed by Eliot to speak repeatedly. In fact, the Chorus of *Murder in the Cathedral* becomes the drama's most fully developed "character," a coherent personality that articulates Eliot's "first voice" as defined in his essay "The Three Voices of Poetry."[15] One of the powerful outcomes of Eliot's employment of this personal, intimate voice is that it often expresses itself through the first-person pronoun and helps demonstrate Cixous's point that one way the feminine text can subvert and transcend the controlling masculine discourse is through the personal, through its use of pronouns that create a new language that woman can inhabit.[16] Despite Eliot's uneasiness early in his career with both female discourse and personal poetic utterance, it was female language that most interested him when he first envisioned a play about Becket. For example, textual evidence shows the writer composed a number of choral odes for the Women of Canterbury before any other parts of the play and then built up the subsequent action around the choral poetry. Not only was the Chorus the first part of the play to take shape, according to Eliot's July 1934 letter to Rupert Doone, but in essays like "The Three Voices of Poetry" and "The Aims of Poetic Drama," respectively, Eliot spoke of identifying the Chorus with himself and remarked upon how easy he found writing choral poetry compared to dramatic dialogue.[17] In accord with Irigaray's model, the Chorus's language, which is the most open, elusive, and "fluid," provides the basic structure for the play.[18] That fluidity is actually advanced, as I argue below, by the collective makeup of the choral body. No longer a threat, the group is celebrated for the power that derives from an alliance of individuals. Far from fearing engulfment by the feminine, as illustrated in "Hysteria," by 1935 Eliot is seeking it, embracing it, and even writing it.

Whereas Eliot's earlier nondramatic verse offered the potential belittlement of female speech in mocking rhymes like "In the room the women come and go / Talking of Michelangelo" (*CPP*, 14), the Chorus's lines contain some of the best poetry in the drama, an illustration of Eliot's increasing comfort with female discourse and an implicit endorsement of its role. Notably, although *Murder in the Cathedral* accepts the abovementioned binaries as cultural givens, it also seeks actively to revalue feminine speech in a way that undermines those polarities. Fifteen years after *Murder in the Cathedral*, Eliot argued in "Poetry and Drama" that the Women of Canterbury were "reflecting in their emotion the significance of the action." This foregrounding of the language of emotion as crucial to the understanding of the play represents a profound departure from Eliot's earlier models. Later in that same discussion, when advocating the particular advantages of verse drama over the prose drama of Ibsen and Chekhov, Eliot explains that "dramatic poetry, at its moment of greatest intensity," allows artists to "touch the border of those feelings which only music can express." In another essay, he associates music with a "deeper" level of communication, less rational, less controlled, less complete, but utterly necessary. Eliot does this, not surprisingly, during an examination of the Chorus, which "intensifies the action by projecting its emotional consequences, so that we as the audience see it doubly" because "underneath the action . . . there should be a musical pattern which intensifies our excitement by reinforcing it with feeling from a deeper and less articulate level."[19] Notably, this comment reveals Eliot in the process of working through the dilemma presented by hysterical discourse: a language that is not "masculine" is also not fully comprehensible (not even to its speaker), since it rejects phallogocentric structures such as reason and logic. Although Becket does step in to challenge the Priests' hostile characterization of choral speech – "[t]hey speak better than they know, and beyond your understanding. / They know and do not know, what it is to act or suffer" (*CPP*, 245) – Eliot's own description of how the Chorus functions in the drama rejects the notion that feminine discourse is inaccessible by presenting it as the key to experiencing the play fully. Here, Eliot radically departs from theories of impersonality in the earlier work that reveal a bias against personal emotion. In the plays, while working within the traditional binary alignment of women with emotion, Eliot revalues the discourse that grows out of such culturally determined oppositions by valorizing its meaning. "Feminine" speech becomes the music that ultimately gives the play value as art.

Indeed, Eliot seems to be embracing a "semiotic" language, characterized by Kristeva as a "surge of instinctual drive: a panting, a breathlessness, an acceleration of verbal utterance, concerned not so much with finally reaching a global summing up of the world's meaning, as, to the contrary, with revealing, within the interstices of predication, the rhythm of a drive that remains forever unsatisfied."[20]

The Chorus embodies this instinctual drive, not only in its "breathlessness," but also in its penchant for open-ended discourse and experience. This "open-endedness" serves as the antithesis of the type of closure the drama associates with the male, whether it be through murder (by the Knights) or election to heaven (of Becket), for male speech and action is always tied to specific outcomes. Eliot's male characters are incessantly preoccupied with telos. The Chorus, on the other hand, offers impressionistic visions of its surroundings, for its members are content to wait and to witness. Some of its odes evolve into poetic, almost preverbal, stuttering: "O late late late, late is the time, late too late, and rotten the year; / Evil the wind, and bitter the sea, and grey the sky, grey grey grey" (*CPP*, 243). The lines continue to press forward, not because they are driving to an end, but because they represent immediate responses to experience. As such, the poetry can simply sputter to a halt, as it does here, without reaching a formal end beyond the line break. Contrast Becket's response to a physical threat, as when he faces the Four Tempters and ponders his next move. The result is a rational, controlled, concise, and balanced rhetoric: "Can I neither act nor suffer / Without perdition?" (*CPP*, 255). The Chorus delivers its alternative version of these fears in stark language that places those conceptual ideas in terms of physical, worldly images, as when its members complain: "Thick and heavy the sky. And the earth presses up against our feet," or when they ask: "What is the sickly smell, the vapour? [T]he dark green light from a cloud on a withered tree? The earth is heaving to parturition of issue of hell. What is the sticky dew that forms on the back of my hand?" (*CPP*, 256). The Chorus insistently views and articulates experience through its own body and repeatedly returns to rhetorical devices – like the question – that emphasize open-endedness over closure. In fact, Eliot often pairs the discourses of Thomas and the Chorus to achieve the effect of rhetorical contrast. This pairing occurs when Becket concludes Part I of the drama with a couplet – implying closure, balance, reason – and the Chorus opens Part II with a series of questions about the seasons – signaling open-endedness.

The Chorus's verbal representations of Becket's quest for sainthood are also central to the success of the play as a whole. Through their discourse the women measure and articulate the suffering of Canterbury's martyr, a role that corresponds to the conception of the chorus in Attic drama as reflector of onstage action.[21] Yet this status embodies not the negative, Woolfian version in *A Room of One's Own* of woman as mirror, but a positive model that allows the Chorus to sift through the stage action, interpret it, and finally present, in the communal format of a group, what it takes to be the most meaningful message of the events that make up the drama. In effect, the women become a more fully realized version of Tiresias, whose visions, Eliot claimed in a note, were "the substance" of *The Waste Land* (*CPP*, 78). The language used by the Chorus to describe its situation represents the tenuous female position in medieval England. Full of violent metaphors and images of stasis, paralysis, and dryness, the women's discourse betrays a resignation over their banishment to an environment marked by its lack of fertility. They are doomed to "wander in a land of barren boughs" (*CPP*, 275) or to "wait in barren orchards for another October" (*CPP*, 240). That violent discourse reflects a physical pain that seems quite remote from Becket's more cerebral existence, thus enacting thematically Eliot's separation of the theatrical experience into two levels. The play balances discussions of history, theology, philosophy, and ethics with an emotionally charged poetry of the body expressed by the Women of Canterbury. While the

Archbishop pontificates in dry, dispassionate language "[t]hat the pattern may subsist, for the pattern is the action / And the suffering, that the wheel may turn and still / Be forever still" (*CPP*, 245), the Chorus cries out that "our hearts are torn from us, our brains unskinned like the layers of an onion" (*CPP*, 244) and fears that "a new terror has soiled us, which none can avert . . . flowing in at the ear and the mouth and the eye" (*CPP*, 257). Becket may talk cerebrally about suffering, but it is the Chorus that is living that burden.

In stressing the women's language of physicality versus Becket's discourse of reason, Eliot has created a group of female characters that, in effect, literally speaks the body. We could expect this linguistic dichotomy to be used by Eliot to devalue women along the lines of flesh/spirit hierarchies, or other binary oppositions common since Plato, like emotion/reason, disorder/order, and poetry/prose.[22] But that is not the case here, for that very difference results in the appeal, both to Eliot and to audiences, of the Women of Canterbury. This conflict can be better understood in light of Cixous's observation that woman

has constituted herself necessarily as that "person" capable of losing a part of herself without losing her integrity. But secretly, silently, deep down inside, she grows and multiplies . . . Unlike man, who holds so dearly to his title and his titles, his pouches of value, his cap, crown, and everything connected with his head, woman couldn't care less about the fear of decapitation (or castration), adventuring, without the masculine temerity, into anonymity, which she can merge with, without annihilating herself.[23]

Cixous's reading of female power stresses woman's ability to become stronger through a negation of identity, at least as it is constructed culturally. Eliot highlights a similar anonymity in the Chorus throughout the play: a collective body, its unnamed, identically costumed members move back and forth seamlessly between singular and plural first-person pronouns,[24] from the collective "us" in the lines above, to the singular "ear," "mouth," and "eye" (*CPP*, 257). In Irigaray, the fluidity between the "You" and "I" allows for transcendence: "We – you/I – are neither open nor closed. We never separate simply: *a single word* cannot be pronounced, produced, uttered by our mouths. Between our lips, yours and mine, several voices, several ways of speaking resound endlessly, back and forth. One is never separable from the other. You/I: we are always several at once." This characteristic allows the Chorus of women to approach that state identified by Irigaray as an expression of "multiplicity," which members of the patriarchy do not teach because it threatens "their compartments, their schemas, their distinctions." The goal, instead, is to "shake off the chain of these terms, free ourselves from their categories, rid ourselves of their names," and overthrow accusations like those of the Priests.[25]

Becket, on the other hand, seems to embody fully the "masculine temerity," returning recklessly from exile to a sure death, daring his enemies to strike him down, flaunting his lone identity. The Chorus possesses the characteristic Cixous locates as a paradoxical "propriety," woman's

capacity to depropriate unselfishly, body without end, without appendage, without principal "parts." If she is a whole, it's a whole composed of parts that are wholes, not simple partial objects but *a moving, limitlessly changing ensemble*, a cosmos tirelessly traversed by Eros, an immense astral space not organized around any one sun that's any more of a star than the others.[26]

This passage might be describing the makeup of the Chorus, its ensemble nature highlighted even more starkly by its opposite, Becket, the exile, the singular, "the still point of the turning world" (*CPP*, 173) or "wheel" in this version, an image staged literally as the murderers circle the Archbishop, their swords poised spoke-like toward their target. The collective makeup of the Chorus validates its position aurally, as well, for in speaking together the Women of Canterbury create a powerful wall of sound that will have the most pronounced effect upon the audience and will be what theatergoers remember about the performance. It offers an effective counterpoint to the long-winded Knight-murderers who address the audience one-by-one in prose.

Ironically, some of Eliot's earlier work helped establish conditions that allowed him eventually to embrace the Chorus (and Celia), for in that poetry Eliot associates legitimate martyrdom with violence. In a series of poems about sainthood and martyrdom written in 1914–15, for example, Eliot's fascination with the subject matter tended usually to focus, as Lyndall Gordon observes, upon the "savage joy in pain." In a 1914 letter to Conrad Aiken, Eliot refers to one of those treatments, "The Love Song of St. Sebastian," a monologue consisting of two dramatic scenes in which the primary motivation seems a revulsion of the physical resulting in various mistreatments of the body via the wearing of a hair shirt, flogging of the self, and ultimately murder of a lover.[27] In his letter, Eliot makes the overt connection between the speaker of the poem, who wants to ensure permanently his lover's devotion by freezing the moment through murder and keeping the corpse at his side, and artists who try to fix the beauty of youthful spirituality on the canvas. The violence, toward the bodily self and in the form of murder, is attractive and erotic. In both cases, like the arrows piercing the body, the speakers metaphorically capture the objects of devotion, albeit in different media. The gruesomeness of the Women of Canterbury's bodily discourse, then, serves to authenticate their role by, in effect, verifying its members as sacrificial victims and martyrs. This quality permitted Eliot to identify with their cause. The violence that surrounds the women operates not as a manifestation of Eliot's misogyny, but as a validation of the earnestness of their journey.

Not until twenty years later would he explore the linkage between the spiritual and the feminine in the creation of the Chorus, whose members do not imagine an erotic union in tentative conditional terms, but describe vividly in active verbs a kind of violent ecstasy. To the Archbishop they confess to being "torn away, subdued, violated, / United to the spiritual flesh of nature, / Mastered by the animal powers of spirit" (CPP, 270–1). They are also "dominated by the lust of self-demolition, / By the final utter uttermost death of spirit, / By the final ecstasy of waste and shame" (CPP, 271). In speaking the body, the Women of Canterbury's references to "flesh," "animal," "lust," "ecstasy," and being "torn" insist on maintaining a bodily language even when characterizing the spirit. The rape imagery highlights the women's subjugation to a patriarchal system that seeks to "master" and "dominate" even as their charged imagery concurrently emphasizes the Chorus's resistance to it. The Archbishop tries to calm and control the women by offering them an alternative vision to a discourse marked by "overflow," "tumult," "waves," "floods."[28] He does so, however, in a logocentric text that attempts to contain their ecstatic vision in the methodical, controlled, teleological framework that is his hallmark: "This is your share of the eternal burden, / The perpetual glory." Although "[t]his is one moment," he continues, "know that another / Shall pierce you with a sudden painful joy / When the figure of God's purpose is made complete" (CPP, 271). Such painfully static language only serves to highlight the dramatic power of the choral verse that precedes it.[29]

Despite the Priests' earlier attempts to minimize the presence of the Chorus because they see the women as inconsequential peasants with little knowledge of the intricate workings of the Church, it is the Chorus's very engagement with the physical world that gives their words so much weight in the audience's eyes as well as in Becket's. The women's experiential language anticipates Cixous's claims that the "flesh speaks true" and woman "physically materializes what she's thinking; she signifies it with her body."[30] The Chorus processes and understands the world through bodily sensation and seasonal cycles: "Winter shall come bringing death from the sea," worry the women. After the passing of that season, they fear that "[r]uinous spring shall beat at our doors, / Root and shoot shall eat our eyes and our ears, / Disastrous summer burn up the beds of our streams." All they have to look forward to at the conclusion of the destructive sequence is "another decaying October" (*CPP*, 240). This signification occurs to such a degree that at times the Women of Canterbury merge with the landscape that surrounds and threatens them: "I have tasted / The living lobster, the crab, the oyster, the whelk and the prawn; and they live and spawn in my bowels, and my bowels dissolve in the light of dawn" (*CPP*, 270). The startling final image, with its evaporation of boundaries between the body and the physical world, is reminiscent of the dematerialization of the self at the end of Whitman's *Song of Myself*.[31] In both cases, identity vanishes as a means to transcendent expansion. Speech characterizing such moments is never "linear or 'objectified,'" according to Cixous. Thus the Chorus's lines are the least controlled of the play, the least reined in, the most syntactically complex and oblique, and the longest.[32] It is this very nonlinearity that the Priests attack.

In the Christian universe of *Murder in the Cathedral* and in Eliot's post-conversion mind, suffering can be understood as a positive trait. The physical pain of the Chorus substantiates its mission and elevates its role as a Christian model for other characters, for readers, and for Eliot. In a book on witnessing called *Testimony*, Shoshana Felman points out that legitimate witnessing is validated only through the physical: the experience "requires one to live through one's own death, and paradoxically, bear witness to that living through one's dying."[33] The Chorus's seeing privileges its knowing. So when the women begin their final ode before Becket's sermon by explaining that they "know of oppression and torture," and they "know of extortion and violence, / Destitution, disease, / The old without fire in winter" (*CPP*, 257), we are meant to understand that, in Eliot's world, such suffering certifies their point of view as meaningful, authentic, and compelling. This contextualization helps broaden readings by feminist critics such as Sandra Gilbert and Susan Gubar that perceive female physical suffering solely in negative terms. Laura Severin's discussion of *The Cocktail Party*'s misogynist social agenda, for example, observes that "Celia, the story's Circe, is the most dangerous threat and therefore receives [from Eliot] the most violent sentence . . . Not only is she killed, but her story of martyrdom is erased . . . Alex, who possesses her story, tells only the barest of details."[34] Indeed, textual evidence reveals that Eliot had intended to share more of those details, with references to decomposing flesh and the body's juices, but early audiences found the graphic language too distasteful, and Eliot was persuaded by his director, Martin Browne, to tone down the account.[35] As in "The Love Song of St. Sebastian," violence here serves not as a punishment, but as a vehicle allowing Eliot to identify with and ultimately sympathize with its victim. Celia, like the Chorus, is the character on whom Eliot pinned his hopes and fears. Rather than feeling threatened by Celia's tragic story, Eliot embraces it.

Like *Murder in the Cathedral*, a play dominated by polarities, *The Cocktail Party* focuses upon contrasts, options, and opportunities. That play sets Celia Coplestone's choice of an ascetic life among nuns in a British colony against the stagnant marriage of Lavinia and Edward Chamberlayne, and finally exalts her death as a martyr crucified near an ant-hill over shallow, modern-day representations of love. Furthering the symbolism is Celia's earlier abandonment of an affair with the married Edward and a failure to pursue a more conventional relationship with the single Peter Quilpe. The lengthy plot of *The Cocktail Party* introduces various well-to-do society types enjoying a party at the Chamberlaynes' London flat, traces the collapse of their own marriage and eventual reconciliation, and ends where it began, with the couple once again preparing to entertain guests. Although the (temporary) repairing of their marriage might seem a triumph for Edward and Lavinia – the reconciliation ironically evokes the classic happy ending of traditional comedy – all they have really done is assent tacitly to return as a superficial couple to the frivolous world of the cocktail party, a place where guests continually retell stories "about Lady Klootz and the wedding cake" and "how the butler found her in the pantry, rinsing her mouth out with champagne" (*CPP*, 353). Indeed, this is a marriage in which after five years the husband is not sure he would be able to describe his wife accurately for a missing person's report (*CPP*, 364).

Celia is at first intrigued and even excited by this climate. She acts on that attraction by having an affair with Edward, and her first line encourages the telling of a familiar party tale. Yet Celia recognizes slowly that the environment in which she operates is "humiliating" (*CPP*, 379). Although Celia has difficulty locating the cause of that feeling and stumbles in search of words to articulate her predicament, she alone among all her friends senses that her world lacks substance. The metaphor of the cocktail party, which frames and thus controls the stage action, is a world of logos and telos, a world marked by linear anecdotes that climax in punch lines and by social conventions requiring participants to follow prescribed modes of talking, thinking, and acting. Like drama itself, the cocktail party consists of carefully orchestrated roles and scripted discourse, of entrances and exits, beginnings and ends. As such, it follows Kristeva's model of "a culture where the speaking subjects are conceived of as masters of their speech, they have what is called a 'phallic' position."[36] This model unfolds at the very opening of *The Cocktail Party*, with the magisterially named Alexander MacColgie Gibbs firmly in control, mastering the particular discourse that greets the audience with the opening of the curtain: "You've missed the point completely, Julia: / There *were* no tigers. *That* was the point," explains Alex. "Then what were you doing, up in a tree," asks Julia, "You and the Maharaja?" Then, in reply to Peter's suggestion that he clear up the confusion by recounting the story again, Alex confidently declares, "I never tell the same story twice" (*CPP*, 353). Such an environment publicly glorifies discourse that is linear, a linearity that in this case ends up literally at a fixed "point." Participants move from point A to point B, with each level of understanding predicated on the previous stage. In the case of Alex, he flaunts his authoritative position by first relating his anecdote and subsequently withholding its retelling from one confused auditor.

Like the Women of Canterbury, Celia attacks this logical/rational system by constructing her own version of speaking the body, a discourse marked by conditionals, pauses, and silences. As Kristeva notes, such "fragmentation of language in a text calls into question the very posture of this mastery."[37] Elsewhere, Kristeva points out how semiotic communication – a "poetic language" – can "in its most disruptive form" show "the constraints of a civilization dominated by transcendental rationality."[38] Such moments occur most often when Celia sets herself against the ultra-rational cocktail-party environment and ends up deeply questioning her standing in that world. At those instants, Celia realizes that accepting the "good life" where everyone remains comfortable with the "common routine" might not satisfy internal longings for spiritual and self-fulfillment: "I know I ought to be able to accept" it, she explains to Sir Henry Harcourt-Reilly, "[i]f I might still have it. Yet it leaves me cold. / Perhaps that's just a part of my illness, / But I feel it would be a kind of surrender." Upon further consideration, she decides, "no, not a surrender – more like a betrayal. / You see, I think I really had a vision of something / Though I don't know what it is. I don't want to forget it." This vision helps her decide that she "could do without everything, / Put up with anything," if she were just able to "cherish" it. "In fact," she continues, "I think it would really be dishonest / For me, now, to try to make a life with *any*body! / I couldn't give anyone the kind of love" that is part of the common, everyday world. At the end of this speech, she finally declares: "Oh, I'm afraid this sounds like raving! / Or just cantankerousness . . . still, / If there's no other way . . . then I feel just hopeless" (*CPP*, 418: ellipses in original). Like that of the Chorus, Celia's language threatens to collapse upon itself during these moments of intense awareness. Marked by sudden reversals, sentences broken off abruptly, and elliptical pauses that embrace silence rather than fear it, the speech struggles to contain the sentiments expressed by its speaker. Celia seems at this point almost paralyzed by her own discourse, by the abundance of conditionals, qualifications, and halting conclusions. Her struggle to articulate the meaning of her existence is as messy and bumpy as the cocktail-party prattle is clean and smooth. But that is, in effect, the point; for in scrutinizing the self and acting upon what she finds, Celia has forever divorced herself from the static group. Cixous's "The Laugh of the Medusa" argues that because the structure of language validates men and diminishes women, the goal must then be to collapse that oppressive linguistic system from within and to invent a new language for women to inhabit: not to manipulate language to serve some larger end, but to operate within its possibilities. This is the very situation in which Celia finds herself. She enacts Cixous's call to speak through the body by "invent[ing] the impregnable language that will wreck partitions, classes, and rhetorics, regulations and codes," the effect of which is to "get beyond the ultimate reserve-discourse, including the one that laughs at the very idea of pronouncing the word 'silence.'"[39] Celia makes real Cixous's dream of "perform[ing] the gesture that jams sociality" and "punctur[ing] the system of couples and opposition."[40] I agree with Severin that Celia is a "threat," but not to Eliot; instead, her disruptive discourse acts as a positive counterpoint to the dominant model established at the start of the drama.

Celia, alone of the characters in *The Cocktail Party*, speaks a language that possesses semiotic meaning. Conditioned by cultural models that reject discourse that does not seem comprehensible on its surface, Celia believes that Reilly might dismiss her words as "raving." Also, she does not have the luxury of a collective choral body, the authority that comes with the communal and that consequently allows the Women of Canterbury to embrace a "nonsense" discourse that threatens signification, as when they exclaim, "[t]he forms take shape in the dark air: / Puss-purr of leopard, footfall of padding bear" and "[p]alm-pat of nodding ape, square hyaena waiting / For laughter, laughter, laughter" (*CPP*, 257). Celia lives under the threat of institutional condemnation of the types offered by Canterbury's Priests, who dismiss such discourse as "babbling" (*CPP*, 245). Her transgressions are limited by her solitary circumstances and thus take the form of having an affair with a married man, refusing to participate in linear discourse, and, finally, actively establishing conditions that lead to her martyrdom. When set within Kristeva's model, Celia also represents the inherent dangers of the semiotic, a language whose instability can lead to self-annihilation of the type catalogued at the conclusion of "About Chinese Women." Although not an actual suicide, Celia's death does suggest that she shares a certain complicity in her own destruction, of the type that all martyrs must confront when faced with the notion that halting their transgressive behavior will often assure their (physical) survival.

While we repeatedly see and hear the plight of the Chorus in *Murder in the Cathedral*, Celia's struggle occurs much more obliquely and subtly. Eliot had abandoned the choral device by his third play, so Celia's subversions necessarily take place in a quieter and much less public fashion. Even Celia's martyrdom occurs offstage (she makes no appearance in the third act) and its particulars are delivered verbally amongst the social trappings she had previously fled. Alex relays the details of Celia's death to the other guests, and it is a story that will no doubt recirculate through the party circuit for many years to come, despite his early pronouncement forbidding the retelling of tales. By making her death known in this way, Eliot further separates Celia from the Prufrockian world of tea and polite chatter. This separation in effect signals and endorses her escape, for the play concludes by accenting both the decaying marriage of Edward and Lavinia and the vacuous cocktail-party environment they inhabit as failures. Thus while the power of the Women of Canterbury hinges on the verbalization of their discourse, it is Celia's very lack of words at the end of the play that signifies her transcendence above and beyond the phallogocentric atmosphere of the cocktail party. Of all the characters, only Celia feels the need to explore the self and discover a role more fulfilling than wife, lover, or good conversationalist, occupations that depend on another person for validation. Only she is able to "invite the unexpected, release a new force, / Or let the genie out of the bottle" and "start a train of events / Beyond . . . [her] control" (*CPP*, 361), a plan of action Reilly unsuccessfully attempts to inflict upon Edward. Thus condemnations of Celia's inability to speak her story in the third act get it backwards – this verifies her success. Her silence, or in Cixous's terms "aphonic revolt,"[41] (and eventual physical absence) amidst the pointless banter acts as a foil and thus provides dignity to her quest in the way that witnessing validated the Women of Canterbury. It is akin to Susan Gubar's association of the "Blank Page" and female creativity, whereby "blankness" can serve as "an act of defiance, a dangerous and risky refusal to certify purity."[42] Only Celia willingly tries to make sense of these feelings "of emptiness, of failure / Towards someone, or something, outside of myself; / And I feel I must . . . *atone* – is that the word?" (*CPP*, 416: ellipsis in original). Significantly, at this turning point in the drama,

Celia struggles for the appropriate language to describe her condition, for she has cast off the insecurities that previously controlled her actions in the environment of the cocktail party, where casual banter functioned as a kind of substitute religion. This revolutionary discourse rejects the privileging of the phallic position by flaunting its nonlinearity, and its incessant proximity to syntactical collapse.

Edward and Lavinia are the perfect symbols of stasis. We find the couple at the end of the play evading the problems of their troubled marriage and looking forward to yet another evening of inane talk. Celia, on the other hand, experiences significant growth during the course of *The Cocktail Party*. In contrast to the clever rhetorical evasions of all the other characters, Celia eventually articulates a harsh reading of her companions. She terminates her affair with Edward because she realizes he is "only a beetle the size of a man" (*CPP*, 382). In many respects, Celia's ability to separate herself from those worldly companions endows her with a certain strength necessary for achieving martyrdom, itself a privileged position in Eliot's oeuvre for male and female characters.[43] When Celia finally verbalizes her discomfort with the culture she has inhabited, she locates its *discourse* as the fundamental flaw that reveals its uselessness, despite the fact that many other characters romanticize this element. Celia confesses this new understanding to Reilly, when she notices her solitude for the first time: "I mean that what has happened has made me aware / That I've always been alone. That one always is alone." Yet this isolation extends not only to her relationship with lovers but to her "relationship / With *everybody*. Do you know – / It no longer seems worth while to *speak* to anyone!" Here, Celia calls into question the very mode of communication of characters like Edward and Lavinia, and she concludes her outburst with a stinging critique of their verbal method: "They make noises, and think they are talking to each other; / They make faces, and think they understand each other. / And I'm sure that they don't. Is that a delusion?" (*CPP*, 414). Even though this moment of revelation signals a new awareness for Celia, her language continues to turn against itself, contradict itself, and pull back from closure each time it appears on the horizon. As with the Chorus, seeing and acting are intimately connected for Celia; as the one true "witness" in *The Cocktail Party*, she recognizes that activities like a cocktail party only offer the illusion of action and personal growth. Unlike the stagnant characters around her, Celia alone will challenge "the common routine" (*CPP*, 417). She is the only passionate, emotional character, a disruption in the face of the Chamberlaynes' frigid marriage. Whereas the Chorus achieves a kind of Cixousian transcendence through the anonymity provided by the group,

Celia "adventures" forward by embracing silence specifically because the drama highlights public, verbal communication as the culturally privileged action. Again, Eliot is attacking the very foundation of such polarities by embracing the element typically situated by cultural norms in the inferior position.

The drama finally approves Celia's choice of martyrdom – and the poetic language employed on her way to that martyrdom – because she has chosen the opposite path from the Chamberlaynes. After acknowledging that Celia "will go far," Reilly contrasts her choice with that of Edward and Lavinia, who will return at the end of the play to "[t]he stale thoughts mouldering in their minds. / Each unable to disguise his own meanness / From himself, because it is known to the other" (*CPP*, 420). The play circles back to where it began, a geometrical demonstration of linearity, unity, and reconciliation. Yet these qualities have been entirely subverted by this point – through Celia's revolt – so that the closing of the curtain on this symbol of marriage highlights the deficiencies of a culture that endorses it as a fit model and projects a grotesque hollowness, as the specter of Celia hovers above that couple. The great irony of the drama is that Celia's heroic silence allows her, alone among the characters, to act. For the Chamberlaynes, numb to their surroundings and their own inner thoughts, life becomes a series of evasions designed to avoid self-examination and intimate communication. As Eliot pointed out in an early essay for the *Athenæum*, "most people are too unconscious of their own suffering to suffer much."[44] Celia, on the other hand, like the Chorus before her, recognizes that the way to growth and redemption leads through the pain of self-recognition that results from any authentic witnessing ("martyr" means witness in Greek). Although some might want to read Celia's crucifixion as just another Eliotic femicide sanctioned by the trappings of Christian martyrdom, within the model I have drawn that privileges absence, lack, and silence, Celia, despite her tragic end, is the only "successful" character. As Margaret Higgonet writes of the act of self-destruction: "Some choose to die in order to shape their lives as whole." Such a choice "force[s] others to read one's death," or, in the case of *The Cocktail Party*, forces others to talk about it.[45] Instead, Celia's absence at the end of *The Cocktail Party* operates as a foil to highlight the shallowness of those characters left on stage, wasting away in their presence. Although many critics have read Eliot's work with drawing-room, comedic verse dramas as rather stale, traditional exercises, my positing of a semiotic language in these early plays proposes a far more subversive text that extends Eliot's experimental tendencies in the early poetry, just in drastically different, and sometimes more humane, ways.

NOTES

1. Joseph Bentley, "Some Notes on Eliot's Gallery of Women," in *Approaches to Teaching Eliot's Poetry and Plays*, ed. Jewel Spears Brooker (New York: Modern Language Association, 1988), 39; Sandra M. Gilbert and Susan Gubar, *No Man's Land: The Place of the Woman Writer in the Twentieth Century*, vol. 1: *The War of the Words* (New Haven: Yale University Press, 1988), 37; and M. Teresa Gibert-Maceda, "T. S. Eliot on Women; Women on T. S. Eliot," in *T. S. Eliot at the Turn of the Century*, ed. Marianne Thormählen (Lund, Sweden: Lund University Press, 1994), 105.

2. T. S. Eliot, *The Complete Poems and Plays* (London: Faber and Faber, 1969), 38; hereafter referred to as *CPP*.

3. Emphasis added. Marianne DeKoven, *Rich and Strange: Gender, History, Modernism* (Princeton: Princeton University Press, 1991), 192.

4. Eliot tended to view drama structurally in terms of two "levels," which allowed audiences to approach drama either intellectually or emotionally. See, for example, T. S. Eliot, "John Marston" (in *Selected Essays* [London: Faber and Faber, 1934] and *Poetry and Drama* [London: Faber and Faber, 1951]).

5. Domna C. Stanton, "Language and Revolution: The Franco-American Dis-Connection," in *The Future of Difference*, ed. Hester Eisenstein and Alice Jardine (New Brunswick, N. J.: Rutgers University Press, 1990), 73.

6. It is useful to recall the Greek origin of this word, which equates "word" or "speech" with "reason."

7. Julia Kristeva, "From One Identity to an Other," in *Desire in Language: A Semiotic Approach to Literature and Art*, ed. Leon Roudiez, trans. Thomas Gora, Alice Jardine, and Roudiez (New York: Columbia University Press, 1980), 125.

8. Andreas Huyssen, *After the Great Divide: Modernism, Mass Culture, Postmodernism (Theories of Representation and Difference)* (Bloomington: Indiana University Press, 1986).

9. Carolyn Burke, "Getting Spliced: Modernism and Sexual Difference," *American Quarterly* 39 (1987): 99.

10. Maud Ellmann, *The Poetics of Impersonality: T. S. Eliot and Ezra Pound* (Cambridge, Mass.: Harvard University Press, 1987), 94–5; Wayne Koestenbaum, *Double Talk: The Erotics of Male Literary Collaboration* (New York: Routledge, 1989), chapter 4.

11. Hélène Cixous, "The Laugh of the Medusa," in *New French Feminisms: An Anthology*, ed. Elaine Marks and Isabelle de Courtivron (Amherst: University of Massachusetts Press, 1980), 247 n. 1.

12. Ibid., 250.

13. Jacques Derrida, "'This Strange Institution Called Literature': An Interview with Jacques Derrida," in *Acts of Literature*, ed. Derek Attridge (New York: Routledge, 1992), 59; Jonathan Culler, *On Deconstruction: Theory and Criticism after Structuralism* (Ithaca, N. Y.: Cornell University Press, 1982), 172.

14. Cixous, "The Laugh of the Medusa," 251.

15. For a discussion of the Chorus as a single expressive voice, see Richard Baden-hausen, "'When the Poet Speaks Only for Himself': The Chorus as 'First Voice' in *Murder in the Cathedral*," in *T. S. Eliot: Man and Poet*, ed. Laura Cowan (Orono, Maine: National Poetry Foundation, 1990), 239–52.

16. In "The Laugh of the Medusa," Cixous writes of woman that "once she blazes *her* trail in the symbolic, she cannot fail to make of it the chaosmos of the 'personal' – in her pronouns, her nouns, and her clique of referents" (258).

17. E. Martin Browne traces Eliot's early conception and writing of the choral passages and prints Eliot's letter to Doone (Browne, *The Making of T. S. Eliot's Plays* [Cambridge: Cambridge University Press, 1969], 39–55). T. S. Eliot, "The Three Voices of Poetry," in *On Poetry and Poets* (London: Faber and Faber, 1957), 91; T. S. Eliot, "The Aims of Poetic Drama," *Adam: International Review* 200 (November 1949): 11.

18. See Luce Irigaray's chapter on "The 'Mechanics' of Fluids" (106–18), particularly 111–12, in *This Sex Which Is Not One*, trans. Catherine Porter with Carolyn Burke (Ithaca, N. Y.: Cornell University Press, 1985). For a useful summary and contextualization of Irigaray, to which I am indebted, see Temma Berg, "Suppressing the Language of Wo(Man): The Dream as a Common Language," in *Engendering the Word: Feminist Essays in Psychosexual Poetics*, ed. Berg (Urbana: University of Illinois Press, 1989), 8–9, 25 n. 4. John J. Winkler discusses the chorus in early Greek drama as the thematic and structural center of the action. Winkler, "The Ephebes' Song," in *Nothing to Do with Dionysos?: Athenian Drama in Its Social Context*, ed. Winkler and Froma I. Zeitlin (Princeton: Princeton University Press, 1990), 20–62.

19. T. S. Eliot, "Poetry and Drama," in *On Poetry and Poets*, 81, 87; T. S. Eliot, "The Need for Poetic Drama," *Listener* (November 25, 1936): 995, 994.

20. Kristeva, "From One Identity to an Other," 142.

21. Oddone Longo cites as the "essence of the chorus" in Greek drama "its role as 'representatives of the collective citizen body.'" Longo, "The Theater of the Polis," in *Nothing to Do with Dionysos?*, ed. Winkler and Zeitlin, 17.

22. The famous attack on poetry in Book X of *The Republic* is perhaps the best early example of this. It delineates reason, civic order, and prose as male.

23. Cixous, "The Laugh of the Medusa," 259.

24. See, for instance, as one of many examples, the choral ode that accompanies Becket's murder: "The land is foul, the water is foul, our beasts and ourselves defiled with blood. / A rain of blood has blinded my eyes" (*CPP*, 275).

25. Irigaray, *This Sex Which Is Not One*, 209, 210, 212.

26. Emphasis added. Cixous, "The Laugh of the Medusa," 259.

27. Lyndall Gordon, *Eliot's Early Years* (New York: Farrar Straus Giroux, 1977), 59; T. S. Eliot, *The Letters of T. S. Eliot*, ed. Valerie Eliot (San Diego: Harcourt Brace Jovanovich, 1988), vol. 1: 43–7. "The Love Song of St. Sebastian" is published in *Inventions of the March Hare: Poems 1909–1917*, ed. Christopher Ricks (New York: Harcourt Brace, 1996), 78.

28. Cixous, "The Laugh of the Medusa," 246.

29. I see far more tension between Becket and the Chorus than Michael Beehler, whose exploration of lines like those in the previously cited passage expresses his primary concern with investigating how *Murder in the Cathedral* resolves the difference between temporal and sacramental notions of time and history; Becket's death results, he argues, in "an ahistorical reality beyond interpretation." Beehler, *T. S. Eliot, Wallace Stevens, and the Discourses of Difference* (Baton Rouge: Louisiana State University Press, 1987), 101.

30. Cixous, "The Laugh of the Medusa," 251.

31. On Eliot's complicated attitude toward Whitman, see Richard Badenhausen, "In Search of 'Native Moments': T. S. Eliot (Re)Reads Walt Whitman," *South Atlantic Review* 57, no. 4 (1992): 77–91.

32. Cixous, "The Laugh of the Medusa," 251. Cixous also locates the "sweeping away [of] syntax" as that which will allow women to "go right up to the impossible" (256).

33. In Shoshana Felman and Dori Laub, *Testimony: Crises of Witnessing in Literature, Psychoanalysis, and History* (New York: Routledge, 1992), 109.

34. Laura Severin, "Cutting Philomela's Tongue: *The Cocktail Party*'s Cure for a Disorderly World," *Modern Drama* 36 (1993): 403–4.

35. Browne, *The Making of T. S. Eliot's Plays*, 226.

36. Julia Kristeva, ["Oscillation between Power and Denial"], interview by Xavière Gauthier, trans. Marilyn A. August, in *New French Feminisms*, ed. Marks and de Courtivron, 165.

37. Ibid.

38. Kristeva, "From One Identity to an Other," 140.

39. Cixous, "The Laugh of the Medusa," 256.

40. Ibid., 258.

41. Ibid., 256.

42. Susan Gubar, "'The Blank Page' and the Issues of Female Creativity," *Critical Inquiry* 8 (1981): 259.

43. Rudolph M. Bell argues that as many as half of the women designated saints by the Roman Catholic Church from the thirteenth century up to today exhibited signs of anorexia. He asserts that self-starvation, *like martyrdom*, became one of the few ways for woman to assert the self in the face of dominance by patriarchal social structures, even though "victory leads to self-destruction." Bell, *Holy Anorexia* (Chicago: University of Chicago Press, 1985), 56.

44. T. S. Eliot, "Beyle and Balzac," *Athenæum* (May 30, 1919): 392.

45. Margaret Higonnet, "Speaking Silences: Women's Suicide," in *The Female Body in Western Culture*, ed. Susan Rubin Suleiman (Cambridge, Mass.: Harvard University Press, 1986), 69, 68.

CHAPTER 10

T. S. Eliot, women, and democracy

Rachel Potter

This chapter explores two points of literary departure. First there are women, whose voices echo vacuously through domestic interiors and whose bodies straddle men and give promise "of pneumatic bliss," women who consolidate ideas of male subjectivity in modernist writing.[1] Second there is the debate between a politicized romanticism, which "made the revolution" and is linked to ideas of liberty, humanism, progress, democracy, and liberalism, and the new classicism in the arts, characterized alternatively by a reactionary politics of authority and discipline.[2] Although both departures are crucial for Anglo-American modernist writing and for Eliot's work, they have only rarely been brought into dialogue with each other. However, Eliot's depiction of women as a shifting vehicle for his evolving political critique, initially of an individualistic liberal humanism, and later of mass democracy, recurs throughout his poetry and criticism.

A number of important discussions have addressed Eliot's poetic representation of women, including Albert Gelpi's detailed analysis of the way that "fear of women as the stimulants of an enslaving, defiling sexual passion is obsessive" in Eliot's early poems, Carol Christ's discussion of gender and voice in his early poems, and Lyndall Gordon's biographical analyses of Eliot's poems in relation to the women in his life.[3] Michael Levenson, Jeffrey Perl, Michael North, and Kenneth Asher have discussed the importance of romanticism, classicism, liberalism, and democracy for modernist aesthetics.[4] Yet these accounts have ignored the relation of modernist aesthetics to one of the key aspects of the shift toward democracy in the period: the political and cultural position of women in British and American society. Michael Tratner, in *Modernism and Mass Politics: Joyce, Woolf, Eliot, Yeats*, does discuss the relationship between Eliot's politics and his representation of women. Focusing particularly on the way that the crowd is figured as "feminine" in *The Waste Land*, Tratner's analysis of Eliot's poetry forms part of a wider discussion of the modernist response to the "transformations of English, European, and American politics that occurred in the early

twentieth century," and specifically "the shift from individualism (or liberalism) to collectivism." He examines Eliot's poetry in relation to what he
calls the "modern" premise "that individuals cannot control their own lives"
and the attendant belief that "vast collective entities such as classes, genders,
and nationalities shape the individual mind." Tratner thus focuses primarily on the connections between Eliot's women and mass politics, exploring
how "women are involved in mysterious ways in the emergence of anarchic
mobs."[5] In this chapter I argue that Eliot consistently employed women as
signifiers of the contemporary political moment, a contemporaneity which
by turns encompassed "liberal" individualism, and, later, notions of mass
democracy.

Before turning to Eliot's shifting configurations of women and democracy, it would be useful to outline the debates surrounding definitions of liberal democracy in the rapidly changing social, political, and literary climate
of the early twentieth century. It has become a commonplace to argue, like
Tratner, that nineteenth-century individualist liberalism was supplanted by
a new kind of collective politics in the early twentieth century. As John Gray
puts it, "The decline of the classical system of liberal thought coincided
with, and was in very significant measure occasioned by, the arrival of a
mass democracy in which the constitutional order of the free society soon
came to be alterable by the processes of political competition." While the
Reform Bill of 1918, which gave the vote to all men and to women over thirty,
changed the constitutional order of politics in Britain, Gray argues, by 1914
the notion of liberal government as "the guardian of the framework within
which individuals may provide for themselves" gave way to a "conception of
government as the provider of general welfare."[6] Indeed, debates about the
relationship between liberal individualism and collectivism had been a key
feature of late nineteenth-century politics. Many liberal theorists argued
that basic liberal beliefs such as the "moral primacy of the individual person against the claims of any social collectivity" might be destroyed, rather
than furthered, by the political mechanisms of mass democracy. In the
early decades of the twentieth century such debates became more acute.
In 1911, L. T. Hobhouse, one of the most influential and perceptive political theorists of the period, argued that liberalism was in crisis. Could a
liberalism based on the desire to free the individual from the institutional
shackles of Church and State, he asked, meet the new political demands of
twentieth-century mass politics, most importantly, the needs of the newly
powerful working classes? Liberalism needed to become what he called a
"constructive" political ideology to compete with the communitarian ideals
of the emerging Labour Party.[7] Moreover, it needed to deal with gender;

the impact of women's enfranchisement on liberal beliefs was an important feature of prewar political debates. Andrew Chadwick asserts that, in the prewar period, the suffragettes' claims that the Liberal Party had reneged on its commitment to women's enfranchisement destroyed "the 'natural link' between liberalism and its institutional base in the Liberal Party and government."[8]

If Hobhouse believed that liberalism was being undermined by the very economic and democratic forces it had created, in Britain, World War I radically altered the relationship between the individual and the State. Such pieces of legislation as repressive policies on freedom of information undermined basic liberal values and were not revoked once the war ended. Despite the enfranchisement of all individuals, then, the State's authority over the individual had been significantly and permanently extended. In the 1920s, the example of authoritarian mass politics in Italy and of Communism in Russia caused debates about liberalism and democracy to shift ground, suggesting that liberal ideals might be redundant in the context of the new totalitarian democracies of postwar politics. This crisis intensified in the 1930s, when the totalitarian states of Europe forced politicians and writers to confront the prospect of a complete disintegration of basic liberal beliefs. In Britain, before World War I, the Liberal Party had dominated parliamentary politics for three decades. By the 1930s, it had "dwindled to a rump of a mere twenty-one MPs," prompting George Dangerfield famously to claim in 1935 that middle-class English liberalism died a "strange death" between 1910 and 1913.[9]

These social changes profoundly affected Eliot, who was an astute, if selective, commentator on political affairs. This chapter will consider four key moments in his career when he engaged with wider political events or arguments and their impact on his shifting representations of women. First, in Oxford in 1916, Eliot delivered a series of lectures on Modern French literature in which he discussed the politicized categories of romanticism and classicism. The attack on the "egoism" of romanticism in these lectures serves as a starting point for considering his equation between women and solipsism in poems written from 1909–1915. Second, from 1918 to the early 1920s, Eliot occupied an ambivalent position in relation to postwar mass politics. While he declared triumphantly that liberal individualism had been succeeded by new forms of authority, he simultaneously expressed worries about the cultural impact of the displacement of liberal values by the newly powerful democratized masses. This ambivalence appears in his negative depictions of "femininity" in *Ara Vos Prec* and *The Waste Land*. Third, in 1928, Eliot's "Commentaries" for the *Criterion* became insistently concerned with the "dilution" of individual agency in modern democracy. Reversing his earlier position, he began to defend the rights of the individual in the context of what he saw as a feminized tyranny of the majority. Finally, in Eliot's famous attack on liberalism in *After Strange Gods* (1933), the triumphalism of his postwar declarations gave way to a pessimistic account of the cultural dominance of liberal values, values he associates with the feminine.

ROMANTICISM AND CLASSICISM

In Eliot's syllabus notes summarizing his lectures on Modern French Literature (1916), he uses the oppositional terms "romanticism" and "classicism" he had inherited from French literary debates. In these debates, the "romantic" progressive ideals of the French Revolution were pitted against a reinvigorated classicism connected to monarchism and authority. Rousseau was seen as the most important "romantic" philosopher and the proponent of the egalitarian ideals of the French Revolution. These ideals were challenged by a group of disparate contemporary intellectuals which included Charles Maurras, who organized the group *L'Action Française*, as well as Auguste Barrès and Georges Sorel.

Accepting the terms of this French opposition, Eliot's lecture notes on French literature and culture connect political democracy to ideas of cultural democratization and adopt the broad categories of romanticism and classicism to summarize complex political and cultural debates: "Rousseauistic" political and literary values are described as the "purely personal expression of emotion" in literature and are contrasted with a new classicism based on a defense of *"form* and *restraint* in art, *discipline* and *authority* in religion, *centralization* in government (either as socialism or monarchy)."[10] Eliot connects socialism and monarchism here because within France the syndicalist Sorel and the monarchist Charles Maurras had a common enemy in the liberal politics of the Third Republic and the system of democracy: "Both currents express revolt against the same state of affairs, and consequently tend to meet."[11]

Despite the fact that the liberal tradition was rather different in France than in England and America, these lectures also map out the coordinates of an Anglo-American literary agenda in which the aesthetic is accorded a crucial role in resolving the contradictions and dislocations of modern politics. Romanticism, Eliot asserts, involves three things: the "purely personal expression" in literature, excessive emotion, and excessive realism or "devotion to brute fact." Modern classicism departs from all three of these things through a "growing devotion to form." Eliot's claims about the literary consequences of romanticism and classicism were the basis for subsequent important critical essays. In "Tradition and the Individual Talent," for example, he discussed in more detail the need for the "extinction" of personality and emotion in literature.

Eliot was not the only Anglo-American writer to define what he was doing by means of the French intellectual context and to use the broad categories of romanticism and classicism to criticize liberal values and to politicize the modern preoccupation with form. T. E. Hulme had set out a similarly politicized program for modern art in his essays "A Tory Philosophy" and "Romanticism and Classicism." In "Romanticism and Classicism" he insists that politics cannot be divorced from arguments about aesthetics: "I make no apology for dragging in politics here; romanticism both in England and France is associated with certain political views." For Hulme, the difference between romanticism and classicism is largely focused on different understandings of human nature: the romantics believe in liberty because they believe that "man, the individual, is an infinite reservoir of possibilities," while the classicists see man as "an extraordinarily fixed and limited animal whose nature is absolutely constant. It is only by tradition and organization that anything decent can be got out of him."[12] These different understandings of human nature produce distinct kinds of poetry. The romantic aspiration toward "infinite possibility" produces abstraction and extravagant bursts of imagination, while, by contrast, the classical emphasis on man's limitations induces aesthetic restraint and formal control. Thus, for Hulme, the new classicism will be defined by the power of its "visual concrete" language.

In his *Masters of Modern French Criticism*, Irving Babbitt, Eliot's Harvard tutor, traces a similar genealogy of ideas. He connects "Rousseauist democracy" to the democratization of culture and advocates a return to order and impersonal standards of political, moral, and literary value.[13] Babbitt's later 1919 volume, *Rousseau and Romanticism*, further characterizes Rousseau as "the great modern romancer," and argues that romanticism involves an extreme form of what he calls "naturalistic individualism," based on a degraded positivism in which the individual believes that "his own private and personal self is to be the measure of all things."[14]

Finally, of particular relevance to this chapter is how such modernist attacks on romanticism, democracy, and legalism implicated women's recent attainment of political, social, and cultural freedoms. Changes in women's political position in the nineteenth century were fundamentally connected to two kinds of liberal argument: first, a liberal egalitarianism arguing that all persons should be accorded the same moral status and denying the relevance to the legal and political order of differences among human beings; second, the argument that liberty involves an entitlement to take part in the collective decision making of government. The latter argument, that individual liberty involves civic participation, was foundational to John Stuart Mill's defense of women's emancipation in *The Subjection of Women* (1869), in which he argued that equal political, educational, and financial rights were central to women realizing themselves as full human beings. Many key rights, such as rights to ownership of property and income, and to higher education, had been won during the late nineteenth century. In the years 1900–10, women's rights, particularly the issue of women's suffrage, were insistently debated, not only in the British and American presses, but also in journals such as the *New Age*, for which Hulme wrote extensively, and the *Egoist*, which Eliot helped edit from 1917.

The new political and literary program of anti-liberal reaction in France and Anglo-America embraced by Eliot, Hulme, and Babbitt, and many other intellectuals, questioned both egalitarian and libertarian arguments for individual freedom. The focus on what Hulme sees as a "static" human nature refutes the idea that political participation will create enlightened subjects. The anti-liberalism of this diverse group of intellectuals was also a critique of the legalism, or formalism, of liberal accounts of human agency and emancipation. This chapter examines, among other things, the extent to which such attacks on egalitarian and libertarian belief in individual freedom implicated a reaction against women's recent political advances.

While Eliot does not mention women in his notes to his Oxford lectures, he consistently associates legalism, formalism, and "verbalism" with women in his poetry and prose. His early poems, written from 1909 to 1915, present us with a series of gendered dramas in which men assert control over a feminized environment equated with the "romanticism" he defined in the syllabus to the lectures: in these poems, the egoism Eliot associates with romanticism is attributed primarily to women; and women are agents of excess, in terms both of emotion and of an unreflective, engulfing physicality. Above all, women function as key signs of the modern "liberal" moment in Eliot's poems and essays, a modern moment severed from a meaningful history or tradition.

BOURGEOIS WOMEN IN ELIOT'S EARLY POEMS

Individual alienation from the political, legal, or social sphere is often a starting point for European and Anglo-American modernist writing, and it is central to Eliot's first poetic achievements. Notably, Eliot sexualizes both the estrangement and fragmentation central to his poetry and the idea of cultural power. In "The Love Song of J. Alfred Prufrock," originally entitled "Prufrock among the Women," the opening simile, likening the sky to "a patient etherised upon a table," powerfully conjures the image of a helpless and unconscious individual, whose fate lies in the hands of a scientist or surgeon; this image hovers over the entire poem. Prufrock, like the patient, is controlled by and estranged from the exact, scientific judgments of others and struggles to free himself from an etherized or drugged existence. Prufrock will make a beginning by spitting out the formulated phrases of his cultural milieu, awakening from the sleepy, sensual afternoons, and risking his overwhelming question.

By implication he is also struggling to awake and to differentiate himself from a vacuous bourgeois society. Such visions of estrangement, which Pound described as being "out of key" with one's time, are common in modernist writing. However, while Joyce and Kafka depict forms of civic alienation related to law, work, commodification, religion, or family, Eliot configures alienation as a gendered issue: it is women who fix Prufrock in formulated phrases, whose sensual perfume makes him digress, whose smooth fingers induce a soporific inaction, who insist that he has misunderstood their meaning. Focusing on the relationship between the sexes, Eliot appears to identify the cause of alienation with the cultural and sexual power of bourgeois women.

A similar dynamic of female cultural power and male estrangement controls "Portrait of a Lady," in which the poet shrinks away from the lady's claim upon his friendship, recoiling from her suggestion that their relationship should involve a meaningful form of recognition. This withdrawal is connected to the idea that her demand, like her words and her gestures, are insincere, as they merely parrot received opinions about friendship, rather than recognize the poet's individuality. Eliot is here being ironic about the disjunction between the lady's social ideas of friendship and the false note of the poet's solipsistic reality. For their relationship to work, the poet would have to perform a rather absurd social personality. Notwithstanding the "hammering" invocation of their "friendship," a word repeated ten times in the poem, the poet and the hostess remain in the dark when it comes to understanding each other. The poet's withdrawal into a tentative and incomplete self-possession and the lady's insistence on their friendship produce each other: her words force him to shrink into himself; and the more he recoils, the more she invokes the idea of friendship they have failed to attain.

In both poems, bourgeois women are depicted as being outside a cultural language they use and abuse. In "Tradition and the Individual Talent" Eliot distinguishes between the poet, who has "absorbed" the texts and beliefs of a tradition, and the individual who sees knowledge merely as a "useful" tool for examinations and the drawing room. The drawing rooms of Eliot's early poems are, of course, largely populated by bourgeois women who do precisely that, "come and go / talking of Michelangelo." Similarly, the hostess in "Portrait of a Lady" talks "of" rather than through friendship. Both are poetic images of humans who use words as symbols of cultivation or intimacy, rather than as meaningful forms of communication or recognition. Their words thereby remain external to their ostensible referent, a painting by Michelangelo or the particular friend of the poem, and rebound back onto the speaker, creating a linguistic and emotional egotism. This modern egotism, which Eliot associated with romanticism, constitutes a particularly dangerous kind of fragmentation, in which the stability of language itself is threatened.

Eliot saw this individualistic use of language, which he links to bourgeois women in both poems, as a key feature of the modern moment. In "The Perfect Critic" he claims that "words have changed their meanings. What they have lost is definite, and what they have gained is indefinite."[15] He describes indefinite language, in which words have become severed from their objects, as a "verbalism," or "abstraction" he elsewhere associates with contemporary "feminine" culture. In a letter to Pound of 1915, he bemoans the "monopolisation of literature by women," although he suggests that it is "imprudent" to admit it.[16] In his essays he is less direct, but the impulse to characterize contemporary culture as feminine is similar. In "Reflections on *Vers Libre*," for example, he paints a picture of contemporary cultural exchange. The essay begins tellingly with a lady's pronouncements on modern poetry; she claims that she can no "longer read any verse but *vers libre*," thus reducing her to a sign of the modern moment. *Vers libre* is *the* modern verse form, and the lady is modern because of her susceptibility to fashion. Further, her interest in *vers libre* is equated with "abstraction" because she is fascinated by its novelty and fashionableness, not by the thing itself. To understand the thing itself, the essay argues, she would need to know about the history of poetry. Without this knowledge, the woman is interested in novelty for the sake of novelty, and "freedom" for the sake of freedom. Just as the romantics believe in the illusion of free will and liberals believe in the illusory freedoms of the individual, so the "freedom" of *vers libre* is an illusion. When Eliot insists that "there is no freedom in art," it is because he believes more generally that freedom involves individual expression in the context of a meaningful "artificial limitation," restraint, authority, or formal control.[17]

If Eliot is critical of a feminine abstraction, he is equally critical of the unreflective realism or "devotion to brute fact" of romanticism, as he describes it in his Extension lectures. In each of Eliot's poems and essays, he asks how pattern, form, structure, and order can be generated out of the "chaotic, irregular, fragmentary" experience of the ordinary man, a "mass" of perceptions, and "the chaos of contemporary history."[18] Significantly, his early texts often connect chaos to women and form to men. Eliot's focus on women's sexual invasiveness, as a chaos which defeats formal self-possession, is perhaps most startlingly illustrated in his 1915 prose piece "Hysteria," in which an overwhelmingly physical femaleness vies with the writer's desire for autonomy: the poet is "drawn in," "inhaled," "lost," and "bruised" by a female body. The text ends: "I decided that if the shaking of her breasts could be stopped, some of the fragments of the afternoon might be collected, and I concentrated my attention with careful subtlety to this end."[19] The writing bluntly dramatizes the movement of dissociation, the shift from a moment of female engulfment to the writer's fastidious withdrawal. Here, rather than the textual and political fragments of *The Waste Land*, it is the afternoon, or perhaps the man's mind, which is in fragments, and which must be "collected" through "concentration," "attention," and "careful subtlety."

Eliot has transposed a language of fragmentation and formal organization, implicit in the shift from erratic to regular prosody in "The Love Song of J. Alfred Prufrock" and present in the ideas of discord and musical arrangement in "Portrait of a Lady," onto a moment of physical exchange between a man and a woman. In all three texts, the man, whether Prufrock, the poet, or the writer, withdraws in the face of the woman's physical or intellectual demands. In all three texts, only his withdrawal allows space for poetic reflexivity, particularly on the nature of poetic form.

DEMOCRATIZED VOICES: *ARA VOS PREC* AND *THE WASTE LAND*

The individualized dramas of Eliot's early poems are displaced by more collective concerns in *The Waste Land*, with its images of the crowd on London Bridge and the revolutionary hordes over distant mountains. This shift from a concern with romantic solipsism to an interest in wider historical forces is mirrored in his essays of the early 1920s, where he triumphantly announced, on a number of occasions, that liberal individualism was dying and became increasingly concerned with the status of art in the context of the new era of mass democracy.

Many commentators have discussed Eliot's feminization of the working classes in *The Waste Land* and his disdain for them. In this section I want to explore in more detail Eliot's ambivalence toward the contemporary moment, paying particular attention to relations he draws among ideas of individuality, collectivity, and gender difference in *The Waste Land*.

The first of Eliot's "Reflections on Contemporary Poetry," published in the *Egoist* in 1917, suggests how we might discuss the politics of the new poems he was writing, which were published in *Ara Vos Prec* in 1919. He describes modern poetry's departure from a liberal literary sensibility: "One of the ways in which contemporary verse has tried to escape the rhetorical, the abstract, the moralizing, to recover (for that is its purpose) the accents of direct speech, is to concentrate its attention upon the trivial or accidental or commonplace objects."[20] Eliot suggests that moralism is a kind of abstraction. He argues that contemporary verse escapes abstraction and moralism by attending to the particularity of the contemporary object, in all its accidental, commonplace dimensions. The corollary of attending to the particularity of the object is a recognition of the particularity of people, a particularity he locates in voice. Direct speech, then, will involve both an object-centered language and the cadences of contemporary class- and gender-specific voices. Paradoxically, Eliot appears to embrace a liberal position here, suggesting that the poetic revolt against bourgeois culture will produce a form of democratization of voice, or linguistic inclusiveness, in modernist poetry. Eliot's pluralism of voices, however, contributed to yet another gendered critique of liberalism.

Eliot's early poems depend on the farcical distance between linguistic registers. In "The Love Song of J. Alfred Prufrock," for example, the prosaic, conversational register of women's voices is contrasted to the literary register of Prufrock's imagination. Eliot continued to focus on the significance of voices through 1910, but their meaning was to change. Thus, in the early poems – "The Love Song of J. Alfred Prufrock," "Portrait of a Lady," "Mr Appolinax," and "Cousin Nancy" – the cadences and sentiments of pretentious Boston drawing rooms are mocked by means of a clash of linguistic registers. As Eliot's work developed, however, he became interested in incorporating a much wider range of human voices into his poems, removing the quotation marks that frame these voices and thereby making them integral to the language of the poem.

This difference corresponds to a radical change of register, form, and direction of satire in Eliot's new poems of 1917. His poetic characters,

Burbank, Sweeney, and Pipit, are vehicles for basic rhymes and scatological detail, and the satire shifts from the vacuity of polite Boston chitchat to the "broadbottomed," "straddled" bodies of sensual individuals, from the drawing room to the boarding house, and from the literary dressing up of empty emotions to the attempt to capture working-class idioms. In "Sweeney Erect," for instance, Eliot includes the idiomatic, "Mrs Turner intimates / It does the house no sort of good," and in "A Cooking Egg" he rhymes "Sir Philip Sidney" with "heroes of that kidney."

The deliberate tastelessness to this sequence of poems, which flouts the diction Eliot had ironized in earlier poems, now targets the empty tastefulness of women. In "Sweeney Erect," for instance, he mocks refinement by depicting a vulgar female body and by ridiculing a female sense of propriety. It is a female body that is caught in the convulsive seizures, which are the result of either epilepsy or the sexual act. And it is women who are ridiculed for characterizing this violent confusion of images as a question of taste:

> The ladies of the corridor
> Find themselves involved, disgraced,
> Call witness to their principles
> And deprecate the lack of taste.

The female body is the site of a repulsive violence, and women lack a meaningful moral register by which to understand this violence. Their reversion to farcically inadequate principles signals both their inability to deal with the particularity of the situation and the redundancy of their moral beliefs. In addition, however, Eliot smuggles in a reflexive reference to his poem's "lack of taste," indicating that the shocked audience for Eliot's poem will resemble the disgraced witnesses to Sweeney's erection.

Eliot described himself as "intensely serious" about these poems, claiming that "Sweeney Among the Nightingales" and "Burbank" were "among the best" that he had ever done.[21] Although Eliot worried, in a note to his brother (1920), that his mother would be shocked by "Sweeney Erect," on some level the poem's vulgarity is designed to offend a refined, feminine, literary sensibility. Other modernist and avant-garde writers also violated good taste by means of sexually explicit detail and nonpoetic registers. When Laforgue compares the sun to a "gobbet of pub-spit" in his late poem "L'hiver qui vient," for instance, he uses the simile ironically to undermine an inflated notion of poetic language.[22] Avant-garde writers such as Apollinaire and Marinetti took such shock tactics to new levels,

envisioning their tastelessness as a direct challenge to the dominant bourgeois, sentimental culture.

The attempt to capture the linguistic dimensions of class-, race-, and
gender-inflected idioms is important for other modernist writers such as
Gertrude Stein and James Joyce, and Eliot's own concern with direct speech
certainly forms part of this wider interest. The language and structure of
The Waste Land, particularly the first draft of the poem, collects together the
class- and gender-inflected voices of a fragmented contemporary moment.
Such voices include the words of Marie, Madame Sosostris, the woman
whose nerves are bad, the women in the pub, the typist, and the "murmur of
maternal lamentation." However, while these voices represent the different
forms of direct speech that constitute the contemporary moment, they also
illustrate Eliot's pervasive association of contemporaneity with "femininity."
Madame Sosostris dishes out a debased and secondhand form of spiritual
knowledge; the woman in "A Game of Chess" mis-recognizes what the man
is thinking; the women in the pub are in states of extreme physical decay;
and the typist is unconscious of her own state of sexual degradation. Such
secondhand knowledge, mis-recognition, physical decay, sexual degradation, and unconsciousness have broken apart the language and beliefs of a
common culture.

Eliot's essay on the music hall actress Marie Lloyd (1923) praises her
embodiment of the moral virtues of the working class – "that part of the
English nation which has perhaps the greatest vitality and interest" – citing her use of the same idiomatic, class-inflected cadences he attached to
the voices in *The Waste Land*. He points to her "tone of voice" and her
employment of particular objects as signifiers of class, age, and gender.[23]
He attributes her success to the fact that she understood and sympathized
with the working classes, and was recognized by them in turn. For Eliot,
this mutual recognition amounts to a form of embodied, cultural morality.
By contrast, Eliot attacks the middle class he perceives as aspiring toward
democratization in England and as gradually inheriting cultural and political authority on the grounds that they lack both a distinct morality and a
specific form of cultural expression. Thus Marie Lloyd forms an important
symbol of Englishness and a crucial component of the English nation in
this review. Any attempt to represent the totality of the English nation
would need to incorporate her voice, as *The Waste Land* may be seen to
do. Yet, Eliot's idea of embodiment is dependent on the maintenance of
a steady sense of class distinctions. Class mobility, in the form of Brad-
ford millionaires and young house agents' clerks, creates a confusion and
dislocation in which an embodied, aestheticized morality is impossible.

These comments on Marie Lloyd are extremely revealing for an under-standing of the way that Eliot represents democracy and gender difference in *The Waste Land*. As in his early poems and essays, Eliot attacks the ego-tistical, "vacuous" nature of the cultured class. Yet, rather than embrace a new classicism or authority to order these vacuous and disconnected egos, he attacks liberal individualism by defending the "vitality" of working-class expression, precisely the kind of "direct speech" he incorporates into his poems after 1917.

Thus, two contradictory impulses direct the composition of *The Waste Land*, one seeking to incorporate the modern voices constituting contem-porary history, and another aiming to represent the disintegration of class and gender hierarchies. This incongruity may be explained by Eliot's objects of attack in the poem: the tasteful poetic language of a liberal feminized culture, and the mass politics of the crowd unleashed after the war. The contemporary voices, therefore, are hollowed out and morally bankrupt, estranged from the sources of aesthetic value located firmly in the past. Is the language of the poem, then, controlled by the very voices Eliot believes to be morally and culturally vacant? And if so, have the democratic masses destroyed the poetic object which sought to contain them? These are the questions Eliot began to engage with after the publication of *The Waste Land* in 1922.

"AUTHORITY NOT DEMOCRACY"

In 1923, Eliot declared that the humanist values informing the work of a writer such as George Bernard Shaw were dying. Instead, a new set of values, "of authority not democracy, of dogmatism not tolerance, of the extremity and never the mean," were taking their place.[24] A year later, Eliot used his review of T. E. Hulme's posthumously published book, *Speculations*, to declare a new set of values. In this review, Eliot polemically reiterates the dichotomies of the debate he had discussed in his lectures on modern French literature, stating that "Hulme is Classical, reactionary, and revolutionary; he is the antipodes of the eclectic, tolerant, and democratic mind of the last century." Notwithstanding the fact that Hulme had died in the war in 1917, and that Eliot is reviewing his work retrospectively, it is significant that he wants to define Hulme's modern classicism in relation to a histori-cal moment which has already been politically displaced, the "democratic mind of the last century." Eliot uses this retrospective idea of democracy as a foundation for a definition of modern art and culture, equating the democratic "mind" with dislocation from authority and belief: "We say democracy advisedly: that meanness of spirit, that egotism of motive, that incapacity for surrender or allegiance to something outside oneself, which is a frequent symptom of the soul of man under democracy." In the absence of authority, he concludes, art is rejected in favor of a debased culture: "[The] aversion for the work of art, [the] preference for the derivative, the marginal, is an aspect of the modern democracy of culture."[25]

Eliot's rhetorical strategy of moving quickly from the democratic mind of the last century to a general description of that democratic mind and, abruptly, to a comment about the modern democracy of culture renders the phrase "modern democracy of culture" ambiguous. It could refer to a nineteenth-century liberal democracy, or to the mass democracy of postwar Anglo-America, but notably, while Eliot himself saw these two kinds of democracy as different, here he fuses them together. Eliot's rhetorical slip from the past to the present thus allows him to define modern art in connection to issues of authority, and to link a democratized culture with notions of the self that consolidate the individual ego at the expense of authority. His criticism of "the incapacity for surrender, or allegiance to something outside oneself" seems to attack classically liberal notions of the self as a grounded entity which exists prior to articulated and historically specific ends.

Eliot's attacks on democracy were to become increasingly strident through the 1920s, but his focus on the individual was to shift dramatically toward the mass democracy he studiously sidesteps in his review of Hulme. In this new context, he no longer worries about the individual's incapacity for surrender or "allegiance to something outside oneself," but rather about the individual's ready surrender to the wrong forms of authority. Obeying a sinister kind of dialectical logic, Eliot fears that the masses themselves will start to occupy the position of external authority controlling the individual. This ambiguous allegiance would both destabilize Marie Lloyd's embodied, aestheticized morality and render Eliot's own cultural authority rather tenuous. The terms of his critique of democracy, then, become complicated, as he persists in criticizing liberal definitions of the subject, while simultaneously attacking mass democracy.

Eliot's 1928 essay "The Humanism of Irving Babbitt," which was a review of Babbitt's 1924 book *Democracy and Leadership*, marks an important moment in Eliot's attempt to bring together these two different impulses. Here he criticizes Babbitt's own reversion to a liberal idea of the individual subject in order to criticize mass democracy: "For the conscience that is felt as a still small voice," Babbitt writes, "and that is the basis of real justice, we have substituted a social conscience that operates rather through a megaphone."[26] Babbitt's humanist philosophy is based on an idea of a secular ethical will, which he identifies with a vigorously individualist conception of justice, right action, and the work ethic. While Eliot agrees with Babbitt's criticisms of the tyrannical aspects of mass democracy, he disagrees with Babbitt's humanism, which Eliot argues is an abstraction dislocating the subject from "their contexts of race, place, and time." Eliot argues that the ethical will cannot be grounded in the self, and that only religion can provide the authority and structure for ethical belief. He proclaims that Babbitt's sharp distinction between inner and outer belief is untenable: profoundly experienced religious belief has already become a form of "inner control." Thus for Eliot the religious individual is so saturated in the beliefs of the Church that the boundary between individual belief and religious authority dissolves. Eliot's critique of his old tutor, Babbitt, is important because it captures his ongoing sense of the limitations of a self-grounded moral consciousness, but does so within the new context of an engagement with the mass democracy of the megaphone.

Yet it was hard not to revert to liberal categories of the self in the context of the realities of mass politics in the 1920s and 1930s, and at times we find Eliot doing precisely this. In his "Commentary" for April 1931, for instance, he criticizes democracy for the way it allows for the invasion of privacy: "The extreme of democracy – which we have almost reached – promises greater and greater interference with private liberty . . . In complete democracy, everyone in theory governs everyone else, as a kind of compensation for not being allowed to govern himself."[27]

This fragile balance Eliot struck between a defense of private liberty in the context of the invasions of mass democracy and an attack on liberal categories of the individual subject is also integral to his comments about women in this period. In his review of "The Literature of Fascism," published in December 1928, the same year Eliot announced that he was a "classicist in literature, royalist in politics, and anglo-catholic in religion," Eliot insists that British democracy has been destroyed by mass enfranchisement, has been "watered down to nothing," as he puts it: "With every vote added, the value of every vote diminishes."[28] Eliot is responding specifically to the gender imbalance created by the large number of votes recently added to the British electorate through the "Representation of the People Act" of 1928. The Act extended the franchise from women over thirty to women over twenty-one and removed the remaining property qualifications of the 1918 Act, making women the majority of the electorate for the first time, comprising "52.7 percent of the potential voters."[29]

In "The Literature of Fascism" Eliot's defense of the "idea of Democracy" against a "watered-down democracy" criticizes the language of individual rights central to feminist arguments for equality in the 1920s: "from the moment when suffrage is conceived as a *right* instead of as a privilege and a duty and a responsibility, we are on the way merely to government by an invisible oligarchy instead of government by a visible one."[30]

Three years later, Eliot returned to this question and explicitly injected it with the gender categories that lie just beneath the surface in 1928. In his *Criterion* commentary of January 1931, he returns to the question he had posed in December 1928 by mocking the insistence that women's full participation in the democratic process is essential to a modern democracy: *The Times* has put forward "the irresistible contention that the framework of democracy would not be complete without – without what? – without the young women of twenty-one." He goes on to ask, "what, now that this tasteful piece of joinery, the 'framework of democracy,' is complete, is the character of the canvas to be found within it?"[31] Eliot's language not only implies that democracy has been destroyed by women's inclusion in its framework, but also links together ideas of democracy, women, and taste. Here we seem to have returned to the logic animating "Sweeney Erect," in which democratization, women, and a tasteful, empty bourgeois culture produce each other. As in his poems, then, Eliot's prose comments represent women both as a particularly potent symbol of democratization and as the embodiments of an enfranchised, but disconnected citizenry.

AGAINST LIBERALISM: *AFTER STRANGE GODS*

Eliot's notorious critique of a society "worm-eaten by liberalism" in his 1932 lectures, published as *After Strange Gods* in 1933, again implicates feminine writing as a cause of society's demise. In the second lecture, Eliot analyzes three short stories, *Bliss* by Katherine Mansfield, *The Shadow in the Rose Garden* by D. H. Lawrence, and *The Dead* by James Joyce, all of which deal with the issue of "disillusionment." He uses these stories to illustrate his wider argument about the relationship between tradition and individualism, terms which he injects with a moral and religious register by re-naming them as orthodoxy and heresy. While Lawrence is "an almost perfect example of the heretic" and Joyce is "ethically orthodox," Mansfield, in contrast to both writers, is described as "feminine."[32] The significance of Eliot's evaluation of Mansfield's writing is elucidated by his discussion of the three texts' "differences in moral implication." In *Bliss*, according to Eliot, the "moral implication is negligible" because the story restricts its focus to the "wife's feeling." In contrast to this "limited" aesthetic, a word Eliot uses twice in his discussion of Mansfield's story, Lawrence's and Joyce's stories have moral significance because they function on both an emotional and an intellectual level. Despite the fact that Eliot criticizes Lawrence's story as an example of literary heresy, then, it nevertheless offers us a "great deal more than" Mansfield's story. The feminine is mentioned very briefly in this text, yet it functions as a crucial conceptual foundation for moral and, he implies, literary value. Eight pages later, Eliot makes this connection explicitly: without moral "struggle," he argues, art will be "inoffensive" and characters will be "vaporous." In the third lecture, in the context of another discussion of Lawrence's writing, Eliot states that the "insensibility to ordinary social morality" is so alien to his mind that he is "completely baffled by it as a monstrosity." It is Mansfield's text, not Lawrence's, that ultimately lacks a social morality, and that expresses the "Liberalism, Progress and Modern Civilisation" both Lawrence and Eliot criticize.[33] Eliot claims further that her writing is confined by a limited focus on feeling. Thus, for Eliot, "feminine" writing is an example of liberalism and progress because of its disconnection from and unconsciousness of the historical and political forces which nevertheless control its terms of reference and its aesthetic ambition.

CONCLUSION

Eliot's target for political attack altered, from the liberal individualism he associated with a particular kind of literature to the tyranny of the majority in the late 1920s. Eliot associates women with both of these political formations: as potent instances of liberal egoism in the early poems and as key agents of the tyranny of the masses in essays of the 1920s. *The Waste Land* incorporates both of these registers, as Eliot used the "vitality" of working-class culture to destabilize middle-class values, while trying to maintain rigid forms of class distinction. Finally, in *After Strange Gods* Eliot attacks a "feminine" liberalism, claiming that it has created dangerous forms of modern heresy. Despite the changing nature of the political landscape and the kinds of historical agency with which they are associated, women remain negative signifiers of contemporary modern democracy. Thus, in Eliot's work, women become culturally significant when a homogeneous bourgeois culture is destabilized, and women become citizens at the historical moment when citizenship becomes politically insignificant.

NOTES

1. T. S. Eliot, "Whispers of Immortality," in *T. S. Eliot: The Complete Poems and Plays* (London: Faber and Faber, 1969), 52.

2. T. E. Hulme, "Romanticism and Classicism," in *Speculations* (1924; 2nd edn. London: Routledge and Kegan Paul, 1960), 179.

3. Albert Gelpi, "T. S. Eliot: The Lady between the Yew Trees," in *A Coherent Splendor: The American Poetic Renaissance, 1910–50* (Cambridge: Cambridge University Press, 1987), 93; Carol Christ, "Gender, Voice and Figuration in Eliot's Early Poetry," in *T. S. Eliot: The Modernist in History*, ed. Ronald Bush (Cambridge: Cambridge University Press, 1991), 23–40; Lyndall Gordon, *T. S. Eliot: An Imperfect Life* (London: Vintage, 1998).

4. Michael Levenson, *A Genealogy of Modernism* (Cambridge: Cambridge University Press, 1984); Jeffrey M. Perl, *Skepticism and Modern Enmity: Before and after Eliot* (Baltimore: Johns Hopkins University Press, 1989); Michael North, *The Political Aesthetic of Yeats, Eliot and Pound* (Cambridge: Cambridge University Press, 1991); Kenneth Asher, *T. S. Eliot and Ideology* (Cambridge: Cambridge University Press, 1995).

5. Michael Tratner, *Modernism and Mass Politics: Joyce, Woolf, Eliot, Yeats* (Stanford: Stanford University Press, 1995), 172, 3, 171.

6. John Gray, *Liberalism: Concepts in the Social Sciences* (Milton Keynes: Open University Press, 1986), 92.

7. L. T. Hobhouse, *Liberalism* (London: Williams and Norgate, 1911).

8. Andrew Chadwick, *Augmenting Democracy: Political Movements and Constitutional Reform during the Rise of Labour, 1900–1924* (Aldershot: Ashgate, 1999), 120.

9. George Searle, *The Liberal Party* (Basingstoke: Palgrave, 2001), 1.

10. The lecture notes are reproduced in A. D. Moody, *Thomas Stearns Eliot, Poet* (Cambridge: Cambridge University Press, 1979), 41–9, 44.

11. Ibid., 45.

12. T. E. Hulme, *Speculations*, 115, 116.

13. Irving Babbitt, *Masters of Modern French Criticism* (London: Constable, 1913).

14. Irving Babbitt, *Rousseau and Romanticism* (Boston: Houghton Mifflin, 1919), 5, xii.

15. T. S. Eliot, "The Perfect Critic," in *Selected Prose of T. S. Eliot* (London: Faber and Faber, 1975), 55.

16. T. S. Eliot to Ezra Pound, April 15, 1915, in *The Letters of T. S. Eliot*, ed. Valerie Eliot, vol. 1: *1898–1922* (San Diego: Harcourt Brace Jovanovich, 1988), 96.

17. T. S. Eliot, "Reflections on *Vers Libre*," in *Selected Prose*, 31, 32.

18. T. S. Eliot, "The Metaphysical Poets," "The Perfect Critic," "Ulysses, Order and Myth," in *Selected Prose*, 64, 58, 177.

19. T. S. Eliot, "Hysteria," in *T. S. Eliot: Collected Poems and Plays* (London: Faber and Faber, 1969), 32.

20. T. S. Eliot, "Reflections on Contemporary Poetry," *Egoist* 4, no. 8 (September 1917): 118.

21. T. S. Eliot to Henry Eliot, February 15, 1920, in *The Letters of T. S. Eliot*, vol. 1: 363.

22. Jules Laforgue, "L'hiver qui vient," *Dernier Vers*, in *Selected Poems*, trans. Graham Dunstan Martin (Harmondsworth: Penguin Books, 1998), 218.

23. T. S. Eliot, "In Memoriam: Marie Lloyd," *Criterion* 1, no. 2 (January 1923): 192, 193.
24. T. S. Eliot, "A Commentary," *Criterion* 3, no. 9 (October 1924): 4.
25. T. S. Eliot, "A Commentary," *Criterion* 2, no. 7 (April 1924): 231, 235.
26. Irving Babbitt, *Democracy and Leadership* (Boston: Houghton Mifflin, 1924), 200.
27. T. S. Eliot, "A Commentary," *Criterion* 8, no. 32 (April 1931): 379.
28. T. S. Eliot, "The Literature of Fascism," *Criterion* 8, no. 31 (December 1928): 281.
29. Harold L. Smith, *The British Women's Suffrage Campaign, 1866–1928* (London: Longman, 1998), 81.
30. The feminist groups agitating for equal franchise extended across the political spectrum in the 1920s. They included the Conservative Party women's organization and Labour Party women, as well as the "National Union of Societies for Equal Citizenship," run by Eleanor Rathbone, Lady Rhondda's "Six Point Group," and Lady Astor's "Consultative Committee for Women's Organisations"; T. S. Eliot, "The Literature of Fascism," 287.
31. T. S. Eliot, "A Commentary," *Criterion* 10, no. 39 (January 1931): 307.
32. T. S. Eliot, *After Strange Gods* (New York: Harcourt Brace, 1959), 41.
33. Ibid., 38, 46.

CHAPTER II

Vipers, viragos, and spiritual rebels: women in T. S. Eliot's Christian society plays

Elisabeth Däumer

A cursory glance at the female characters in T. S. Eliot's later plays leaves one with the disconsolate impression that they were modeled, not on living women, but on stock figures of female neurosis and maternal excess popularized in Philip Wylie's misogynist bestseller *Generation of Vipers* (1942).[1] Presiding over the conventional world of the English drawing room and invested with the stereotypic identities of dominating matron, discontented wife, hardened spinster, and poor cousin, they inhabit a world seemingly untouched by the social and political eruptions of the time, from women's suffrage to war, whose impact on the lives of women and men had been trenchantly analyzed by Eliot's friend Virginia Woolf. In contrast to such flat characterization, however, is the startling fact that many of these female characters undertake crucial tasks in the protagonists' spiritual transformation, functioning as intercessors, spiritual guides, and stern priestesses.[2] Thus Eliot's women lead double lives: on the naturalist surface of the plays, they are custodians of a world of stifling civility and banality, whose pretensions to social authority are comically exaggerated or farcically dismissed; in the symbolic subpattern of the plays, they emerge as pursuing and hieratic figures representing the disruptive claims of a higher spiritual reality, to which only the elect few find access.

This double life of Eliot's female characters is a product of the plays' multilayered construction: a surface plot drawn from popular forms of theater dealing with conventional social settings and a spiritual subplot steeped in wide-ranging mythic sources overlaid with Christian meanings. Following Eliot's own ruminations on poetic drama, early critics of his plays, notably Carol Smith, have read them as coherent, self-enclosed dramatic worlds in which surface events and spiritual subplot forge a seamless whole – dramatic worlds, that is, in which a character's social behavior is firmly, even if frequently ironically, anchored in a hidden mythic or spiritual function, with the promise that once that function is revealed, any incongruities in the character's behavior or fate will be laid to rest.[3] In

234

more recent critical readings of the plays, focused on Eliot as conservative ideologue, such earlier assumptions of formal and religious coherence have been supplanted with an emphasis on ideological continuity. Thus both Kenneth Asher and John Xiros Cooper approach the plays as more or less unmediated reflections of Eliot's ideological position, articulated, most conspicuously, in *The Idea of a Christian Society* (1939) and *Notes towards the Definition of Culture* (1948).[4] Since neither Asher nor Cooper expresses interest in gender as an ideological category, the clash between the indifference to women discernible in Eliot's cultural criticism and the preoccupation with women's transformative spiritual agency in his plays has gone largely unnoticed.

The approach taken in this chapter questions such assumptions of dramatic, religious, or ideological coherence by foregrounding the discontinuities and contradictions both between the plays' naturalist surface and symbolic substructure and between Eliot's avowed ideological positions and his drama's implied spiritual and social agendas. More specifically, I shall argue that the paradoxes besetting Eliot's female characters testify to his uncertainty about women's role in the spiritual and social resuscitation of the modern world. That he shared contemporary male anxieties about the social advances of the New Woman is indicated by his female characters' fate on the naturalist level of his plays.[5] Further complicating such anxieties, however, was Eliot's emotional debt to his mother, Charlotte Stearns Eliot, and her spiritually based feminism, which was rooted in the Victorian belief that women had a sacred calling as moral and spiritual authorities. Aware that Charlotte Stearns Eliot appealed to this belief in her struggle for reforming women's social position, he himself remained ambivalent about the social implications of women's spiritual centrality. Thus the formidable authority wielded by women within the symbolic order of Eliot's drama coexists with misogynist forces designed to reinstate traditional gender arrangements within the social order of the plays.

While much recent critical attention continues to be directed toward Eliot's first wife, Vivienne, as a central influence on his life, my chapter draws attention to the enduring, and so far neglected, emotional and creative impact of Charlotte Eliot on her son long after he left his home in St. Louis.[6] I shall argue that she embodied for him a formidable and deeply problematic model of female authority which remained to shape Eliot's response to women until the end of his life.[7] An apparently stern and high-minded woman, Charlotte Eliot raised her children to heed the example of their illustrious grandfather, the missionary and founder of St. Louis's Washington University, whose life she immortalized in a biography dedicated to her children, "Lest they forget." Charlotte Eliot was also the author of numerous devotional poems, including two longer works devoted to the martyrs Giordano Bruno and Girolamo Savonarola, as well as a successful social reformer, who was hailed, at one time, as the "mother" of St. Louis's juvenile court.[8] As head of a household dominated by women – herself and four daughters, all of whom were older than Thomas – Charlotte Eliot conducted herself as an exemplary Victorian mother whose first duty, as she herself put it, was "to her own household," and the momentous task of raising her children.[9] Her assiduous, sometimes overly anxious, care for her youngest and gifted child was shaped by Victorian notions of maternal responsibility that endowed mothers with an exalted mission as the molders and creators of the human character.[10] Yet like other educated women of her time, Charlotte Eliot was not content with the narrow confines of women's appointed sphere; in both her poetry and articles on social issues, she expressed her desire for women to play a more energetic part in the cultural and political life of their country.

Born when his mother was forty-five years of age and on the verge of her career as a social reformer, T. S. Eliot grew up very much aware of his mother's accomplishments. During the impressionable years of his childhood, his mother was his first model of a person seriously engaged with poetry. Her long poem, the dramatic monologue *Bruno in Prison*, appeared in 1890, when T. S. Eliot was just two years old. Her numerous hymns and religious poems were published, intermittently, in such widely read religious journals as the *Christian Register* and the *Unitarian*. In 1926, three years before her death, her most ambitious work, the closet drama *Savonarola*, was issued by Cobden-Sanders with an introduction by her son. The family attributed T. S. Eliot's poetic gifts to his mother's inheritance. He himself knew, at an early age, "what [his mother's] verse meant to her," and sought her advice on the poems he began writing as a young man.[11] After his departure from America, his mother remained an unflagging, critical guardian of her son's career, a role that he encouraged by sending her carbon copies of forthcoming works.[12] The weight of her opinion persisted beyond her death, prompting, as Ronald Bush proposed, her son's concern for a socially responsive kind of literature that "any educated person's mother could understand."[13]

Growing up under the protective, at times stifling, wings of as ambitious a mother as Charlotte Eliot, T. S. Eliot realized that her dearest hope was to see him succeed where she had failed. She was distressed when her 27-year-old son, then living in London, procured his living as a schoolteacher, and she called upon Bertrand Russell's assistance in persuading him to complete his Ph.D. in Philosophy. To coerce Tom into the service of secondary education was, she lamented, "like putting Pegasus in harness," a deeply felt analogy that touches upon her own experiences as a young woman who found herself obliged to teach small children instead of pursuing a course in higher education, as she had desired.[14] Yet never a woman to linger on her regrets, Charlotte Eliot directed her energies into changing the world which "had denied her the full use of her gifts."[15] Once relieved from the day-to-day care of small children, she joined two of St. Louis's women's clubs to pour her considerable intellect and managerial skill into reforming St. Louis's prison system.[16] She also championed women's rights when she petitioned for their access to the traditionally male *sancta* of higher education and national affairs. In an article on "The Higher Education of Women," she expressed her impatience with the Victorian dictum that "man is the head and woman the heart," reminding readers that "the heart is very unreliable if its impulses are not controlled by reason." Thus education "is useful in proportion as it enables [women] to labor intelligently, not as the slave who bows under the yoke, but as one who goes forth to achievement and victory."[17]

Like other bourgeois matrons of her time, Charlotte Eliot found much sustenance in faith for her struggles to expand the narrow confines of women's appointed sphere.[18] As a Unitarian, she belonged to a notoriously progressive church, which counted among its leaders such well-known defenders of women's public lecturing and preaching as William H. Channing and Theodore Parker. In her devotional poetry, Charlotte Eliot followed the counsel of the nineteenth-century transcendentalist Margaret Fuller, whose model of emancipated womanhood, Miranda, attributes her self-reliance to the power of religion which awakened in her the "sense that what the soul is capable to ask it must attain."[19] The conviction that faith in God will strengthen a believer's inner voice in opposition to clerical and social orthodoxy is articulated most incisively in Charlotte Eliot's longer works devoted to the sixteenth-century philosopher, astronomer, and poet Giordano Bruno and the fifteenth-century religious reformer and political leader Girolamo Savonarola. Both men serve as evocative examples of a heretical self-assertion legitimated by Christian piety that would have been especially appealing to a woman like Charlotte Eliot who ventured into politics and poetry as a Christian mother charged by God with an exalted moral and spiritual task. Thus when Charlotte Eliot's Bruno prophesies the world's awaking from the tyranny of clerical dogma, he sounds much like the ill-fated prophet Cassandra from Florence Nightingale's tract against the paralyzing strictures of Victorian femininity:[20]

> O! Soul of man, that beats with idle wing,
> Like some imprisoned bird against its cage,
> Be patient, 'tis the world's awakening,
> Thy bars expand in each succeeding age.
> Thy gaze is ever towards the dim unknown,
> The center of a universe thou art,
> Around thee endless realms to make thine own,
> And all is thine – thou hast in all a part.[21]

T. S. Eliot's uneasy awareness of the radical strain in his mother's thinking sometimes surfaces in his prose when he links her favorite martyrs with his own ideological antagonists: anti-clericalism, romanticism, liberal protestantism, and middle-class feminism.[22] The evocative figures of spiritually incisive women in his plays, however, intimate an abiding, if complex, debt to his mother's spiritually based feminism, whose impact on his work has been slighted in biographical approaches that favor the notion of Charlotte Eliot as the archetypal domineering mother. Thus Tom Matthews, in the most venomous account, describes her as a "clucking," "protective," "apprehensive," and overly possessive mother, whose dislike for small children poisoned her son's beginnings.[23] Guided by a psychological framework deeply ambivalent toward maternal authority and intellect, such critics as Matthews, Beer, and Drexler have tended to look upon Charlotte Eliot's literary and social aspirations as evidence of maternal discontent and the source of her son's Prufrockian insecurities as a grown man.[24] They have done so, moreover, without consulting Charlotte Eliot's writing or the Victorian cult of motherhood that unabashedly advocated the sort of zealous investment in the child's life that twentieth-century commentators have found so reprehensible in Charlotte Eliot's mothering.

To be sure, the depictions of maternal negligence and excess in Eliot's plays have done much to lend credibility to such vilifying portraits. Indeed, when Matthews portrays Charlotte Eliot as "one of those admirable women who have strict standards of conduct and no intimate friends, and who are admired, disliked, and feared by all who know them" (*Great Tom*, 9), he appears to have had in mind Dowager Amy Monchensey, the mother figure in Eliot's first and most autobiographical society play, *The Family Reunion* (1939), whose disastrous stranglehold over her son Harry is linked to his murderous rage against his first wife. Amy Monchensey is not the only one of Eliot's female characters to evoke the vipers and viragos of Wylie's 1942 diatribe against modern Moms, which accused socially ambitious mothers of undermining the social fabric of society by precipitating "a massive flight from manhood" among helpless husbands and sons.[25] Offshoots of this stock figure of female narcissism and powermongering are apparent, as well, in Julia Shuttlethwaite's tireless meddling with the lives of Edward, Lavinia, and Celia in *The Cocktail Party* (1949); in Lavinia's control over her husband, who complains, "Must I become after all what you would make me?" (*TCP*, 343); in Lady Elizabeth's dictatorial self-absorption; and in Mrs. Guzzard's abuse of maternal responsibility in *The Confidential Clerk* (1954).[26]

By suggesting a deep-seated resentment at female domination, these stereotypical invocations of feminine excess do much to underwrite critical portraits of Charlotte Eliot. However, such efforts at extrapolating the mother's true nature from the evidence of her son's fictional women are complicated by the plays' simultaneous insistence that women's authority is not only monstrous or comically inept but transformative as well. Thus when Agatha and Mrs. Guzzard reveal to the male protagonists of each play the story of their origin, providing them with knowledge of their biological and, by extension, heavenly father, they facilitate the young men's apprehension of a different order of reality and of the requirements of their special destiny. Working in the Christian tradition of female intercession, they free them to realize their vocation. Julia, similarly, functions as a comic, if ominous, divine agent whose strategic forgetfulness reminds Celia to open her eyes to her true destination in life, not with an apron in Edward's kitchen, but as a solitary traveler bent on atonement. Finally, through her gruesome martyrdom, Celia is the only character of the drawing room plays endowed with the symbolic centrality of Christ. Her crucifixion not only replicates Christ's sacrifice on the cross, but also effects a resurgence of spirituality within the cocktail-party world that she left behind and, as an earlier draft indicates, among the natives who crucified her.[27]

If nothing else, the ambiguous double life of Eliot's female characters as domestic vipers and agents of spiritual transformation calls for a revaluation of Charlotte Eliot's legacy to her son. More than the model for the domineering wives and mothers of her son's plays, Charlotte Eliot exemplified a kind of incipient feminism that envisioned women's spirituality as a central force in nourishing female autonomy and reforming traditional gender relations. While Eliot's society plays betray an uneasy ambivalence toward his mother's radicalized spiritual agenda, they also, in the figures of Agatha, Julia, Celia, and Mrs. Guzzard, suggest his indebtedness to her particular brand of spiritually based feminism. In fact, as if in response to his mother's insurgent desires, the double structure of Eliot's plays invites audiences to reflect upon the relationship between women's spiritual function, indicated on the mythic level of Eliot's plays, and their social roles, depicted on the naturalistic surface.

Initially, it appears that Eliot's drama elevates women spiritually while disempowering them socially. Women's spiritual authority releases the protagonists from the burden of social expectations, directing them to a metaphysical world beyond human comprehension; at the same time, however, women's emotional and social dominance has to be curbed before the protagonists can find their true vocation. Thus, at the end of the plays, women's power on the social playing field is contained: Dowager Monchensey from *The Family Reunion* is dead; strong-willed Lavinia from *The Cocktail Party* is pregnant and stripped of the social ambitions that threatened her marriage; Lavinia's rival, Celia, has been crucified; and Julia, whose hilarious, anti-domestic antics provided much of the comic relief in Act I of this play, has succumbed to silence.[28] Similarly, the end of *The Confidential Clerk* presents audiences with a social world in which traditional norms have been restored: Lucasta's flightiness is to be cured by marriage to Barnabas Khagan, while Lady Elizabeth, admitting that she always "wanted to inspire an artist" (*TCC*, 107), finds new contentment in her marriage to Sir Claude.

One implication of this design is, of course, that women's spiritualization operates as a means of channeling their disturbing authority into more acceptable, and to the male protagonists more beneficial, paths.[29] The fact that in at least three of the plays women's supernatural agency serves to restore traditional social order lends credence to this inference. Yet a closer look at such divinely inspired figures as Agatha, Julia, Celia, and Mrs. Guzzard reveals an alternate, implicitly female-centered, pattern, in which women's spiritualization entails not social compliance but, on the contrary, a curious autonomy whose impact tends to be disruptive before it becomes a force for renewal.

Significantly, in the case of each of these characters, spiritual authority is linked to the assumption of nontraditional female roles. Agatha, a "spinster," is also the president of a women's college; Julia is an apparently unattached single woman of independent means who acts as a "guardian" – a member of a religious secret service; Celia, in turn, abandons the socially condoned aspiration of becoming Edward's wife for the terrors of an uncharted, and to her world incomprehensible, spiritual journey; and finally, the suburban housewife Mrs. Guzzard's farcically distorted sense of maternal duty indicates a curious indifference to the requirements of her gender. Reinforcing such insurgent reverberations of female spirituality, moreover, is the seldom noted fact that Eliot's supernaturally empowered women characters evoke pre-Christian, at times pre-Hellenic, archetypes, who subtly resist seamless integration with the avowed Christian direction of the plays. With the exception of Monica from Eliot's final play *The Elder Statesman* (1958), and, to a limited extent, Celia, none of Eliot's spiritualized female figures persuasively embodies such Christian ideals as forgiveness, humility, or love. And although they work as agents of an elusive divine power understood to be the heavenly Father, their association with pursuing witch figures such as the Furies and pagan goddesses such as Athena and the Moirae betrays a startling amount of spiritual autonomy – not the humility of Mary, mother of Christ, but the hieratic authority of pagan fertility goddesses like Ishtar or Isis.[30]

A legacy of his mother's late-Victorian feminism, this hidden nexus between a female-centered spirituality and a certain kind of social autonomy surfaces most distinctly in Eliot's first society play, *The Family Reunion*, in which the two sisters Amy and Agatha embody his complex response to female authority: Amy epitomizes the stifling impact of a mother's vicarious investment in her child, while Agatha, whose educational accomplishments echo Charlotte Eliot's own capacities and aspirations, dramatizes the transformative potential of a liberated motherhood anchored in a woman's sense of her autonomous agency. With Agatha, Eliot created a female character of passion and wisdom who attained her spiritual authority in the course of a difficult life marked by a host of untraditional choices: she flouted the conventions of marriage by engaging in a passionate affair with her brother-in-law; she renounced this attachment, not because it was adulterous, but because it threatened the life of her as yet unborn nephew; she pursued a degree in higher education and achieved a publicly influential position as president of a women's college; and she mentors her niece, Mary, to follow in her footsteps, delivering her from a destructively reductive notion of womanhood embodied by her aunt Amy.

Of course, by referring to her as a "spinster," Eliot did much to obscure Agatha's intellect and autonomy, presenting her instead as the stock figure of a woman condemned to assume an uncongenial profession because she could not marry the man she loved. More decisive in eliding the transformative role of Agatha's spiritual and social independence, however, is the Orestian subtext of the play, which invites readers to compare Agatha to Athena – the goddess not of woman born who, presiding over the contest between ancient matriarchal divinities and the ascendant gods of the Greeks, casts her ballot for Orestes. Thus Martha Carpentier, in the most cogent analysis of the play's Aeschylean parallels, maintains that "Agatha, like Athena, is aligned throughout the play with a patriarchal godhead" and "able to find life after death in the spiritual eternity promised by God the Father."[31] Yet in her single-minded focus on Agatha's association with Athena, Carpentier overlooks the depth of Agatha's ties to a matriarchal spirituality, manifest in cryptic invocations of a richly pagan world of natural forces:

> The world around the corner
> The wind's talk in the dry holly-tree
> The inclination of the moon.
> (*TFR*, 231)

There lingers, moreover, an unmistakable air of witchcraft – an ancient form of magic, reaching back to shamanism – over Agatha and her ritualistic chants, described by Martin Browne as "rune-like."[32] Accused by Amy of putting a spell on Harry that induces him to leave the family estate, Agatha rebukes her sister by avowing, "I have only watched and waited" (*TFR*, 284). Yet earlier in the play Agatha appears to intervene directly on Harry's behalf, when, in a trance, she steps in the place that the Eumenides had occupied and delivers him from his family's curse:

> O my child, my curse,
> You shall be fulfilled:
> The knot shall be unknotted
> And the crooked made straight.
> (*TFR*, 279)

Agatha's association with ancient matriarchal rituals is corroborated in the play's final scene when she and her niece Mary ceremoniously proceed around the table that holds, as if on an altar, the birthday cake of Harry's by then deceased mother. "At each revolution," Eliot's stage directions specify, "they blow out a few candles, so that their last words are spoken in the dark" (*TFR*, 292). With these last words, Agatha, as high priestess, assisted by Mary as her acolyte, absolves Harry from the curse. The ritual both women administer is a strange mixture of Christian liturgy and pagan rites, a celebration of Harry's spiritual rebirth through an invocation of the forces of darkness – "the nether world," the "under side of things / Behind the smiling mirror / And behind the smiling moon" (*TFR*, 292) – as agents of Harry's conversion.[33]

At the level of the submerged female-centered plot, then, Eliot's adaptation of the *Oresteia* reverses the Orestian drive toward matricide. For Harry's transformation requires not his liberation from the maternal archetype, as

Carpentier and others have suggested, but his reconnection with the creative spirituality of the Great Mother, who, because of her curious position both within and on the margins of the social world presented in the play, is able to reveal to him his father's, and thus his own, identity.[34] Enacting the revolutionizing power of maternal autonomy and resistance is the unsettling presence of the Furies, "those ill-fated figures," as Eliot would later call them, whose central role in Harry's transmutation had already been indicated by the play's earlier title, "Follow the Furies."[35] Confusing critics and audiences alike, Eliot insisted from the start that these monstrous witch figures, associated with the rage of the injured earth mother, were "*divine* instruments, not simple hell-hounds," and thus, in the play, referred to them as "Eumenides" – the kindly ones.[36] In Aeschylus' trilogy, they attain this name only after Athena wins them over by offering to them an honored place of their own in the bowels of the earth. In Eliot's version of the play, however, the Furies' inherently kind nature is revealed to Harry once Agatha helps him understand his mother's tragically loveless life. In the beginning, Harry fears the Furies in their mythic role as avengers of the injured mother, in this case Amy, whom both husband and son have rejected. He loses his fear of the Eumenides only after Agatha initiates him into the secret of his parents' unhappy marriage, of his father's violent wish to do away with his mother, and of her own passionate love for Harry's father, crystallized, in her memory, as "a summer day of unusual heat / For this cold country" (*TFR*, 274). This revelation leads to Harry and Agatha's recognition scene, their lyrical "duet," a moment of spiritual and semi-erotic passion, in which Harry and Agatha are (re)joined as mother and son. That Harry would accept the Eumenides as his guides, his "bright angels" (*TFR*, 281), when they reappear at the end of his love duet with Agatha, suggests not only their persecutive, but also their clarifying function in the play. Harbingers of memory, and especially of a past both he and his biological mother, Amy, sought to hold at bay, they are aligned with the authority of the speaking mother, Agatha, who embodies a modernized version of the late-Victorian feminist ideal of an articulate, socially and spiritually active motherhood.

We might think of the Furies, in the words of Elizabeth Grosz, as the "unrepresented residue in maternity . . . that refuses to conform, as Christianity requires, to masculine, Oedipal, phallic order."[37] The fact that Eliot's play refers to them as Eumenides, rather than Furies, marks his recognition of the spiritually vital role of maternal resistance and autonomy. Thus, in this play, Eliot found a way of reconciling matricidal impulses with a recognition of the mother's centrality in human development. The play rejects the patriarchal mother, for whom the son is the only legitimate access to social participation and power, and advocates a liberated, and thus liberating, motherhood that resists the subordination of female desire and subjective agency to the needs of fathers and children.

By investing Charlotte Eliot's spiritual feminism with archetypal, pagan meanings and thus freeing it from the fetters of Victorian, middle-class respectability, *The Family Reunion* dramatizes the disruptive force of a female-centered spirituality that drives elect individuals, both female and male, to transcend their socially appointed place in society. In Eliot's subsequent two plays, *The Cocktail Party* and *The Confidential Clerk*, women's spiritual authority retains its disruptive potential, even as it restores the promise of authentic communion rooted in a traditional way of life that approximates the ideal advanced in Eliot's cultural criticism of a "life in conformity with nature."[38] Both of these plays indicate that Eliot was a social conservative when it came to the vast majority of human beings whom he saw as best served by a return to tradition and order. Yet extraordinary individuals, like Celia Coplestone from *The Cocktail Party*, were permitted, even required, to transcend the bounds of social mores and define themselves exclusively in relation to God. Eliot's most successful Christian drama, *The Cocktail Party*, is also his most disturbing articulation of the relation between women's social and spiritual calling. The play features a young woman of superior character and literary talent, who was bound to appeal to the New Women in the female audiences of the time, and then asks audiences to embrace as exemplary her portentous decision to sacrifice her hopes and ambitions for a religious devotion leading to painful suffering and death.

Given such paradoxical coexistence of women's social marginalization and spiritual exaltation, it is not surprising that one of the few explicitly feminist readings of the play has approached it as a misogynist fable targeting the cultural aspirations of educated, middle-class women. Thus Laura Severin argues that Celia, both Circe and poet at once, is too powerful a woman for the play's timid and dependent male characters, and must be "destroyed": "She is sent off by Sir Henry to be a missionary, where she is condemned to the ghastly fate of being eaten by ants."[39] Yet Celia's conversion does not, as Severin's interpretation suggests, shatter the fulfillment of the heroine's literary strivings so much as the rather more conventional wish of being Edward's wife once he has freed himself from Lavinia. Unhesitating in her willingness to conduct an affair with a married man, Celia is nevertheless bent on becoming the properly married wife of Edward, a desire signaled by the apron she dons to rescue the remnants of Edward's burned meal. It is, moreover, after Julia's initially tiresome interventions rather than after Reilly's "cure," as Severin maintains, that Celia comes to reject the role she had so far desired. Her refusal to help Edward search the kitchen for Julia's spectacles – fitting symbols of the need for insight – marks her own traumatically accomplished awakening. "You look for [the spectacles]," she commands Edward, "I shall never go into your kitchen again" (*TCP*, 327).[40]

The transformative impact of Julia's intervention in Celia's life has rarely been recognized in readings that privilege the significance of Sir Henry, the play's psychoanalyst *cum* confessor. Julia's role in this play is closest to that of Agatha in *The Family Reunion* and Mrs. Guzzard in *The Confidential Clerk*, even if the function of unhinging and then reconstructing the self is shared, in important ways, with the other two members of the play's religious secret service, the "guardians" Alex and Sir Henry. A precursor of comically absent-minded Lady Elizabeth from *The Confidential Clerk*, Julia uses her forgetfulness strategically, to probe, rattle, and supervise. That the result of her meddling should prove to be so life-altering for Celia might be linked to the incursion of female-identified mythic material not dramatized in Euripides' *Alcestis*, the play from which Eliot took the nucleus of his comedy. For even as the role of the guardians has been compared to that of ministers who serve the higher power of God the Father,[41] their ritualistic prayer to the "holy ones," at the end of Act 2, is rife with the lunar symbolism belonging to the Great Mother (*TCP*, 369). Such matriarchal symbolism is even more distinct in an earlier draft of the ritual, in which all three guardians repeatedly invoke the powers of the moon.[42] Celia will be fetched for her journey in the evening, "When the full moon has risen" (186). In "the prayer for the building of the hearth," Alex appeals to "the protection of the Moon," while Julia and Reilly call for the moon to "influence the bed" of the newly reunited couple, Edward and Lavinia (187). In addition, "The four higher protectors" and, especially, "The two winged ones," called up to watch over house and roof, can be linked to spirits of the earth goddess. That the guardians might be agents of the Great Mother, as much as of God the Father, is further indicated in Alex's graphic account of Celia's death, excised from the play's final version, where he recalls a "touching" incident that links her martyrdom explicitly to pagan goddess worship: after crucifying her, the natives "Had erected a sort of shrine for Celia / Where they brought offerings of fruit and flowers, / Fowls, and even sucking pigs" (227).

By eliminating many of the matriarchal references from the scene's final draft, Eliot may have wanted to strengthen the Christian meaning of the guardians' ritual as much as of Celia's martyrdom itself. These excised passages confirm the interpretation recently advanced by Grover Smith that Celia is a type of Kore, whose voluntary journey toward death echoes Persephone's abduction by Hades, god of the underworld.[43] Worshipping at the shrine of Celia, then, the natives might be said to propitiate not only Celia/Kore's wrath, but also that of her mother, Demeter, on whose abundant goodwill and fertility they depend. Despite Alex's rather patronizing account of native behavior – "The native is not, I fear, very logical" (*TCP*, 375) – the elided version of this scene does indicate that the inhabitants of Kinkanja have a more profound grasp of the meaning of Celia's death than the members of the cocktail party. Their ritualistic offerings at Celia's shrine convey an awareness of the transfiguring nature of Celia's horrible death; for now they worship Celia as a goddess, a type of Demeter, the author of all being.

What cure for modern disorder and alienation does the play propose, then? The literal and figurative mutilation of women, as Severin has argued, or the resuscitation of female divinity, accomplished by Celia's death and transfiguration into Demeter? Elicited by Celia's alarming martyrdom, the question is complex and not easily answered, since this comedy implies the contradictory presence of both impulses – to eliminate, or somehow contain, women's social authority on the one hand, and to retrieve women's spiritual power on the other. The paradoxical coexistence of misogyny and female advocacy in Eliot's drama reaches a final, farcical elaboration in *The Confidential Clerk*, a play in which a community's peace is restored by a mother's intervention and subsequent self-abdication. In this farce, it is Mrs. Guzzard, this play's pagan goddess, fairy godmother, and wise woman, who resolves the mysteries of identity troubling the major characters: Lady Elizabeth and her husband Sir Claude, both of whom claim the play's protagonist, Colby, as their child from a previous marriage; Sir Claude's illegitimate daughter Lucasta, a confused young woman; her suitor Barnabas Khagan, who is revealed at the play's end to be Lady Elizabeth's lost son; and of course Colby himself, who finds out that he is neither Lady Elizabeth's lost child, nor Sir Claude's illegitimate son, but the disavowed offspring of Mrs. Guzzard's marriage to a modestly successful musician. As the force that clarifies and restores, Mrs. Guzzard's formidable oracular authority is connected to the mother's privileged access to the truth of parentage, a fact reluctantly acknowledged by Sir Claude when he accuses her of fabricating the "fiction" of Colby's musician father (*TCC*, 149). Equally decisive, however, is Mrs. Guzzard's ability to remember and articulate the truth, an ability that reveals the extent of her spiritual and psychological autonomy in a social world largely unequipped to accept reality.

Mrs. Guzzard's associations with the Great Mother archetype are not developed poetically, as in the case of Agatha from *The Family Reunion*, but structurally. The farce recapitulates key components of the earlier play's mother-centered design according to which the male protagonist is freed to know his father, and thus his calling, only through the intervention of a spiritualized, semi-magical, mother figure who, because of her peculiar psychological and spiritual autonomy, is able to provide him with insight and self-knowledge. Thus, although knowledge of the heavenly father is the ultimate objective of both Harry's and Colby's quests, such knowledge can only be obtained by remembering, and thereby reconnecting with, the mother. Only through the speaking, authorial mother can the father be known.

Like Agatha, Mrs. Guzzard is modeled on Athena in her role as prophetess and intercessor in questions of parenthood. In the *Eumenides*, Athena casts her ballot in favor of Apollo's argument that "the mother is no parent of that which is called / her child . . . The parent is he who mounts";[44] in *Ion*, which provided the nucleus of Eliot's farce, she speaks as Apollo's mouthpiece, verifying that Ion is indeed an offspring of the god's rape of Creusa, a daughter of the earth. Yet when Eliot's "suburban Pallas Athene" makes her appearance, she is entirely her own oracle:[45] for even as her entrance as *dea ex machina*, deployed to untangle the mysteries of parentage, furthers the Christian direction of the play, Mrs. Guzzard's intercession is curiously self-generated and autocratic. More of a magical figure than a spiritual one, she does not appear to act directly as agent of God the Father. By contrast, the rapacious connotation of her name, her formidable appearance, clothed in "black or dark grey," and the revelations of her earlier heartless conduct toward her infant son, call to mind the annihilating aspects of the Great Mother, the goddess "of life and death at once."[46] Mrs. Guzzard's power to also bestow identity, and thus new life, is manifest in her role as fairy godmother, "Come to gratify everyone's wishes" (*TCC*, 145). She grants Colby two wishes. First, he can choose to know either his father or his mother. Then, when Colby decides in favor of the father, she offers him a second, equally remarkable choice: "Whose son would you wish to be, Colby: / Sir Claude's – or the son of some other man / Obscure and silent?" (*TCC*, 148).

By granting Colby his wishes, Mrs. Guzzard confers upon him a new identity. Yet by subsequently rebuking his question, "and who was my mother?" with the curt reminder that he wished to have no mother (*TCC*, 148–9), she abdicates the very power as arbiter of the self that made Colby's newly gained self-knowledge possible. In curious ways, then, the recognition between Colby and his mother echoes Christ's famous rebuke to his mother, "Why did you seek me? Did you not know that I must be about my Father's business?" (Luke 2:7). In Eliot's rendition of the scene, however, the mother willing to release her child to pursue his vocation is not the self-abnegating, silent vessel of God, idolized in Christian iconography, but a fearsome, articulate mother, whose identity-bestowing authority invokes the power of the Great Mother to both create and revoke life.

That for Eliot the benefit of such matriarchally focused spirituality was not to empower women socially, but, instead, to return them to a way of life designed to foster social harmony, even at the cost of women's creative and intellectual development, is evident at play's end when Lady Elizabeth's consistently lampooned intellectual aspirations and Lucasta's confused desire to create for herself a liberated sexual identity are laid to rest by their renewed commitment to the bonds of marriage. The play's restored social world "in conformity with nature" depends upon women's acquiescence to the traditional roles of wives and mothers. Yet, as the force that disrupts a sickened world and restores it to some level of emotional and spiritual health, women function as unusual intercessors, endowed with the archetypal authority of pagan goddesses and permitted to pursue vocations that transcend the narrow bounds of gendered propriety. Thus, despite Eliot's rather uninspired views on women's material lives and social aspirations, conveyed as well in his cultural criticism, his Christian society plays offer a surprisingly complex exploration of women's function as autonomously acting subjects in the spiritual renewal of the modern world. Eliot's comment in a footnote to *The Idea of a Christian Society* that "no normal married woman would prefer to be a wage-earner if she could help it" has a decidedly Victorian ring.[47] It is to his credit, however, that as a dramatist Eliot did not stoke contemporary anxieties about female subjectivity, whipped to a frenzied height in such misogynist classics as Wylie's *Generation of Vipers*. Instead, his plays' melodramatically exaggerated, farcically distorted, or simply denaturalized, antimimetic portrayals of women make visible, and thus open to reflection, his culture's ambivalence toward female agency.

What ultimately interests Eliot is not women's actual material existence and individuality, but their distinctively female power to save men, who are the truly hollow and confused characters of his drama. Salvation in Eliot's plays is possible only through the intervention of women. This is, of course, a traditional theme of Western literature – from Dante to Goethe and Wagner. The uniqueness of Eliot's treatment of this theme lies in his emphasis not on female love (only in his last play, *The Elder Statesman*, does he focus on the redemptive power of a daughter's love for her father), but on women's chilling and awe-inspiring authority as arbiters of truth and self-knowledge. In *The Idea of a Christian Society*, Eliot spoke of the need "to recover the sense of religious fear, so that it may be overcome by religious hope."[48] It is perhaps Eliot's most startling contribution to the modern discourse on femininity that he allocated this task of reawakening our "sense of religious fear" to women.

NOTES

I would like to thank the curators of the Houghton Library and the Missouri Historical Society for permission to quote from Charlotte Eliot's poetry and prose. I also wish to thank Donald Lawniczak for his valuable responses to successive drafts of this essay and Jacque Saunders for inspiring my interest in taking a more serious look at Eliot's society plays. Finally, I would like to express my gratitude to Sandra Gilbert and Susan Gubar for their bold revisions of modern literary history which have freed me to pursue my own understanding of T. S. Eliot's poetry and plays.

1. Philip Wylie, *Generation of Vipers*, rev. edn. (New York: Pocket Books, 1955). Another classic work in this vein is Ferdinand Lundberg and Marynia Farnham, *Modern Woman: The Lost Sex* (New York: Grosset and Dunlap, 1947). The misogynist implications of both works are discussed in Mari Jo Buhle's *Feminism and Its Discontent: A Century of Struggle with Psychoanalysis* (Cambridge, Mass.: Harvard University Press, 1998), especially chapters 4 and 5.

2. See Susan Robertson, "T. S. Eliot's Symbolic Woman: From Temptress to Priestess," *Midwest Quarterly* 24 (1986): 476–86.

3. See, above all, Carol Smith, *T. S. Eliot's Dramatic Theory and Practice* (Princeton: Princeton University Press, 1963).

4. Originally published by Faber and Faber, both works were reprinted in *Christianity and Culture* (New York: Harcourt Brace Jovanovich, 1968); Kenneth Asher, *T. S. Eliot and Ideology* (Cambridge: Cambridge University Press, 1995) and John Xiros Cooper, *T. S. Eliot and the Ideology of* Four Quartets (Cambridge: Cambridge University Press, 1995).

5. The standard reference for such modernist male anxieties about women's social and authorial gains remains, of course, Sandra Gilbert and Susan Gubar's *No Man's Land: The Place of the Woman Writer in the Twentieth Century*, 3 vols. (New Haven: Yale University Press, 1988–94).

6. For recent explorations of Vivienne Eliot's role in her husband's creative and spiritual life, see Ronald Schuchard, *Eliot's Dark Angel: Intersections of Life and Art* (New York: Oxford University Press, 1999) and Carole Seymour-Jones, *Painted Shadow: The Life of Vivienne Eliot, First Wife of T. S. Eliot, and the Long-Suppressed Truth about Her Influence on His Genius* (New York: Doubleday, 2002).

7. Thanks to Herbert Howarth's pioneering work on Charlotte Stearns Eliot in *Notes on Some Figures behind T. S. Eliot* (Boston: Houghton Mifflin, 1964) and Lyndall Gordon's exhaustive account in *Eliot's Early Years* (New York:

Oxford University Press, 1977), revised and reprinted in *T. S. Eliot: An Imperfect Life* (New York: Norton, 1998), a fuller assessment of the mother's place in T. S. Eliot's emotional and creative development has become possible. What remains to be sufficiently acknowledged, however, is the extent to which the poet's lifelong effort at understanding his mother shaped his creative work, in particular his frequently hostile, and, in later works, increasingly complex, depictions of strong-willed women. For a beginning in this direction, see my "Charlotte Stearns Eliot and *Ash-Wednesday*'s Lady of Silences," *English Literary History* 65 (1998): 479–501, and my dissertation, "A Literary Mother and a Literary Son: Charlotte Eliot and T. S. Eliot" (Indiana University, 1989).

8. See Howarth, *Notes on Some Figures behind T. S. Eliot*, 22–35, and his entry on Charlotte Eliot in *Notable American Women 1607–1950*, ed. Edward T. James (Cambridge, Mass.: The Belknap Press of Harvard University Press, 1971), vol. 1: 568–9. Charlotte Eliot's poetry and other writings, both published and unpublished, are preserved in the Houghton Library and the Missouri Historical Society. She collected many of her publications – poems and articles, as well as letters to the editor – in a scrapbook (Eliot collection, Houghton Library), yet frequently without indicating the date or place of publication. A printed copy of *Bruno in Prison*, dated 1890, is pasted in this scrapbook. The Missouri Historical Society has three notebooks of Charlotte Eliot's poems, all handwritten: an early one, which she kept as a young woman before her marriage, and two later ones. In addition, Charlotte Eliot published the biography of her father-in-law, *William Greenleaf Eliot: Minister, Educator, Philanthropist* (Boston: Houghton Mifflin, 1904), a small book of poems, *Easter Songs* (Boston: James H. West, n.d.), and the closet drama *Savonarola* (London: R. Cobden-Sanders, 1926).

9. Charlotte Eliot, "Woman's Interest in National Affairs" (ts., Eliot collection, Houghton Library), n. pag.

10. For analyses of nineteenth-century maternal rhetoric, see Ann Douglas, *The Feminization of American Culture* (New York: Alfred A. Knopf, 1977) and my dissertation, in particular chapter 1, "'Next to the Creator': The Mother as Author."

11. See Valerie Eliot's introduction to Eliot's *Poems Written in Early Youth* (New York: Farrar Straus Giroux, 1967), v–vi.

12. See Ronald Schuchard's introduction to T. S. Eliot, *The Varieties of Metaphysical Poetry*, ed. Schuchard (New York: Harcourt Brace, 1993), 24.

13. Ronald Bush, *T. S. Eliot: A Study in Character and Style* (Oxford: Oxford University Press, 1984), 161.

14. Charlotte Eliot to Bertrand Russell, St. Louis, January 18, 1916, in *The Letters of T. S. Eliot*, vol. 1: *1898–1922*, ed. Valerie Eliot (New York: Harcourt Brace Jovanovich, 1988), 131.

15. Peter Ackroyd, *T. S. Eliot: A Life* (New York: Simon and Schuster, 1984), 20.

16. Howarth, *Some Figures behind T. S. Eliot*, chapter 1.

17. Charlotte Eliot, "The Higher Education of Women" (ts., Eliot collection, Houghton Library), n. pag.

18. On American women's revisionary engagement with religion see, for instance, *Immaculate & Powerful: The Female in Sacred Image and Social Reality*, ed. Clarissa W. Atkinson, Constance H. Buchanan, and Margaret R. Miles (Boston: Beacon Press, 1985); Donna A. Behnke, *Religious Issues in Nineteenth Century Feminism* (Troy, N.Y.: Whitston, 1982); and Nancy Cott, *The Bonds of Womanhood: Woman's Sphere in New England, 1780–1835* (New Haven: Yale University Press, 1977).

19. Margaret Fuller, *Woman in the Nineteenth Century* (1855; reprint, New York: Norton, 1971), 40.

20. Florence Nightingale, *Cassandra: An Essay*, intro. Myra Stark (New York: Feminist Press, 1979).

21. Charlotte Eliot, *Bruno in Prison*, n. pag.

22. That Bruno, in Eliot's judgment, was afflicted with the flaws of romanticism – an emphasis on personality, lack of discipline, and immaturity – is suggested in a 1916 review, in which he asserts that the martyr's work has proven to be of "slight" value; only his "personality and career," in particular, his "violent, somewhat undisciplined temperament," his "varied wanderings," and his "spectacular death" have endured. T. S. Eliot, "Review of *Giordano Bruno: His Life, Thought, and Martyrdom* by William Boulting," *New Statesman* (October 21, 1916): 68. Three years later, Eliot reiterated these objections in another review, "Humanist, Artist, and Scientist," *Athenaeum*, (October 10, 1919): 1014–15. In his introduction to Charlotte Eliot's closet drama, he describes Savonarola as a "disciple of Schleiermacher, Emerson, Channing and Herbert Spencer," and compares her treatment of the moral reformer to Shaw's dramatization of St. Joan which made her into "a disciple of Nietzsche, Butler and every chaotic and immature intellectual enthusiasm of the later nineteenth century": "Savonarola has escaped from the cloister to the parsonage; St. Joan has escaped from the parsonage to a studio in Chelsea . . . In both is perceptible a certain opposition to ecclesiasticism." T. S. Eliot, introduction to *Savonarola*, by Charlotte Eliot, X. The smooth transition from an apparently neutral discussion of his mother's poem to a condemnation of Shaw's St. Joan suggests that part of the criticism leveled at Shaw belongs to the author of *Savonarola* as well. Eliot's animosity against Shaw was longstanding. "Mr. Shaw," he proclaimed in the *Criterion*, represents "the great middle-class liberalism"; his Joan of Arc, he continued, "is perhaps the greatest sacrilege of all Joans: for instead of the saint or the strumpet of the legends to which he objects, he has turned her into a great middle-class reformer, and her place is a little higher than Mrs. Pankhurst." T. S. Eliot, "A Commentary," *Criterion* 3 (1924): 5.

23. Tom Matthews, *Great Tom: Notes toward the Definition of T. S. Eliot* (New York: Harper and Row, 1973), 12.

24. Ernst Beer, *Thomas Stearns Eliot und der Antiliberalismus des XX. Jahrhunderts* (Wien: Wilhelm Baumüller, 1953) and Peter Drexler, *Escape from Personality: Eine Studie zum Problem der Identität bei T. S. Eliot* (Frankfurt am Main: Peter D. Lang, 1980).

25. See Mari Jo Buhle's discussion of Momism in *Feminism and Its Discontent*, 125–64.

26. Quotations from Eliot's drawing room plays are cited in the text with the abbreviations listed below.

> TFR: *The Family Reunion*, in *The Complete Poems and Plays 1909–1950* (New York: Harcourt, Brace and World, 1971), 223–93.
> TCP: *The Cocktail Party*, in *The Complete Poems and Plays*, 295–387.
> TCC: *The Confidential Clerk* (London: Harcourt Brace Jovanovich, 1954).
> TES: *The Elder Statesman* (New York: Farrar, 1959). ·

27. Martin Browne, *The Making of T. S. Eliot's Plays* (Cambridge: Cambridge University Press, 1969), 227. This earlier draft will be discussed below.

28. For a discussion of Julia's diminished role at the end of play, see Laura Severin, "Cutting Philomela's Tongue: *The Cocktail Party*'s Cure for a Disorderly World," *Modern Drama* 36 (1993): 396–408.

29. See A. David Moody, "Being in Fear of Women," in his *Tracing T. S. Eliot's Spirit* (Cambridge: Cambridge University Press, 1996), 182–95. With regard to the spiritualization of women in Eliot's post-conversion work, Moody writes: "It is only so far as they assume these spiritual roles [as spiritual sister and mother] that women are associated with anything other than fear and anxiety. Spiritualized, they provide in an acceptable form what was found inadequate and even threatening when offered by real women" (187).

30. For the archetype of the Great Goddess in Eliot's depictions of sacred women, see my "Charlotte Stearns Eliot and *Ash-Wednesday*'s Lady of Silence" and John Gatta's *American Madonna: Images of the Divine Woman in Literary Culture* (New York: Oxford University Press, 1997), especially chapter 6, "Eliot's Archetypal Lady of Sea and Garden: The Recovery of Myth," 116–37.

31. Martha Carpentier, "Orestes in the Drawing Room: Aeschylean Parallels in T. S. Eliot's 'The Family Reunion,'" *Twentieth Century Literature* 35 (1989): 17–41, 21.

32. Browne, *The Making of T. S. Eliot's Plays*, 94.

33. That Eliot may have intended Agatha's association with magic and witchcraft is supported by a marginal comment in an earlier draft of the play's final section: "Great uncle Harry was cursed by a witch?" (Browne, *The Making of T. S. Eliot's Plays*, 94).

34. See Carpentier, "Orestes in the Drawing Room," and Maud Bodkin, *The Quest for Salvation in an Ancient and a Modern Play* (London: Oxford University Press, 1941). In *T. S. Eliot's Poetry and Plays*, 2nd edn. (Chicago: University of Chicago Press, 1974), Grover Smith argues that "on one level, not the naturalistic one, Amy's death shows the subsidence of the obsolete idea of domineering motherhood so that the idea of liberating motherhood may stand unimpeded" (209).

35. Gordon, *An Imperfect Life*, 552.

36. Browne, *The Making of T. S. Eliot's Plays*, 107.

37. Elizabeth Grosz, *Sexual Subversions: Three French Feminists* (Sydney: Allen and Unwin, 1989), 84.
38. Eliot, *Christianity and Culture*, 48.
39. Severin, "Cutting Philomela's Tongue," 403.
40. Severin points out that both Celia and Alex, her admirer, had artistic ambitions. While the play gives Alex a chance to realize his ambition to become a Hollywood screenwriter, it does not permit the fulfillment of Celia's poetic aspirations. Yet within the moral and spiritual context of the comedy, Celia's decision to sacrifice her personal and literary ambitions for an arduous spiritual journey is not only the exemplary, saintly, choice, but also an expression of her single-minded pursuit of a vision "of something / Though I don't know what it is" (364). Challenging Severin's reading, then, we might point out that, unlike Alex and Edward, Celia is not willing to compromise her dream. And surely, it is this single-minded, courageous pursuit of her vision that makes Celia such an unusual female character in Eliot's work.
41. See David Jones, *The Plays of T. S. Eliot* (Toronto: University of Toronto Press, 1960), 149–52.
42. This earlier draft is included in Browne, *The Making of T. S. Eliot's Plays.* Subsequent references to this work will be cited in the text.
43. Grover Smith, *T. S. Eliot and the Use of Memory* (London: Associated University Presses, 1996), 128–35.
44. Aeschylus, *Oresteia*, trans. Richmond Lattimore, ed. David Green and Richmond Lattimore (Chicago: University of Chicago Press, 1953), 158.
45. Browne, *The Making of T. S. Eliot's Plays*, 250.
46. Erich Neumann, *The Great Mother: An Analysis of the Archetype*, trans. Ralph Mannheim (New York: Bollingen Foundation, 1955), 45. For Eliot's preliminary description of Mrs. Guzzard, see Browne, *The Making of T. S. Eliot's Plays*, 285.
47. Eliot, *Christianity and Culture*, 54.
48. Ibid., 49–50.

Index

Printed in the United States
47656LVS00002B/172-177

9 780521 806886

SR

Gramley Library
Salem Academy and College
Winston-Salem, N.C. 27108